The Message is a contemporary rendering of the Bible from the original languages, crafted to present its tone, rhythm, events, and ideas in everyday language.

The Message Women's Devotional Bible: The Gospels is excerpted from ***The Message Women's Devotional Bible***. The full Bible will be available from NavPress in summer 2025.

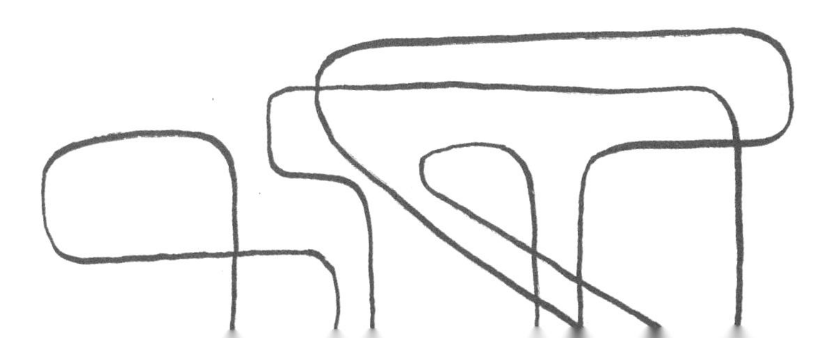

Women's Devotional Bible

THE MESSAGE

THE GOSPELS

EUGENE H. PETERSON

with insights and reflections by women for women

A NavPress resource published in alliance with Tyndale House Publishers

NavPress.com

A NavPress resource published in alliance with Tyndale House Publishers

Published in association with Alive Literary Agency, aliveliterary.com

For information about special discounts for bulk purchases, please contact Tyndale House Publishers at csresponse@tyndale.com, or call 1-855-277-9400.

ISBN 978-1-64158-639-9 Softcover

Printed in China

31 30 29 28 27 26 25
7 6 5 4 3 2 1

CONTENTS

INTRODUCTION TO *THE MESSAGE WOMEN'S DEVOTIONAL BIBLE*

When Eugene Peterson crafted *The Message*, he was a pastor, writing with real women and men he loved in mind. Having invested in his congregation for decades, he found many of them indifferent to the Bible, or bored, or confused. He longed for this family of faith to *encounter* God through the Bible—and, in doing so, find themselves in God's story.

From that longing, *The Message* was born: the words of God in the language of real people, with the metaphors of our modern life.

It was out of a similar longing that we dreamed of creating a devotional Bible for women, drawing on the experiences and insights of women. Our experience parallels Peterson's—but with a twist. We hear women grieving or startled by certain stories they find in the Bible or hear in their churches. We scratch our heads over the lack of women in these pages or feel angered by stories of women's voices silenced and their bodies harmed. Some of us wonder how a book featuring an abundance of male scribes and characters, and centered on a God who came to earth as a *man*, could have good news for women.

Still others have suffered from the Bible being weaponized, misused to suppress or harm women. Many women long for God's Word but are excluded from in-depth study and theology, offered instead shallow teaching, lessons on joyful living and domestic duties.

Yet we are convinced that the Bible *is* good news for women—for *all* women. In this holy, God-breathed book, there is light and life, truth and teaching that is valuable for us today. *Because of this*, the women of the Bible deserve space for their stories to rise to the surface and catch our attention—and women reading the Bible deserve to be better equipped to study it than we historically have been.

We envisioned devotional content that went deep, illuminating and extrapolating the text, interspersed alongside the accessible words of *The Message*. This would be a no-holds-barred project: No question would be silenced, no difficult topic given shallow treatment. We would name the hard things *and* we would be faithful to the text. We would look the painful stories in the eye, and we would not flinch, choosing—like Jacob—to wrestle with God as long as it took until God blessed us, seeking the heart of God from first to last.

To do this, we gathered dozens of women: authors, scholars, ministers, pastors. With one foot in God's Word and the other in our complicated, multidimensional lived experiences, each writer contributed her study, story, and expertise. We endeavored to honor the sacred words of the Bible, the Spirit, who has guarded these words, and the women whose stories they tell. We aimed to be worthy of this description: *thoughtful, soulful, diverse*.

We wrote for women whose guards go up at Christian content marketed specifically to them, expecting caricature and superficial connections. We sought to highlight the biblical women whose courage and conviction—whether in birthing screaming children or assassinating napping generals—form the bedrock of our faith. Digging into the oft-overlooked deep tracks of the Bible, we considered the sometimes-invisible women who are our mothers and sisters in the faith.

We identified women throughout the Bible—some well known, others nameless—and told their stories. There is much of God's truth in their lives that we tend to miss, gloss over, or allow to sit dormant. We sought to bring these women closer to center stage, giving them space and light, asking what we could learn from their lives and the ways God met and used them. We considered what life was like in their shoes and what they have to teach us today.

We identified topics woven throughout the Bible that are especially relevant to women today—but we intentionally did not focus on or limit ourselves to "women's issues." Yes, women look to the Bible for help with female experiences, but we also wanted to consider things common to all humanity—seeking God's presence, finding the courage to stand for justice against oppression, considering the problem of evil.

Furthermore, women bring questions to the Bible that male commentators have not fully understood, much less addressed: How does the male-centered backdrop of the ancient world impact the ways we view women today? What should we make of how often women in the Bible are portrayed predominantly in sexual or reproductive roles: wife, mother, temptress, barren woman? What do we do with the depictions of violence against women? With incidences of degrading or dehumanizing language toward women? How can women see themselves in God's good story when women's voices are so rarely heard there?

What emerged from this effort is beauty, strength, and courage. These devotions hold words that are honoring and challenging, faithful and true.

We pray this project will be a gift to you who pick it up to read. The entries may be written by and for women, but *all* are invited to learn alongside us, men and women alike. We pray that you will see a fresh glimpse of the God who formed all people in God's own image, who has seen and uplifted women from the very beginning. We pray that you will find your own stories told and honored here, your own questions asked. We pray that you will find moments of wrestling and moments of rest. We pray that you will find *God*, fully and joyfully.

From the original Garden in Genesis to the healing leaves of the tree in Revelation, the Bible consistently pushes against patriarchal demands. Over and over again, it is not the firstborn who is chosen (as primogeniture required) but the second; not the stronger but the weaker; not the desired but the unnoticed. The women who appear in these pages boldly and creatively use every tool at their disposal to outwit the powerful who oppress them. It is often these women who turn the tide, whose inspired rebellion forms the foundation of God's redemption: the Hebrew midwives in Exodus, Rahab the spy in Joshua, Mary the mother of Jesus, the woman at the well, and the women who joined Jesus' ministry, who followed him all the way to the empty tomb.

Will you join this mighty throng of God's daughters and take your place in God's kingdom? If you're ready, just turn the page. There's so much we're eager to show you.

THE MESSAGE WOMEN'S DEVOTIONAL BIBLE TEAM

HOW TO GET THE MOST OUT OF *THE MESSAGE WOMEN'S DEVOTIONAL BIBLE*

The Message Women's Devotional Bible is designed to help you read the Bible more deeply and thoughtfully, let the wisdom of the Scriptures seep more fully into your spirit, and consider afresh how the Bible speaks to women in our time. Several features will support your Bible-reading experience.

INTRODUCTIONS. At the beginning of each Bible book (or, in some cases, collection of books) and each section of Scripture is a brief essay by Eugene H. Peterson, pastor, poet, and translator of *The Message*. These have proven over time to give a useful thirty-thousand-foot view of the various Bible books in a literary section.

Added to the section introductions are short paragraphs speaking specifically to where the literary section draws especially near to the experiences and concerns of women. A general introduction to the Bible and its relationship and relevance to women is also included on the preceding pages.

DEVOTIONAL ENTRIES. Our diverse group of contributors has written 320 short meditations inspired by Scripture. They're designed to help you process what's happening in a passage, or what might be happening in you as you read that passage. And many of them speak to realities far beyond the passages themselves—in the family of God and in the world as women. A list of these entries and where they're located is included in the back.

CHARACTER PROFILES. The Bible's people are as helpful to know and understand as its teachings and stories. Our contributors have written fifty profiles of women (and a couple of men) you'll encounter as you engage with the Scriptures. We don't know the names of some of them, but they are known by God, and they help us know God better.

SENSITIVE TREATMENTS OF SENSITIVE PASSAGES. The Bible is filled with stories of people who, in turning away from God, turn toward violence, sexual harm, abuse, oppression, and other dehumanizing acts. The Word of God isn't just true; it's honest. Some of these passages can be difficult to read, and especially so for people who have suffered significant harm through the sin of others. Please know that the writers of these devotional entries and character profiles have taken special care to treat sensitive passages sensitively, allowing space and special concern for those who struggle, allowing space and special concern for you to struggle *with* God, not against God. On each entry that addresses these passages, you'll find this note of caution:

This entry and the passage it addresses involve highly sensitive topics that might be triggering to some readers. If that is you, be gentle with yourself.

You might choose to wait to read these entries until you feel better prepared or skip them altogether. The indexes in the back indicate entries that the editors have determined may be triggering.

▲ ▲ ▲

Of course, the most significant and important feature of this or any Bible is the Bible itself. We open this book and find that on page after page it catches us off guard, surprises us, and draws us into its reality, pulls us into a fuller participation with the God who created us and cares for us. We engage ourselves fully with this text so that we might be transformed and so that God's will may be done on earth as it is in heaven. We hope this resource supports you in this—and every—journey God is inviting you into.

INTRODUCTION TO *THE MESSAGE*

Reading is the first thing, just reading the Bible. As we read we enter a new world of words and find ourselves in on a conversation in which God has the first and last words. We soon realize that we are included in the conversation. We didn't expect this. But this is precisely what generation after generation of Bible readers do find: The Bible is not only written about us but to us. In these pages we become insiders to a conversation in which God uses words to form and bless us, to teach and guide us, to forgive and save us.

We aren't used to this. We are used to reading books that explain things, or tell us what to do, or inspire or entertain us. But this is different. This is a world of revelation: God revealing to people just like us—men and women created in God's image—how God works and what is going on in this world in which we find ourselves. At the same time that God reveals all this, God draws us in by invitation and command to participate in God's working life. We gradually (or suddenly) realize that we are insiders in the most significant action of our time as God establishes his grand rule of love and justice on this earth (as it is in heaven). "Revelation" means that we are reading something we couldn't have guessed or figured out on our own. Revelation is what makes the Bible unique.

And so just reading this Bible, *The Message*, and listening to what we read, is the first thing. There will be time enough for study later on. But first, it is important simply to read, leisurely and thoughtfully. We need to get a feel for the way these stories and songs, these prayers and conversations, these sermons and visions, invite us into this large, large world in which the invisible God is behind and involved in everything visible and illuminates what it means to live here—really live, not just get across the street. As we read, and the longer we read, we begin to "get it"—we are in conversation with God. We find ourselves listening and answering in matters that most concern us: who we are, where we came from, where we are going, what makes us tick, the texture of the world and the communities we live in, and—most of all—the incredible love of God among us, doing for us what we cannot do for ourselves.

Through reading the Bible, we see that there is far more to the world, more to us, more to what we see and more to what we don't see—more to everything!—than we had ever dreamed, and that this "more" has to do with God.

This is new for many of us, a different sort of book—a book that reads us even as we read it. We are used to picking up and reading books for what we can get out of them: information we can use, inspiration to energize us, instructions on how to do something or other, entertainment to while away a rainy day, wisdom that will guide us into living better. These things can and do take place when reading the Bible, but the Bible is given to us in the first place simply to invite us to make ourselves at home in the world of God, God's Word and world, and become familiar with the way God speaks and the ways in which we answer him with our lives.

Our reading turns up some surprises. The biggest surprise for many is how accessible this book is to those who simply open it up and read it. Virtually anyone can read this Bible with understanding. The reason that new translations are made every couple of generations or so is to keep the language of the Bible current with the common speech we use, the very language in which it was first written. We don't have to be smart or well-educated to understand it, for it is written in the words and sentences we hear in the marketplace, on school playgrounds, and around the dinner table. Because the Bible is so famous and revered, many assume that we need experts to explain and interpret it for us—and, of course, there are some things that need to be explained. But the first men and women who listened to these words now written in our Bibles were ordinary, everyday, working-class people. One of the greatest of the early translators of the Bible into English, William Tyndale, said that he was translating so that the "boy that driveth the plough" would be able to read the Scriptures.

One well-educated African man, who later became one of the most influential Bible teachers in our history (Augustine), was greatly offended when he first read the Bible. Instead of a book cultivated and polished in the literary style he admired so much, he found it full of homespun, earthy stories of plain, unimportant people. He read it in a Latin translation full of slang and jargon. He took one look at what he considered the "unspiritual" quality of so many of its characters and the everydayness of Jesus, and he contemptuously abandoned it. It was years before he realized that God had not taken the form of a sophisticated intellectual to teach us about highbrow heavenly culture so we could appreciate the finer things of God. When he saw that God entered our lives as a Jewish servant in order to save us from our sins, he started reading the book gratefully and believingly.

Some are also surprised that Bible reading does not introduce us to a "nicer" world. This biblical world is decidedly not an ideal world, the kind we see advertised in travel posters. Suffering and injustice and ugliness are not purged from the world in which God works and loves and saves. Nothing is glossed over. God works patiently and deeply, but often in hidden ways, in the mess of our humanity and history. Ours is not a neat and tidy world in which we are assured that we can get everything under our control. This takes considerable getting used to—there is mystery everywhere. The Bible does not give us a predictable cause-effect world in which we can plan our careers and secure our futures. It is not a dream world in which everything works out according to our adolescent expectations—there is pain and poverty and abuse at which we cry out in indignation, "You can't let this happen!" For most of us it takes years and years and years to exchange our dream world for this real world of grace and mercy, sacrifice and love, freedom and joy—the God-saved world.

Yet another surprise is that the Bible does not flatter us. It is not trying to sell us anything that promises to make life easier. It doesn't offer secrets to what we often think of as prosperity or pleasure or high adventure. The reality that comes into focus as we read the Bible has to do with what God is doing in a saving love that includes us and everything we do. This is quite different from what our sin-stunted and culture-cluttered minds imagine. But our Bible reading does not give us access to a mail-order catalog of idols from which we can pick and choose to satisfy our fantasies. The Bible begins with God speaking creation and us into being. It continues with God entering into personalized and complex relationships with us, helping and blessing us, teaching and training us, correcting and disciplining us, loving and saving us. This is not an escape from reality but a plunge into more reality—a sacrificial but altogether better life all the way.

▲ ▲ ▲

God doesn't force any of this on us: God's Word is personal address, inviting, commanding, challenging, rebuking, judging, comforting, directing—but not forcing. Not coercing. We are given space and freedom to answer, to enter the conversation. For more than anything else the Bible invites our participation in the work and language of God.

As we read, we find that there is a connection between the Word Read and the Word Lived. Everything in this book is live-able. Many of us find that the most important question we ask as we read is not "What does it mean?" but "How can I live it?" So we read personally, not impersonally. We read in order to live our true selves, not just get information that we can use to raise our standard of living. Bible reading is a means of listening to and obeying God, not gathering religious data by which we can be our own gods.

You are going to hear stories in this book that will take you out of your preoccupation with yourself and into the spacious freedom in which God is working the world's salvation. You are going to come across words and sentences that stab you awake to a beauty and hope that will connect you with your real life.

Be sure to answer.

Eugene H Peterson

The arrival of Jesus signaled the beginning of a new era. God entered history in a personal way, and made it unmistakably clear that he is on our side, doing everything possible to save us. It was all presented and worked out in the life, death, and resurrection of Jesus. It was, and is, hard to believe—seemingly too good to be true.

But one by one, men and women did believe it, believed Jesus was God alive among them and for them. Soon they would realize that he also lived in them. To their great surprise they found themselves living in a world where God called all the shots—had the first word on everything; had the last word on everything. That meant that everything, quite literally every thing, had to be re-centered, re-imagined, and re-thought.

They went at it with immense gusto. They told stories of Jesus and arranged his teachings in memorable form. They wrote letters. They sang songs. They prayed. One of them wrote an extraordinary poem based on holy visions. There was no apparent organization to any of this; it was all more or less spontaneous and, to the eye of the casual observer, haphazard. Over the course of about fifty years, these writings added up to what would later be compiled by the followers of Jesus and designated "the New Testament."

Three kinds of writing—eyewitness stories, personal letters, and a visionary poem—make up the book. Five stories, twenty-one letters, one poem.

In the course of this writing and reading, collecting and arranging, with no one apparently in charge, the early Christians, whose lives were being changed and

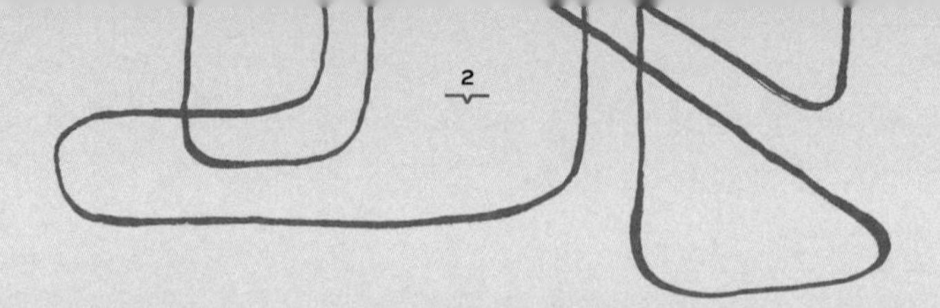

shaped by what they were reading, arrived at the conviction that there was, in fact, Someone in charge—God's Holy Spirit was behind and in it all. In retrospect, they could see that it was not at all random or haphazard, that every word worked with every other word, and that all the separate documents worked in intricate harmony. There was nothing accidental in any of this, nothing merely circumstantial. They were bold to call what had been written God's Word, and they trusted their lives to it. They accepted its authority over their lives. Most of its readers since have been similarly convinced.

A striking feature in all this writing is that it was done in the street language of the day, the idiom of the playground and marketplace. In the Greek-speaking world of that day, there were two levels of language: formal and informal. Formal language was used to write philosophy and history, government decrees and epic poetry. If someone were to sit down and consciously write for posterity, it would of course be written in this formal language with its learned vocabulary and precise diction. But if the writing was routine—shopping lists, family letters, bills, and receipts—it was written in the common, informal idiom of everyday speech, street language.

And this is the language used throughout the New Testament. Some people are taken aback by this, supposing that language dealing with a holy God and holy things should be elevated—stately and ceremonial. But one good look at Jesus—his preference for down-to-earth stories and easy association with common people—gets rid of that supposition. For Jesus is the descent of God to our lives, just as they are, not the ascent of our lives to God, hoping he might approve when he sees how hard we try.

And that is why the followers of Jesus in their witness and preaching, translating and teaching, have always done their best to get the Message—the "good news"—into the language of whatever streets they happen to be living on. In order to understand the Message right, the language must be right—not a refined language that appeals to our aspirations after the best but a rough and earthy language that reveals God's presence and action where we least expect it, catching us when we are up to our elbows in the soiled ordinariness of our lives and God is the furthest thing from our minds.

▲ ▲ ▲

Women are found everywhere in the Gospel stories. Jesus revealed his incarnation, identity, and resurrection first to women, trusting them to proclaim and teach what they knew to the world. Jesus' inner circle included several female disciples—Mary Magdalene, Susanna, Joanna, and others—who traveled with him and the Twelve around Judea and Jerusalem, ministering with and to him. In a world that objectified, sexualized, and marginalized women, Jesus humanized, empowered, and dignified us.

Women are harder to see in the Epistles; letters provide glimpses into the Christian community but cannot tell the full story. Paul praises his colleagues in ministry, Priscilla and Junia, while sending Phoebe to read and teach his letter to the Romans. More broadly, the good news declares that in Christ old dividing walls have fallen, including those between women and men, masters and slaves—all one now, in Christ, postured toward serving *each other*.

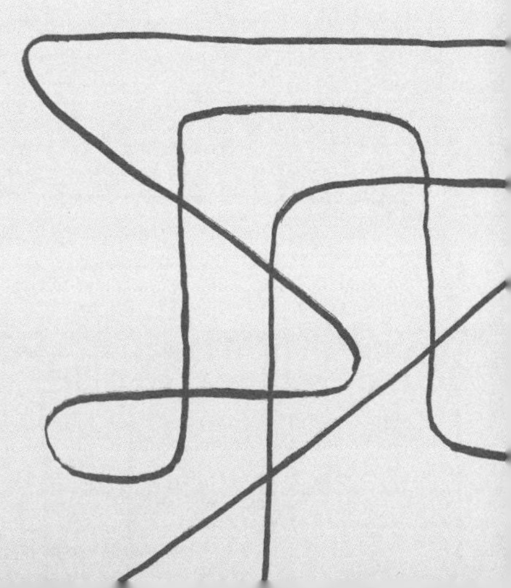

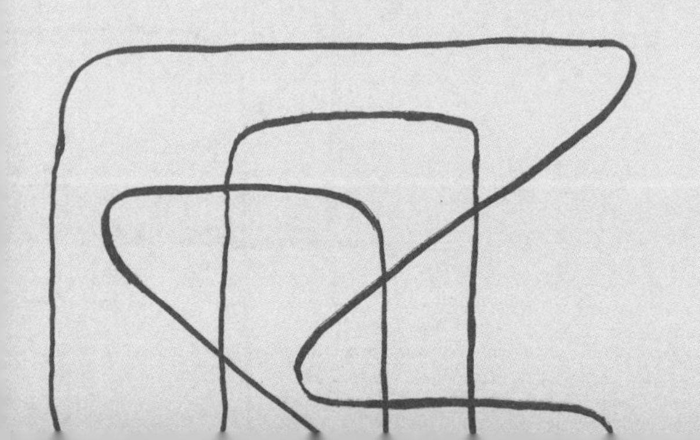

Matthew

FULFILLED

The story of Jesus doesn't begin with Jesus. God had been at work for a long time. Salvation, which is the main business of Jesus, is an old business. Jesus is the coming together in final form of themes and energies and movements that had been set in motion before the foundation of the world.

Matthew opens the New Testament by setting the local story of Jesus in its world historical context. He makes sure that as we read his account of the birth, life, death, and resurrection of Jesus, we see the connections with everything that has gone before. In fact, in his account of Jesus' birth alone, Matthew reminds his readers of two Old Testament prophecies being fulfilled in the coming of the Messiah.

> Watch for this—a virgin will get pregnant and bear a son;
> they will name him Immanuel (Hebrew for "God is with us").
>
> MATTHEW 1:23, QUOTING ISAIAH 7:14

> "It's you, Bethlehem, in Judah's land,
> no longer bringing up the rear.
> From you will come the leader
> who will shepherd-rule my people, my Israel."
>
> MATTHEW 2:6, QUOTING MICAH 5:2

Fulfilled is one of Matthew's characteristic verbs: such and such happened "that it might be *fulfilled*." Jesus is unique, but he is not odd.

Better yet, Matthew tells the story in such a way that not only is everything previous to us completed in Jesus; *we* are completed in Jesus. Every day we wake up in the middle of something that is already going on, that has been going on for a long time: genealogy and geology, history and culture, the cosmos—God. We are neither accidental nor incidental to the story. We get orientation, briefing, background, reassurance.

Matthew provides the comprehensive context by which we see all God's creation and salvation completed in Jesus, and all the parts of our lives—work, family, friends, memories, dreams—also completed in Jesus, who himself said, "Don't suppose for a minute that I have come to demolish the Scriptures—either God's Law or the Prophets. I'm not here to demolish but to complete. I am going to put it all together, pull it all together in a vast panorama" (Matthew 5:17). Lacking such a context, we are in danger of seeing Jesus as a mere diversion from the concerns announced in the newspapers. Nothing could be further from the truth.

1

1 The family tree of Jesus Christ, David's son, Abraham's son:

2-6 Abraham had Isaac,
Isaac had Jacob,
Jacob had Judah and his brothers,
Judah had Perez and Zerah (the mother was Tamar),
Perez had Hezron,
Hezron had Aram,
Aram had Amminadab,
Amminadab had Nahshon,
Nahshon had Salmon,
Salmon had Boaz (his mother was Rahab),
Boaz had Obed (Ruth was the mother),
Obed had Jesse,
Jesse had David,
and David became king.

6-11 David had Solomon (Uriah's wife was the mother),
Solomon had Rehoboam,
Rehoboam had Abijah,
Abijah had Asa,
Asa had Jehoshaphat,
Jehoshaphat had Joram,
Joram had Uzziah,
Uzziah had Jotham,
Jotham had Ahaz,
Ahaz had Hezekiah,
Hezekiah had Manasseh,
Manasseh had Amon,
Amon had Josiah,
Josiah had Jehoiachin and his brothers,
and then the people were taken into the Babylonian exile.

12-16 When the Babylonian exile ended,
Jeconiah had Shealtiel,
Shealtiel had Zerubbabel,
Zerubbabel had Abiud,
Abiud had Eliakim,
Eliakim had Azor,
Azor had Zadok,
Zadok had Achim,
Achim had Eliud,
Eliud had Eleazar,
Eleazar had Matthan,
Matthan had Jacob,
Jacob had Joseph, Mary's husband,
the Mary who gave birth to Jesus,
the Jesus who was called Christ.

17 There were fourteen generations from Abraham to David,
another fourteen from David to the Babylonian exile,
and yet another fourteen from the Babylonian exile to Christ.

THE BIRTH OF JESUS

18-19 The birth of Jesus took place like this. His mother, Mary, was engaged to be married to Joseph. Before they enjoyed their wedding night, Joseph discovered she was pregnant. (It was by the Holy Spirit, but he didn't know that.) Joseph, chagrined but noble, determined to take care of things quietly so Mary would not be disgraced.

20-23 While he was trying to figure a way out, he had a dream. God's angel spoke in the dream: "Joseph, son of David, don't hesitate to get married. Mary's pregnancy is Spirit-conceived. God's Holy Spirit has made her pregnant. She will bring a son to birth, and when she does, you, Joseph, will name him Jesus—'God saves'—because he will save his people from their sins." This would bring the prophet's embryonic revelation to full term:

Watch for this—a virgin will get pregnant
and bear a son;
They will name him Immanuel (Hebrew
for "God is with us").

24-25 Then Joseph woke up. He did exactly what God's angel commanded in the dream: He married Mary. But he did not consummate the marriage until she had the baby. He named the baby Jesus.

SCHOLARS FROM THE EAST

2

1-2 After Jesus was born in Bethlehem village, Judah territory—this was during Herod's kingship—a band of scholars arrived in Jerusalem from the East. They asked around, "Where can we find and pay homage to the newborn King of the Jews? We observed a star in the eastern sky that signaled his birth. We're on pilgrimage to worship him."

3-4 When word of their inquiry got to Herod, he was terrified—and not Herod alone, but most of Jerusalem as well. Herod lost no time. He gathered all the high priests and religion scholars in the city together and asked, "Where is the Messiah supposed to be born?"

5-6 They told him, "Bethlehem, Judah territory. The prophet Micah wrote it plainly:

It's you, Bethlehem, in Judah's land,
no longer bringing up the rear.

The Mothers of Jesus

It's tempting to breeze through this long list of ancestors, often thought of as one of the "boring parts" of the Bible to skim before we get to the good stuff. But if you've ever gone down the rabbit hole of your own genealogy, you know there are countless stories hidden in such a list.

Take just the women mentioned here, these mothers of Jesus. Do you know their stories? Mary's, probably, but what about Tamar's and Rahab's, Ruth's and Bathsheba's (referred to in Matthew 1:6 as "Uriah's wife")? Flipping back to the stories of their lives, we may understand something about the story Matthew is telling. Jesus is no ordinary person—not only because he is the Messiah, but also because of the kind of God-loving, risk-taking lineage he was born into.

Tamar was a granddaughter of Jacob, her two husbands struck dead for their faithlessness. But when the remaining men in the family selfishly abandoned their duty to her, she tricked her father-in-law, Judah, into impregnating her. When her trick was revealed, he declared, "She's in the right" (Genesis 38:26), confirming that Tamar's actions had been faithful and moral when her male relatives' had not.

Rahab was a "harlot" in Jericho (Joshua 2:1) who sheltered the spies sent by Joshua. She believed in the power and mercy of God, courageously saving herself and her family by becoming part of the plan to overthrow the walled city in which she lived.

Ruth, a foreigner and a widow, pledged faithfulness to her bitter mother-in-law with words that sound much like God's own words. Then she risked her reputation in a scandalous move to ensure that she and her mother-in-law would be protected.

Bathsheba's story might be the hardest of all: Her body was taken by the king, David, who then killed her husband to hide his sin. The child conceived by David was condemned to death by God, but after all this, Bathsheba became the mother of Solomon, the wisest king of Israel.

And then there's Mary, who appears in Matthew's story as a mysteriously pregnant fiancée. Meanwhile, imagine how many more women's faithful stories are invisible in this mostly male list.

Each of these women played an important part in God's work—even at great personal cost. For some of them, this cost includes being known primarily by—and judged for—their sexual history and given labels that persist to this day. But in their faithfulness these women paved the way for Jesus' birth—not only through the Holy Spirit, but also through the stories passed down and taught to each generation.

Motherhood may well be the most underestimated tool of God's incoming reign. Who knows what God may do through this generation of mothers raising up children to follow Jesus?

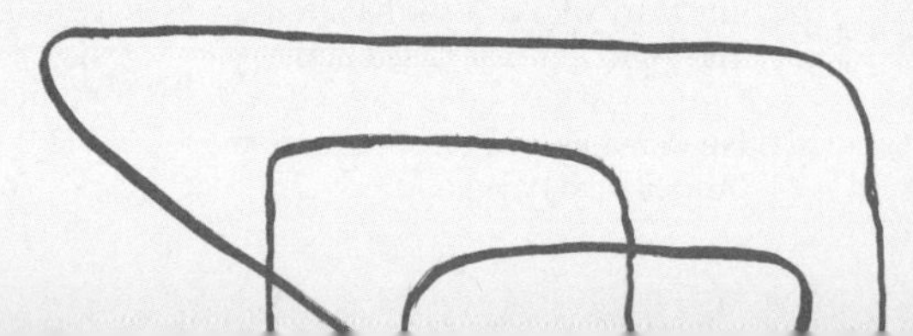

From you will come the leader
who will shepherd-rule my people,
my Israel."

7-8 Herod then arranged a secret meeting with the scholars from the East. Pretending to be as devout as they were, he got them to tell him exactly when the birth-announcement star appeared. Then he told them the prophecy about Bethlehem, and said, "Go find this child. Leave no stone unturned. As soon as you find him, send word and I'll join you at once in your worship."

9-10 Instructed by the king, they set off. Then the star appeared again, the same star they had seen in the eastern skies. It led them on until it hovered over the place of the child. They could hardly contain themselves: They were in the right place! They had arrived at the right time!

11 They entered the house and saw the child in the arms of Mary, his mother. Overcome, they kneeled and worshiped him. Then they opened their luggage and presented gifts: gold, frankincense, myrrh.

12 In a dream, they were warned not to report back to Herod. So they worked out another route, left the territory without being seen, and returned to their own country.

▲ ▲ ▲

13 After the scholars were gone, God's angel showed up again in Joseph's dream and commanded, "Get up. Take the child and his mother and flee to Egypt. Stay until further notice. Herod is on the hunt for this child, and wants to kill him."

14-15 Joseph obeyed. He got up, took the child and his mother under cover of darkness. They were out of town and well on their way by daylight. They lived in Egypt until Herod's death. This Egyptian exile fulfilled what Hosea had preached: "I called my son out of Egypt."

16-18 Herod, when he realized that the scholars had tricked him, flew into a rage. He commanded the murder of every little boy two years old and under who lived in Bethlehem and its surrounding hills. (He determined that age from information he'd gotten from the scholars.) That's when Jeremiah's revelation was fulfilled:

A sound was heard in Ramah,
weeping and much lament.
Rachel weeping for her children,
Rachel refusing all solace,
Her children gone,
dead and buried.

19-20 Later, when Herod died, God's angel appeared in a dream to Joseph in Egypt: "Up, take the child and his mother and return to Israel. All those out to murder the child are dead."

21-23 Joseph obeyed. He got up, took the child and his mother, and reentered Israel. When he heard, though, that Archelaus had succeeded his father, Herod, as king in Judea, he was afraid to go there. But then Joseph was directed in a dream to go to the hills of Galilee. On arrival, he settled in the village of Nazareth. This move was a fulfillment of the prophetic words, "He shall be called a Nazarene."

THUNDER IN THE DESERT!

3 1-2 While Jesus was living in the Galilean hills, John, called "the Baptizer," was preaching in the desert country of Judea. His message was simple and austere, like his desert surroundings: "Change your life. God's kingdom is here."

3 John and his message were authorized by Isaiah's prophecy:

Thunder in the desert!
Prepare for God's arrival!
Make the road smooth and straight!

4-6 John dressed in a camel-hair habit tied at the waist by a leather strap. He lived on a diet of locusts and wild field honey. People poured out of Jerusalem, Judea, and the Jordanian countryside to hear and see him in action. There at the Jordan River those who came to confess their sins were baptized into a changed life.

7-10 When John realized that a lot of Pharisees and Sadducees were showing up for a baptismal experience because it was becoming the popular thing to do, he exploded: "Brood of snakes! What do you think you're doing slithering down here to the river? Do you think a little water on your snakeskins is going to make any difference? It's your life that must change, not your skin! And don't think you can pull rank by claiming Abraham as father. Being a descendant of Abraham is neither here nor there. Descendants of Abraham are a dime a dozen. What counts is your life. Is it green and flourishing? Because if it's deadwood, it goes on the fire.

11-12 "I'm baptizing you here in the river, turning your old life in for a kingdom life. The real action comes next: The main character in this drama—compared to him I'm a mere stagehand—will ignite the kingdom life within you, a fire within you, the Holy Spirit within you, changing you from the inside out. He's going to clean house—make a clean sweep of your lives. He'll place everything true in its proper place before God; everything false he'll put out with the trash to be burned."

▲ ▲ ▲

13-14 Jesus then appeared, arriving at the Jordan River from Galilee. He wanted John to baptize him. John objected, "I'm the one who needs to be baptized, not *you*!"

15 But Jesus insisted. "Do it. God's work, putting things right all these centuries, is coming together right now in this baptism." So John did it.

16-17 The moment Jesus came up out of the baptismal waters, the skies opened up and he saw God's Spirit—it looked like a dove—descending and landing on him. And along with the Spirit, a voice: "This is my Son, chosen and marked by my love, delight of my life."

THE TEST

4 1-3 Next Jesus was taken into the wild by the Spirit for the Test. The Devil was ready to give it. Jesus prepared for the Test by fasting forty days and forty nights. That left him, of course, in a state of extreme hunger, which the Devil took advantage of in the first test: "Since you are God's Son, speak the word that will turn these stones into loaves of bread."

4 Jesus answered by quoting Deuteronomy: "It takes more than bread to stay alive. It takes a steady stream of words from God's mouth."

5-6 For the second test the Devil took him to the Holy City. He sat him on top of the Temple and said, "Since you are God's Son, jump." The Devil goaded him by quoting Psalm 91: "He has placed you in the care of angels. They will catch you so that you won't so much as stub your toe on a stone."

7 Jesus countered with another citation from Deuteronomy: "Don't you dare test the Lord your God."

8-9 For the third test, the Devil took him to the peak of a huge mountain. He gestured expansively, pointing out all the earth's kingdoms, how glorious they all were. Then he said, "They're yours—lock, stock, and barrel. Just go down on your knees and worship me, and they're yours."

10 Jesus' refusal was curt: "Beat it, Satan!" He backed his rebuke with a third quotation from Deuteronomy: "Worship the Lord your God, and only him. Serve him with absolute single-heartedness."

11 The Test was over. The Devil left. And in his place, angels! Angels came and took care of Jesus' needs.

TEACHING AND HEALING

12-17 When Jesus got word that John had been arrested, he returned to Galilee. He moved from his hometown, Nazareth, to the lakeside village Capernaum, nestled at the base of the Zebulun and Naphtali hills. This move completed Isaiah's revelation:

Land of Zebulun, land of Naphtali,
  road to the sea, over Jordan,
  Galilee, crossroads for the nations.
People sitting out their lives in the dark
  saw a huge light;
Sitting in that dark, dark country
    of death,
  they watched the sun come up.

This Isaiah-prophesied revelation came to life in Galilee the moment Jesus started preaching. He picked up where John left off: "Change your life. God's kingdom is here."

18-20 Walking along the beach of Lake Galilee, Jesus saw two brothers: Simon (later called Peter) and Andrew. They were fishing, throwing their nets into the lake. It was their regular work. Jesus said to them, "Come with me. I'll make a new kind of fisherman out of you. I'll show you how to catch men and women instead of perch and bass." They didn't ask questions, but simply dropped their nets and followed.

21-22 A short distance down the beach they came upon another pair of brothers, James and John, Zebedee's sons. These two were sitting in a boat with their father, Zebedee, mending their fishnets. Jesus made the same offer to them, and they were just as quick to follow, abandoning boat and father.

23-25 From there he went all over Galilee. He used synagogues for meeting places and taught people the truth of God. God's kingdom was his theme—that beginning right now they were under God's government,

Watch Out for Twisted Truth

When we're faced with testing or temptation, we often resist only so far; then we fall back on the "I'm not Jesus" reasoning and let ourselves off the hook. It's true that we aren't Jesus. *But Jesus became us.* Jesus had a body, and it was the same kind of body we each have—a body that knew hunger, thirst, pain, loneliness, poverty, and powerlessness.

Out in the hot desert, the newly baptized Son of God felt every bit of our frailty in his human body. And the Devil took advantage! Picture Jesus, weak from hunger and thirst—much like he would be on the way to the cross—taunted, teased, tempted. Yet Jesus did not give in and use his God powers to relieve his own suffering.

Jesus' needs were just like our needs.

Jesus felt the lure of *The end justifies the means.*

Jesus experienced the full pressure of the Devil's "Did God really say . . . ?" just as Eve did in the Garden (see Genesis 3:1). Just as we do today.

Eugene Peterson writes, "Everything that the devil put before Jesus was wrapped in Scripture packaging." Notice that the Devil quoted Psalm 91 (Matthew 4:5-6). What we must watch out for is twisted truth: The real, good, true Word of God in the Devil's mouth entices, claims, and justifies choices that are neither God's desire nor God's intent for us.

This type of temptation is not mundane. We live in a sovereignty-of-self sort of world in which clever and pointed mantras tell us that power, prestige, and security are ours for the taking. We are persuaded to make choices that feel right but aren't right, decisions that look good on paper but are bad for our souls or harmful to those we are called to serve.

Jesus has been in your shoes. He was offered good things that weren't the right things. He was tired of the fight, but he didn't give in. Instead, he faced the Devil's logic head on, meeting "Did God really say . . . ?" with the words we wish Adam and Eve had said in the Garden: "Beat it, Satan!" (Matthew 4:10). *Your offer is rotten to the core.*

We do not have a Savior who is so high above us that he can't relate to our trials and temptations. Jesus became one of us. "He had to enter into every detail of human life. Then, when he came before God as high priest to get rid of the people's sins, he would have already experienced it all himself—all the pain, all the testing—and would be able to help where help was needed" (Hebrews 2:17-18).

a good government! He also healed people of their diseases and of the bad effects of their bad lives. Word got around the entire Roman province of Syria. People brought anybody with a sickness, whether mental, emotional, or physical. Jesus healed them, one and all. More and more people came, the momentum gathering. Besides those from Galilee, crowds came from the "Ten Towns" across the lake, others up from Jerusalem and Judea, still others from across the Jordan.

YOU'RE BLESSED

5 1-2 When Jesus saw his ministry drawing huge crowds, he climbed a hillside. Those who were apprenticed to him, the committed, climbed with him. Arriving at a quiet place, he sat down and taught his climbing companions. This is what he said:

3 "You're blessed when you're at the end of your rope. With less of you there is more of God and his rule.

4 "You're blessed when you feel you've lost what is most dear to you. Only then can you be embraced by the One most dear to you.

5 "You're blessed when you're content with just who you are—no more, no less. That's the moment you find yourselves proud owners of everything that can't be bought.

6 "You're blessed when you've worked up a good appetite for God. He's food and drink in the best meal you'll ever eat.

7 "You're blessed when you care. At the moment of being 'care-full,' you find yourselves cared for.

8 "You're blessed when you get your inside world—your mind and heart—put right. Then you can see God in the outside world.

9 "You're blessed when you can show people how to cooperate instead of compete or fight. That's when you discover who you really are, and your place in God's family.

10 "You're blessed when your commitment to God provokes persecution. The persecution drives you even deeper into God's kingdom.

11-12 "Not only that—count yourselves blessed every time people put you down or throw you out or speak lies about you to discredit me. What it means is that the truth is too close for comfort and they are uncomfortable. You can be glad when that happens—give a cheer, even!—for though they don't like it, *I* do! And all heaven applauds. And know that you are in good company. My prophets and witnesses have always gotten into this kind of trouble.

SALT AND LIGHT

13 "Let me tell you why you are here. You're here to be salt-seasoning that brings out the God-flavors of this earth. If you lose your saltiness, how will people taste godliness? You've lost your usefulness and will end up in the garbage.

14-16 "Here's another way to put it: You're here to be light, bringing out the God-colors in the world. God is not a secret to be kept. We're going public with this, as public as a city on a hill. If I make you light-bearers, you don't think I'm going to hide you under a bucket, do you? I'm putting you on a light stand. Now that I've put you there on a hilltop, on a light stand—shine! Keep open house; be generous with your lives. By opening up to others, you'll prompt people to open up with God, this generous Father in heaven.

COMPLETING GOD'S LAW

17-18 "Don't suppose for a minute that I have come to demolish the Scriptures—either God's Law or the Prophets. I'm not here to demolish but to complete. I am going to put it all together, pull it all together in a vast panorama. God's Law is more real and lasting than the stars in the sky and the ground at your feet. Long after stars burn out and earth wears out, God's Law will be alive and working.

19-20 "Trivialize even the smallest item in God's Law and you will only have trivialized yourself. But take it seriously, show the way for others, and you will find honor in the kingdom. Unless you do far better than the Pharisees in the matters of right living, you won't know the first thing about entering the kingdom.

MURDER

21-22 "You're familiar with the command to the ancients, 'Do not murder.' I'm telling you that anyone who is so much as angry with a brother or sister is guilty of murder. Carelessly call a brother 'idiot!' and you just might find yourself hauled into court. Thoughtlessly yell 'stupid!' at a sister and you are on the brink of hellfire. The simple moral fact is that words kill.

23-24 "This is how I want you to conduct yourself in these matters. If you enter your place of worship and, about to make an offering, you suddenly remember a grudge a friend has against you, abandon your offering, leave immediately, go to this friend and make things right. Then and only then, come back and work things out with God.

Flipping the Script on Blessing

Social media vividly displays what our world considers #BLESSED: Instagram-worthy weddings; jubilant gender reveals; holidays resplendent with family and friends; exclusive-offer letters and VIP invitations; tropical destinations, gadgets, and glam.

When everyone appears to be #TooBlessedToBeStressed, #Winning, and #CrushingIt, our news feeds only feed our fear of missing out. Each swipe or scroll brings further indictment: We can't do, be, or have enough.

Jesus lived anything but #BLESSED. "There was nothing attractive about him, nothing to cause us to take a second look" (Isaiah 53:2)—much less follow him. He never married, raised children, or owned a home you'd see on Pinterest. Bullied and betrayed, his career lasted three years before he was canceled. Publicly shamed, he died naked and abandoned; even his friends failed him.

In God's kingdom economy, *blessing* is simply defined differently. Jesus came to serve, not to be served. He didn't clout chase the religious in-crowd but pursued the outliers, outsiders, and underqualified. Forfeiting every comfort and convenience, he endured the cross to forgive the very haters who trolled him.

Jesus flipped the script on blessing so that we, too, might reappraise ours. If loss is now gain, we're blessed regardless of our net worth or intake or output; with less of us, there is more of God's countercultural currency. We're blessed when we're known and loved for our unfiltered selves; freed from the daily oppression of curating the perfect highlight reel. We're blessed when the holes of grief in our hearts transform into sacred spaces—God-shaped voids only God can fill, to paraphrase Blaise Pascal's *Pensées*.

Anything that drives us to the cross can be a blessing. God can repurpose any lack, loss, or longing into a spiritual scalpel wielded for our sanctification, for God is a redeeming God.

In a world that assigns point values and price tags according to appearances, abilities, and accolades, who is incomparably and exceedingly blessed? The answer is always countercultural: those who find God's strength in weakness. May we ardently follow the only influencer who shapes our souls for eternity. God alone esteems us in immeasurable units of grace.

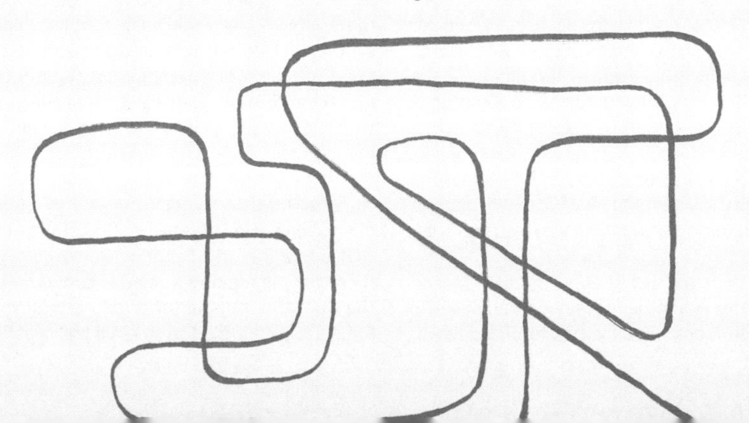

25-26 "Or say you're out on the street and an old enemy accosts you. Don't lose a minute. Make the first move; make things right with him. After all, if you leave the first move to him, knowing his track record, you're likely to end up in court, maybe even jail. If that happens, you won't get out without a stiff fine.

ADULTERY AND DIVORCE

27-28 "You know the next commandment pretty well, too: 'Don't go to bed with another's spouse.' But don't think you've preserved your virtue simply by staying out of bed. Your *heart* can be corrupted by lust even quicker than your *body*. Those ogling looks you think nobody notices—they also corrupt.

29-30 "Let's not pretend this is easier than it really is. If you want to live a morally pure life, here's what you have to do: You have to blind your right eye the moment you catch it in a lustful leer. You have to choose to live one-eyed or else be dumped on a moral trash pile. And you have to chop off your right hand the moment you notice it raised threateningly. Better a bloody stump than your entire being discarded for good in the dump.

31-32 "Remember the Scripture that says, 'Whoever divorces his wife, let him do it legally, giving her divorce papers and her legal rights'? Too many of you are using that as a cover for selfishness and whim, pretending to be righteous just because you are 'legal.' Please, no more pretending. If you divorce your wife, you're responsible for making her an adulteress (unless she has already made herself that by sexual promiscuity). And if you marry such a divorced adulteress, you're automatically an adulterer yourself. You can't use legal cover to mask a moral failure.

EMPTY PROMISES

33-37 "And don't say anything you don't mean. This counsel is embedded deep in our traditions. You only make things worse when you lay down a smoke screen of pious talk, saying, 'I'll pray for you,' and never doing it, or saying, 'God be with you,' and not meaning it. You don't make your words true by embellishing them with religious lace. In making your speech sound more religious, it becomes less true. Just say 'yes' and 'no.' When you manipulate words to get your own way, you go wrong.

LOVE YOUR ENEMIES

38-42 "Here's another old saying that deserves a second look: 'Eye for eye, tooth for tooth.' Is that going to get us anywhere? Here's what I propose: 'Don't hit back at all.' If someone strikes you, stand there and take it. If someone drags you into court and sues for the shirt off your back, giftwrap your best coat and make a present of it. And if someone takes unfair advantage of you, use the occasion to practice the servant life. No more tit-for-tat stuff. Live generously.

43-47 "You're familiar with the old written law, 'Love your friend,' and its unwritten companion, 'Hate your enemy.' I'm challenging that. I'm telling you to love your enemies. Let them bring out the best in you, not the worst. When someone gives you a hard time, respond with the supple moves of prayer, for then you are working out of your true selves, your God-created selves. This is what God does. He gives his best—the sun to warm and the rain to nourish—to everyone, regardless: the good and bad, the nice and nasty. If all you do is love the lovable, do you expect a bonus? Anybody can do that. If you simply say hello to those who greet you, do you expect a medal? Any run-of-the-mill sinner does that.

48 "In a word, what I'm saying is, *Grow up*. You're kingdom subjects. Now live like it. Live out your God-created identity. Live generously and graciously toward others, the way God lives toward you."

THE WORLD IS NOT A STAGE

6 1 "Be especially careful when you are trying to be good so that you don't make a performance out of it. It might be good theater, but the God who made you won't be applauding.

2-4 "When you do something for someone else, don't call attention to yourself. You've seen them in action, I'm sure—'playactors' I call them—treating prayer meeting and street corner alike as a stage, acting compassionate as long as someone is watching, playing to the crowds. They get applause, true, but that's all they get. When you help someone out, don't think about how it looks. Just do it—quietly and unobtrusively. That is the way your God, who conceived you in love, working behind the scenes, helps you out.

PRAY WITH SIMPLICITY

5 "And when you come before God, don't turn that into a theatrical production either. All these people making a regular show out of their prayers, hoping for fifteen minutes of fame! Do you think God sits in a box seat?

6 "Here's what I want you to do: Find a quiet, secluded place so you won't be tempted to role-play before God. Just be there as simply and honestly as you can manage. The focus will shift from you to God, and you will begin to sense his grace.

7-13 "The world is full of so-called prayer warriors who are prayer-ignorant. They're full of formulas and programs and advice, peddling techniques for getting what you want from God. Don't fall for that nonsense. This is your Father you are dealing with, and he knows better than you what you need. With a God like this loving you, you can pray very simply. Like this:

Our Father in heaven,
Reveal who you are.
Set the world right;
Do what's best—
as above, so below.
Keep us alive with three square meals.
Keep us forgiven with you and forgiving others.
Keep us safe from ourselves and the Devil.
You're in charge!
You can do anything you want!
You're ablaze in beauty!
Yes. Yes. Yes.

14-15 "In prayer there is a connection between what God does and what you do. You can't get forgiveness from God, for instance, without also forgiving others. If you refuse to do your part, you cut yourself off from God's part.

16-18 "When you practice some appetite-denying discipline to better concentrate on God, don't make a production out of it. It might turn you into a small-time celebrity but it won't make you a saint. If you 'go into training' inwardly, act normal outwardly. Shampoo and comb your hair, brush your teeth, wash your face. God doesn't require attention-getting devices. He won't overlook what you are doing; he'll reward you well.

A LIFE OF GOD-WORSHIP

19-21 "Don't hoard treasure down here where it gets eaten by moths and corroded by rust or—worse!—stolen by burglars. Stockpile treasure in heaven, where it's safe from moth and rust and burglars. It's obvious, isn't it? The place where your treasure is, is the place you will most want to be, and end up being.

22-23 "Your eyes are windows into your body. If you open your eyes wide in wonder and belief, your body fills up with light. If you live squinty-eyed in greed and distrust, your body is a musty cellar. If you pull the blinds on your windows, what a dark life you will have!

24 "You can't worship two gods at once. Loving one god, you'll end up hating the other. Adoration of one feeds contempt for the other. You can't worship God and Money both.

25-26 "If you decide for God, living a life of God-worship, it follows that you don't fuss about what's on the table at mealtimes or whether the clothes in your closet are in fashion. There is far more to your life than the food you put in your stomach, more to your outer appearance than the clothes you hang on your body. Look at the birds, free and unfettered, not tied down to a job description, careless in the care of God. And you count far more to him than birds.

27-29 "Has anyone by fussing in front of the mirror ever gotten taller by so much as an inch? All this time and money wasted on fashion—do you think it makes that much difference? Instead of looking at the fashions, walk out into the fields and look at the wildflowers. They never primp or shop, but have you ever seen color and design quite like it? The ten best-dressed men and women in the country look shabby alongside them.

30-33 "If God gives such attention to the appearance of wildflowers—most of which are never even seen—don't you think he'll attend to you, take pride in you, do his best for you? What I'm trying to do here is to get you to relax, to not be so preoccupied with *getting*, so you can respond to God's *giving*. People who don't know God and the way he works fuss over these things, but you know both God and how he works. Steep your life in God-reality, God-initiative, God-provisions. Don't worry about missing out. You'll find all your everyday human concerns will be met.

34 "Give your entire attention to what God is doing right now, and don't get worked up about what may or may not happen tomorrow. God will help you deal with whatever hard things come up when the time comes.

A SIMPLE GUIDE FOR BEHAVIOR

7 1-5 "Don't pick on people, jump on their failures, criticize their faults—unless, of course, you want the same treatment. That critical spirit has a way of boomeranging. It's easy to see a smudge on your neighbor's face and be oblivious to the ugly sneer on

Extraordinary Faith

Two men. Two remarkably different backgrounds. Two miraculous healings.

The first thirteen verses of Matthew 8 demonstrate Jesus' authority over sickness and his compassion for all people regardless of their position in society. These stories also invite us to deepen our own faith.

The man with leprosy was an outcast with no status or authority. Not only were lepers shunned, but they also had no hope of getting well. In Jesus' day, people didn't understand what caused this disease. Its symptoms included horrible disfigurement, pain, and ultimately death. The leper's choice to approach Jesus carried great risk: Would this healer turn away like so many others had, reinforcing the man's shame and hopelessness?

This particular event happened shortly after Jesus preached the Sermon on the Mount. Had the leper somehow gotten close enough to hear Jesus' words and rightly discern that proximity offered a once-in-a-lifetime opportunity? The courageous risk paid off. Jesus touched him, and his illness disappeared.

Then a Roman officer also asked Jesus to exert healing power, but from a very different starting point. Unlike the leper, the captain wielded authority and power in the community. He was not in need of physical healing himself but was asking on behalf of his servant who was paralyzed and "in terrible pain" (Matthew 8:6). Jesus granted the captain's request and healed the faraway servant.

The difference in social status between leper and Roman officer spanned the entire spectrum. Yet Jesus saw them both. Some of us are like the leper: We are outsiders with no real status or authority; desperate, we understand that it would take a miracle of someone else's making to meet our need. Some of us are like the Roman officer: We have power, authority, and status; we generously leverage what we have on behalf of others. We are used to having our commands heard and respected.

Regardless of which person best reflects your own station in life, three commonalities unite these stories.

First, these people were vulnerable. They recognized their needs and limitations: Neither had the capacity to heal.

Second, by stating their needs publicly, they displayed humility.

Finally, both believed that Jesus had the authority to heal.

When I was a young Christian, I assumed that extraordinary faith was a prerequisite to asking Jesus for anything—even more so for a miracle. Because I judged my faith to be inadequate, I often didn't ask. These two accounts correct false beliefs such as this one. They affirm that the very process of asking Jesus for something can increase our faith because doing so gives him an opportunity to reveal himself—even if that revelation doesn't look exactly like we've imagined or hoped. In mathematical language:

need + humility + the recognition of Jesus' love and authority = extraordinary faith

May we all walk in this kind of faith.

your own. Do you have the nerve to say, 'Let me wash your face for you,' when your own face is distorted by contempt? It's this whole traveling road-show mentality all over again, playing a holier-than-thou part instead of just living your part. Wipe that ugly sneer off your own face, and you might be fit to offer a wash-cloth to your neighbor.

6 "Don't be flip with the sacred. Banter and silliness give no honor to God. Don't reduce holy mysteries to slogans. In trying to be relevant, you're only being cute and inviting sacrilege.

7-11 "Don't bargain with God. Be direct. Ask for what you need. This isn't a cat-and-mouse, hide-and-seek game we're in. If your child asks for bread, do you trick him with saw-dust? If he asks for fish, do you scare him with a live snake on his plate? As bad as you are, you wouldn't think of such a thing. You're at least decent to your own children. So don't you think the God who conceived you in love will be even better?

12 "Here is a simple, rule-of-thumb guide for behavior: Ask yourself what you want people to do for you, then grab the initiative and do it for *them*. Add up God's Law and Prophets and this is what you get.

BEING AND DOING

13-14 "Don't look for shortcuts to God. The market is flooded with surefire, easygoing formulas for a successful life that can be practiced in your spare time. Don't fall for that stuff, even though crowds of people do. The way to life—to God!—is vigorous and re-quires total attention.

15-20 "Be wary of false preachers who smile a lot, dripping with practiced sincer-ity. Chances are they are out to rip you off some way or other. Don't be impressed with charisma; look for character. Who preachers *are* is the main thing, not what they say. A genuine leader will never exploit your emo-tions or your pocketbook. These diseased trees with their bad apples are going to be chopped down and burned.

21-23 "Knowing the correct password—saying 'Master, Master,' for instance—isn't going to get you anywhere with me. What is required is serious obedience—*doing* what my Father wills. I can see it now—at the Final Judgment thousands strutting up to me and saying, 'Master, we preached the Message, we bashed the demons, our super-spiritual projects had everyone talking.' And do you know what I am going to say? 'You missed the boat. All you did was use me to make your-selves important. You don't impress me one bit. You're out of here.'

24-25 "These words I speak to you are not incidental additions to your life, homeowner improvements to your standard of living. They are foundational words, words to build a life on. If you work these words into your life, you are like a smart carpenter who built his house on solid rock. Rain poured down, the river flooded, a tornado hit—but nothing moved that house. It was fixed to the rock.

26-27 "But if you just use my words in Bible studies and don't work them into your life, you are like a stupid carpenter who built his house on the sandy beach. When a storm rolled in and the waves came up, it collapsed like a house of cards."

28-29 When Jesus concluded his address, the crowd burst into applause. They had never heard teaching like this. It was apparent that he was living everything he was saying—quite a contrast to their religion teachers! This was the best teaching they had ever heard.

HE CARRIED OUR DISEASES

8 1-2 Jesus came down the mountain with the cheers of the crowd still ringing in his ears. Then a leper appeared and dropped to his knees before Jesus, praying, "Master, if you want to, you can heal my body."

3-4 Jesus reached out and touched him, saying, "I want to. Be clean." Then and there, all signs of the leprosy were gone. Jesus said, "Don't talk about this all over town. Just quietly present your healed body to the priest, along with the appropriate expressions of thanks to God. Your cleansed and grateful life, not your words, will bear witness to what I have done."

5-6 As Jesus entered the village of Capernaum, a Roman captain came up in a panic and said, "Master, my servant is sick. He can't walk. He's in terrible pain."

7 Jesus said, "I'll come and heal him."

8-9 "Oh, no," said the captain. "I don't want to put you to all that trouble. Just give the order and my servant will be fine. I'm a man who takes orders and gives orders. I tell one soldier, 'Go,' and he goes; to another, 'Come,' and he comes; to my slave, 'Do this,' and he does it."

10-12 Taken aback, Jesus said, "I've yet to come across this kind of simple trust in Israel, the very people who are supposed to know all about God and how he works. This man is the vanguard of many outsiders who will soon be coming from all directions—streaming in from the east, pouring in from the west, sitting down at God's kingdom banquet alongside Abraham, Isaac, and Jacob. Then those who grew up 'in the faith' but had no faith will find themselves out in the cold, outsiders to grace and wondering what happened."

13 Then Jesus turned to the captain and said, "Go. What you believed could happen has happened." At that moment his servant became well.

14-15 By this time they were in front of Peter's house. On entering, Jesus found Peter's mother-in-law sick in bed, burning up with fever. He touched her hand and the fever was gone. No sooner was she up on her feet than she was fixing dinner for him.

16-17 That evening a lot of demon-afflicted people were brought to him. He relieved the inwardly tormented. He cured the bodily ill. He fulfilled Isaiah's well-known revelation:

> He took our illnesses,
> He carried our diseases.

YOUR BUSINESS IS LIFE, NOT DEATH

18-19 When Jesus saw that a curious crowd was growing by the minute, he told his disciples to get him out of there to the other side of the lake. As they left, a religion scholar asked if he could go along. "I'll go with you, wherever," he said.

20 Jesus was curt: "Are you ready to rough it? We're not staying in the best inns, you know."

21 Another follower said, "Master, excuse me for a couple of days, please. I have my father's funeral to take care of."

22 Jesus refused. "First things first. Your business is life, not death. Follow me. Pursue life."

▲ ▲ ▲

23-25 Then he got in the boat, his disciples with him. The next thing they knew, they were in a severe storm. Waves were crashing into the boat—and he was sound asleep! They roused him, pleading, "Master, save us! We're going down!"

26 Jesus reprimanded them. "Why are you such cowards, such faint-hearts?" Then he stood up and told the wind to be silent, the sea to quiet down: "Silence!" The sea became smooth as glass.

27 The men rubbed their eyes, astonished. "What's going on here? Wind and sea stand up and take notice at his command!"

THE MADMEN AND THE PIGS

28-31 They landed in the country of the Gadarenes and were met by two madmen, victims of demons, coming out of the cemetery. The men had terrorized the region for so long that no one considered it safe to walk down that stretch of road anymore. Seeing Jesus, the madmen screamed out, "What business do you have giving us a hard time? You're the Son of God! You weren't supposed to show up here yet!" Off in the distance a herd of pigs was grazing and rooting. The evil spirits begged Jesus, "If you kick us out of these men, let us live in the pigs."

32-34 Jesus said, "Go ahead, but get out of here!" Crazed, the pigs stampeded over a cliff into the sea and drowned. Scared to death, the swineherds bolted. They told everyone back in town what had happened to the madmen and the pigs. Those who heard about it were angry about the drowned pigs. A mob formed and demanded that Jesus get out and not come back.

WHO NEEDS A DOCTOR?

9 1-3 Back in the boat, Jesus and the disciples recrossed the sea to Jesus' hometown. They were hardly out of the boat when some men carried a paraplegic on a stretcher and set him down in front of them. Jesus, impressed by their bold belief, said to the paraplegic, "Cheer up, son. I forgive your sins." Some religion scholars whispered, "Why, that's blasphemy!"

4-8 Jesus knew what they were thinking, and said, "Why this gossipy whispering? Which do you think is simpler: to say, 'I forgive your sins,' or, 'Get up and walk'? Well, just so it's clear that I'm the Son of Man and authorized to do either, or both. . . ." At this he turned to the paraplegic and said, "Get up. Take your bed and go home." And the man did it. The crowd was awestruck, amazed and pleased that God had authorized Jesus to work among them this way.

9 Passing along, Jesus saw a man at his work collecting taxes. His name was Matthew. Jesus said, "Come along with me." Matthew stood up and followed him.

10-11 Later when Jesus was eating supper at Matthew's house with his close followers, a lot of disreputable characters came and joined them. When the Pharisees saw him keeping this kind of company, they had a fit, and lit into Jesus' followers. "What kind of example is this from your Teacher, acting cozy with crooks and misfits?"

12-13 Jesus, overhearing, shot back, "Who needs a doctor: the healthy or the sick? Go figure out what this Scripture means: 'I'm after mercy, not religion.' I'm here to invite outsiders, not coddle insiders."

KINGDOM COME

14 A little later John's followers approached, asking, "Why is it that we and the Pharisees rigorously discipline body and spirit by fasting, but your followers don't?"

15 Jesus told them, "When you're celebrating a wedding, you don't skimp on the cake and wine. You feast. Later you may need to exercise moderation, but not now. No one throws cold water on a friendly bonfire. This is Kingdom Come!"

16-17 He went on, "No one cuts up a fine silk scarf to patch old work clothes; you want fabrics that match. And you don't put your wine in cracked bottles."

JUST A TOUCH

18-19 As he finished saying this, a local official appeared, bowed politely, and said, "My daughter has just now died. If you come and touch her, she will live." Jesus got up and went with him, his disciples following along.

20-22 Just then a woman who had hemorrhaged for twelve years slipped in from behind and lightly touched his robe. She was thinking to herself, "If I can just put a finger on his robe, I'll get well." Jesus turned—caught her at it. Then he reassured her: "Courage, daughter. You took a risk of faith, and now you're well." The woman was well from then on.

23-26 By now they had arrived at the house of the town official, and pushed their way through the gossips looking for a story and the neighbors bringing in casseroles. Jesus was abrupt: "Clear out! This girl isn't dead. She's sleeping." They told him he didn't know what he was talking about. But when Jesus had gotten rid of the crowd, he went in, took the girl's hand, and pulled her to her feet—alive. The news was soon out, and traveled throughout the region.

BECOME WHAT YOU BELIEVE

27-28 As Jesus left the house, he was followed by two blind men crying out, "Mercy, Son of David! Mercy on us!" When Jesus got home, the blind men went in with him. Jesus said to them, "Do you really believe I can do this?" They said, "Why, yes, Master!"

29-31 He touched their eyes and said, "Become what you believe." It happened. They saw. Then Jesus became very stern. "Don't let a soul know how this happened." But they were hardly out the door before they started blabbing it to everyone they met.

32-33 Right after that, as the blind men were leaving, a man who had been struck speechless by an evil spirit was brought to Jesus. As soon as Jesus threw the evil tormenting spirit out, the man talked away just as if he'd been talking all his life. The people were up on their feet applauding: "There's never been anything like this in Israel!"

34 The Pharisees were left sputtering, "Smoke and mirrors. It's nothing but smoke and mirrors. He's probably made a pact with the Devil."

35-38 Then Jesus made a circuit of all the towns and villages. He taught in their meeting places, reported kingdom news, and healed their diseased bodies, healed their bruised and hurt lives. When he looked out over the crowds, his heart broke. So confused and aimless they were, like sheep with no shepherd. "What a huge harvest!" he said to his disciples. "How few workers! On your knees and pray for harvest hands!"

THE TWELVE HARVEST HANDS

10 1-4 The prayer was no sooner prayed than it was answered. Jesus called twelve of his followers and sent them into the ripe fields. He gave them power to kick out the evil spirits and to tenderly care for the bruised and hurt lives. This is the list of the twelve he sent:

Simon (they called him Peter, or "Rock"),
Andrew, his brother,
James, Zebedee's son,
John, his brother,
Philip,
Bartholomew,
Thomas,
Matthew, the tax man,
James, son of Alphaeus,
Thaddaeus,
Simon, the Canaanite,
Judas Iscariot (who later turned on him).

5-8 Jesus sent his twelve harvest hands out with this charge:

"Don't begin by traveling to some far-off place to convert unbelievers. And don't try to be dramatic by tackling some public enemy.

Go to the lost, confused people right here in the neighborhood. Tell them that the kingdom is here. Bring health to the sick. Raise the dead. Touch the untouchables. Kick out the demons. You have been treated generously, so live generously.

9-10 "Don't think you have to put on a fund-raising campaign before you start. You don't need a lot of equipment. *You* are the equipment, and all you need to keep that going is three meals a day. Travel light.

11 "When you enter a town or village, don't insist on staying in a luxury inn. Get a modest place with some modest people, and be content there until you leave.

12-15 "When you knock on a door, be courteous in your greeting. If they welcome you, be gentle in your conversation. If they don't welcome you, quietly withdraw. Don't make a scene. Shrug your shoulders and be on your way. You can be sure that on Judgment Day they'll be mighty sorry—but it's no concern of yours now.

16 "Stay alert. This is hazardous work I'm assigning you. You're going to be like sheep running through a wolf pack, so don't call attention to yourselves. Be as shrewd as a snake, inoffensive as a dove.

17-20 "Don't be naive. Some people will question your motives, others will smear your reputation—just because you believe in me. Don't be upset when they haul you before the civil authorities. Without knowing it, they've done you—and me—a favor, given you a platform for preaching the kingdom news! And don't worry about what you'll say or how you'll say it. The right words will be there; the Spirit of your Father will supply the words.

21-23 "When people realize it is the living God you are presenting and not some idol that makes them feel good, they are going to turn on you, even people in your own family. There is a great irony here: proclaiming so much love, experiencing so much hate! But don't quit. Don't cave in. It is all well worth it in the end. It is not success you are after in such times but survival. Be survivors! Before you've run out of options, the Son of Man will have arrived.

24-25 "A student doesn't get a better desk than her teacher. A laborer doesn't make more money than his boss. Be content—pleased, even—when you, my students, my harvest hands, get the same treatment I get. If they call me, the Master, 'Dungface,' what can the workers expect?

26-27 "Don't be intimidated. Eventually everything is going to be out in the open, and everyone will know how things really are. So don't hesitate to go public now.

28 "Don't be bluffed into silence by the threats of bullies. There's nothing they can do to your soul, your core being. Save your fear for God, who holds your entire life—body and soul—in his hands.

FORGET ABOUT YOURSELF

29-31 "What's the price of a pet canary? Some loose change, right? And God cares what happens to it even more than you do. He pays even greater attention to you, down to the last detail—even numbering the hairs on your head! So don't be intimidated by all this bully talk. You're worth more than a million canaries.

32-33 "Stand up for me against world opinion and I'll stand up for you before my Father in heaven. If you turn tail and run, do you think I'll cover for you?

34-37 "Don't think I've come to make life cozy. I've come to cut—make a sharp knife-cut between son and father, daughter and mother, bride and mother-in-law—cut through these cozy domestic arrangements and free you for God. Well-meaning family members can be your worst enemies. If you prefer father or mother over me, you don't deserve me. If you prefer son or daughter over me, you don't deserve me.

38-39 "If you don't go all the way with me, through thick and thin, you don't deserve me. If your first concern is to look after yourself, you'll never find yourself. But if you forget about yourself and look to me, you'll find both yourself and me.

40-42 "We are intimately linked in this harvest work. Anyone who accepts what you do, accepts me, the One who sent you. Anyone who accepts what I do accepts my Father, who sent me. Accepting a messenger of God is as good as being God's messenger. Accepting someone's help is as good as giving someone help. This is a large work I've called you into, but don't be overwhelmed by it. It's best to start small. Give a cool cup of water to someone who is thirsty, for instance. The smallest act of giving or receiving makes you a true apprentice. You won't lose out on a thing."

JOHN THE BAPTIZER

11 1 When Jesus finished placing this charge before his twelve disciples, he went on to teach and preach in their villages.

2-3 John, meanwhile, had been locked up in prison. When he got wind of what Jesus was doing, he sent his own disciples to ask, "Are you the One we've been expecting, or are we still waiting?"

4-6 Jesus told them, "Go back and tell John what's going on:

> The blind see,
> The lame walk,
> Lepers are cleansed,
> The deaf hear,
> The dead are raised,
> The wretched of the earth learn that God is on their side.

"Is this what you were expecting? Then count yourselves most blessed!"

7-10 When John's disciples left to report, Jesus started talking to the crowd about John. "What did you expect when you went out to see him in the wild? A weekend camper? Hardly. What then? A sheik in silk pajamas? Not in the wilderness, not by a long shot. What then? A prophet? That's right, a prophet! Probably the best prophet you'll ever hear. He is the prophet that Malachi announced when he wrote, 'I'm sending my prophet ahead of you, to make the road smooth for you.'

11-14 "Let me tell you what's going on here: No one in history surpasses John the Baptizer; but in the kingdom he prepared you for, the lowliest person is ahead of him. For a long time now people have tried to force themselves into God's kingdom. But if you read the books of the Prophets and God's Law closely, you will see them culminate in John, teaming up with him in preparing the way for the Messiah of the kingdom. Looked at in this way, John is the 'Elijah' you've all been expecting to arrive and introduce the Messiah.

15 "Are you listening to me? Really listening?

16-19 "How can I account for this generation? The people have been like spoiled children whining to their parents, 'We wanted to skip rope, and you were always too tired; we wanted to talk, but you were always too busy.' John came fasting and they called him crazy. I came feasting and they called me a boozer, a friend of the misfits. Opinion polls don't count for much, do they? The proof of the pudding is in the eating."

THE UNFORCED RHYTHMS OF GRACE

20 Next Jesus unleashed on the cities where he had worked the hardest but whose people had responded the least, shrugging their shoulders and going their own way.

21-24 "Doom to you, Chorazin! Doom, Bethsaida! If Tyre and Sidon had seen half of the powerful miracles you have seen, they would have been on their knees in a minute. At Judgment Day they'll get off easy compared to you. And Capernaum! With all your peacock strutting, you are going to end up in the abyss. If the people of Sodom had had your chances, the city would still be around. At Judgment Day they'll get off easy compared to you."

25-26 Abruptly Jesus broke into prayer: "Thank you, Father, Lord of heaven and earth. You've concealed your ways from sophisticates and know-it-alls, but spelled them out clearly to ordinary people. Yes, Father, that's the way you like to work."

27 Jesus resumed talking to the people, but now tenderly. "The Father has given me all these things to do and say. This is a unique Father-Son operation, coming out of Father and Son intimacies and knowledge. No one knows the Son the way the Father does, nor the Father the way the Son does. But I'm not keeping it to myself; I'm ready to go over it line by line with anyone willing to listen.

28-30 "Are you tired? Worn out? Burned out on religion? Come to me. Get away with me and you'll recover your life. I'll show you how to take a real rest. Walk with me and work with me—watch how I do it. Learn the unforced rhythms of grace. I won't lay anything heavy or ill-fitting on you. Keep company with me and you'll learn to live freely and lightly."

IN CHARGE OF THE SABBATH

12

1-2 One Sabbath, Jesus was strolling with his disciples through a field of ripe grain. Hungry, the disciples were pulling off the heads of grain and munching on them. Some Pharisees reported them to Jesus: "Your disciples are breaking the Sabbath rules!"

3-5 Jesus said, "Really? Didn't you ever read what David and his companions did when they were hungry, how they entered the sanctuary and ate fresh bread off the altar, bread that no one but priests were allowed to eat? And didn't you ever read in God's Law that priests carrying out their Temple duties break Sabbath rules all the time and it's not held against them?

6-8 "There is far more at stake here than religion. If you had any idea what this Scripture meant—'I prefer a flexible heart to

MARY

It couldn't have been easy being Jesus' mother. His conception seemed scandalous; his birth, difficult. When Jesus was eight days old, a prophet warned Mary that she would feel "the pain of a sword-thrust" because of him (Luke 2:35). Soon she and Joseph fled to Egypt to save their baby from the murderous Herod.

Jesus always had a mind of his own. At twelve he disappeared for three days, scaring her half to death.

When he became an adult, things got worse. She'd heard the hostile talk. The religious leaders resented him, and the Romans eyed the crowds he drew. Mary wanted him safe at home. Besides, she expected her eldest son to take more responsibility for the family. So she brought his brothers to help persuade him. When a disciple interrupted Jesus to say that his family was outside, Jesus replied, "Obedience is thicker than blood. The person who obeys my heavenly Father's will is my brother and sister and mother" (Matthew 12:50).

We're not told what happened next. I assume Jesus did talk with his mother; I also assume he did not go home.

I wonder about the things Mary remembered, the things she held dear deep within herself. Ever since the angel's announcement at conception, ever since she'd declared the Magnificat to her cousin, this woman had been blessed—and burdened.

Later, Mary would watch as her firstborn was crucified. From the cross, Jesus would ask John to take care of her. Mary's son would love her to the end—and she'd know it.

What must it have been like being the mother of God?

an inflexible ritual'—you wouldn't be nitpicking like this. The Son of Man is no yes-man to the Sabbath; he's in charge."

9-10 When Jesus left the field, he entered their meeting place. There was a man there with a crippled hand. They said to Jesus, "Is it legal to heal on the Sabbath?" They were baiting him.

11-14 He replied, "Is there a person here who, finding one of your lambs fallen into a ravine, wouldn't, even though it was a Sabbath, pull it out? Surely kindness to people is as legal as kindness to animals!" Then he said to the man, "Hold out your hand." He held it out and it was healed. The Pharisees walked out furious, sputtering about how they were going to ruin Jesus.

IN CHARGE OF EVERYTHING

15-21 Jesus, knowing they were out to get him, moved on. A lot of people followed him, and he healed them all. He also cautioned them to keep it quiet, following guidelines set down by Isaiah:

Look well at my handpicked servant;
I love him so much, take such delight in him.
I've placed my Spirit on him;
he'll decree justice to the nations.
But he won't yell, won't raise his voice;
there'll be no commotion in the streets.
He won't walk over anyone's feelings,
won't push you into a corner.
Before you know it, his justice will triumph;
the mere sound of his name will signal hope, even
among far-off unbelievers.

NO NEUTRAL GROUND

22-23 Next a poor demon-afflicted wretch, both blind and deaf, was set down before him. Jesus healed him, gave him his sight and hearing. The people who saw it were impressed—"This has to be the Son of David!"

24 But the Pharisees, when they heard the report, were cynical. "Black magic," they said. "Some devil trick he's pulled from his sleeve."

25-27 Jesus confronted their slander. "A judge who gives opposite verdicts on the same person cancels himself out; a family that's in a constant squabble disintegrates; if Satan banishes Satan, is there any Satan left? If you're slinging devil mud at me, calling me a devil kicking out devils, doesn't the same mud stick to your own exorcists?

28-29 "But if it's by *God's* power that I am sending the evil spirits packing, then God's kingdom is here for sure. How in the world do you think it's possible in broad daylight to enter the house of an awake, able-bodied man and walk off with his possessions unless you tie him up first? Tie him up, though, and you can clean him out.

30 "This is war, and there is no neutral ground. If you're not on my side, you're the enemy; if you're not helping, you're making things worse.

31-32 "There's nothing done or said that can't be forgiven. But if you deliberately persist in your slanders against God's Spirit, you are repudiating the very One who forgives. If you reject the Son of Man out of some misunderstanding, the Holy Spirit can forgive you, but when you reject the Holy Spirit, you're sawing off the branch on which you're sitting, severing by your own perversity all connection with the One who forgives.

33 "If you grow a healthy tree, you'll pick healthy fruit. If you grow a diseased tree, you'll pick worm-eaten fruit. The fruit tells you about the tree.

34-37 "You have minds like a snake pit! How do you suppose what you say is worth anything when you are so foul-minded? It's your heart, not the dictionary, that gives meaning to your words. A good person produces good deeds and words season after season. An evil person is a blight on the orchard. Let me tell you something: Every one of these careless words is going to come back to haunt you. There will be a time of Reckoning. Words are powerful; take them seriously. Words can be your salvation. Words can also be your damnation."

JONAH-EVIDENCE

38 Later a few religion scholars and Pharisees cornered him. "Teacher, we want to see your credentials. Give us some hard evidence that God is in this. How about a miracle?"

39-40 Jesus said, "You're looking for proof, but you're looking for the wrong kind. All you want is something to titillate your curiosity, satisfy your lust for miracles. The only proof you're going to get is what looks like the absence of proof: Jonah-evidence. Like Jonah, three days and nights in the fish's belly, the Son of Man will be gone three days and nights in a deep grave.

41-42 "On Judgment Day, the Ninevites will stand up and give evidence that will condemn this generation, because when Jonah preached to them they changed their lives. A far greater preacher than Jonah is here, and you squabble about 'proofs.' On Judgment Day, the Queen of Sheba will come forward and bring evidence that will condemn this generation, because she traveled from a far corner of the earth to listen to wise Solomon. Wisdom far greater than Solomon's is right in front of you, and you quibble over 'evidence.'

43-45 "When a defiling evil spirit is expelled from someone, it drifts along through the desert looking for an oasis, some unsuspecting soul it can bedevil. When it doesn't find anyone, it says, 'I'll go back to my old haunt.' On return it finds the person spotlessly clean, but vacant. It then runs out and rounds up seven other spirits more evil than itself and they all move in, whooping it up. That person ends up far worse off than if he'd never gotten cleaned up in the first place.

"That's what this generation is like: You may think you have cleaned out the junk from your lives and gotten ready for God, but you weren't hospitable to my kingdom message, and now all the devils are moving back in."

OBEDIENCE IS THICKER THAN BLOOD

46-47 While he was still talking to the crowd, his mother and brothers showed up. They were outside trying to get a message to him. Someone told Jesus, "Your mother and brothers are out here, wanting to speak with you."

48-50 Jesus didn't respond directly, but said, "Who do you think my mother and brothers are?" He then stretched out his hand toward his disciples. "Look closely. These are my mother and brothers. Obedience is thicker than blood. The person who obeys my heavenly Father's will is my brother and sister and mother."

A HARVEST STORY

13 1-3 At about that same time Jesus left the house and sat on the beach. In no time at all a crowd gathered along the shoreline, forcing him to get into a boat. Using the boat as a pulpit, he addressed his congregation, telling stories.

3-8 "What do you make of this? A farmer planted seed. As he scattered the seed, some of it fell on the road, and birds ate it. Some fell in the gravel; it sprouted quickly but didn't put down roots, so when the sun came up it withered just as quickly. Some fell in the weeds; as it came up, it was strangled by the weeds. Some fell on good earth, and produced a harvest beyond his wildest dreams.

9 "Are you listening to this? Really listening?"

WHY TELL STORIES?

10 The disciples came up and asked, "Why do you tell stories?"

11-15 He replied, "You've been given insight into God's kingdom. You know how it works. Not everybody has this gift, this insight; it hasn't been given to them. Whenever someone has a ready heart for this, the insights and understandings flow freely. But if there is no readiness, any trace of receptivity soon disappears. That's why I tell stories: to create readiness, to nudge the people toward a welcome awakening. In their present state they can stare till doomsday and not see it, listen till they're blue in the face and not get it. I don't want Isaiah's forecast repeated all over again:

Your ears are open but you don't hear
a thing.
Your eyes are awake but you don't
see a thing.
The people are stupid!
They stick their fingers in their ears
so they won't have to listen;
They screw their eyes shut
so they won't have to look,
so they won't have to deal with me
face-to-face
and let me heal them.

16-17 "But you have God-blessed eyes—eyes that see! And God-blessed ears—ears that hear! A lot of people, prophets and humble believers among them, would have given anything to see what you are seeing, to hear what you are hearing, but never had the chance.

THE MEANING OF THE HARVEST STORY

18-19 "Study this story of the farmer planting seed. When anyone hears news of the kingdom and doesn't take it in, it just remains on the surface, and so the Evil One comes along and plucks it right out of that person's heart. This is the seed the farmer scatters on the road.

20-21 "The seed cast in the gravel—this is the person who hears and instantly responds with enthusiasm. But there is no soil of character, and so when the emotions wear off and

Metaphors and Parables

Throughout Matthew's Gospel, Jesus is always teaching. Wherever he went—synagogues, hillsides, boats on the shoreline—Jesus gave classes, and "God's kingdom was his theme" (Matthew 4:23). His lessons explained the good news that God's heavenly government is setting the world right, bringing about God's righteous, peaceful, and joy-filled purposes for creation.

If you were a student in the crowd, notebook in hand, pen poised to capture important insights into the mind and mission of God, you might wonder what to write down. Jesus didn't recite important facts, give definitions for difficult concepts, or walk through the premises and conclusions of logical arguments. Instead, he asked people to picture things they knew well—and then he drew comparisons. Jesus told stories. Sometimes it seemed that "all Jesus did . . . was tell stories" (Matthew 13:34).

Cognitive scientists tell us that one of the ways our brains make sense of the world is through metaphors. Metaphors take abstract ideas that are hard to explain and connect them to things in our daily human experience. Jesus was a master of metaphors. He used a picture or story that was familiar and easy to understand and then invited his listeners to connect it with something abstract—forgiveness, righteousness, or the kingdom of God.

Jesus' metaphors and parables didn't always make the truth very explicit. He trusted us to draw on our own experiences and imagine the meaning embedded between his word pictures and spiritual truths. When we use our imaginations, we find scenes we have lived in and things we have seen, held, and tasted: salt and yeast, lamps and light, gates and paths, trees and fruit, seeds and soil, wheat and weeds, trash and treasures, birds and flowers. Each of these connects powerfully and immediately to our own memories, feelings, and experiences.

We see something. We feel something. In Jesus' classroom, our lived experience as ordinary women is enough; our imaginations provide the links to God's truth.

John 1:14 tells us, "The Word became flesh and blood, and moved into the neighborhood." Jesus knew how to make spiritual truth come alive in human imaginations because Jesus *had become one of us*. Jesus had a human body and lived a regular life. He felt the same range of emotions we feel, and his senses responded to the world the way our senses do. He walked and napped and went to parties. He cooked and cleaned and got hungry and tired.

The images and stories Jesus chose to show us the kingdom of God with are powerful because he shares our humanity. And we respond to Jesus' teaching like those first-century students in the synagogues, on the hillsides, and along the shores: "They had never heard teaching like this. It was apparent that he was living everything he was saying. . . . This was the best teaching they had ever heard" (Matthew 7:28-29).

some difficulty arrives, there is nothing to show for it.

22 "The seed cast in the weeds is the person who hears the kingdom news, but weeds of worry and illusions about getting more and wanting everything under the sun strangle what was heard, and nothing comes of it.

23 "The seed cast on good earth is the person who hears and takes in the News, and then produces a harvest beyond his wildest dreams."

▲ ▲ ▲

24-26 He told another story. "God's kingdom is like a farmer who planted good seed in his field. That night, while his hired men were asleep, his enemy sowed thistles all through the wheat and slipped away before dawn. When the first green shoots appeared and the grain began to form, the thistles showed up, too.

27 "The farmhands came to the farmer and said, 'Master, that was clean seed you planted, wasn't it? Where did these thistles come from?'

28 "He answered, 'Some enemy did this.'

"The farmhands asked, 'Should we weed out the thistles?'

29-30 "He said, 'No, if you weed the thistles, you'll pull up the wheat, too. Let them grow together until harvest time. Then I'll instruct the harvesters to pull up the thistles and tie them in bundles for the fire, then gather the wheat and put it in the barn.'"

31-32 Another story. "God's kingdom is like an acorn that a farmer plants. It is quite small as seeds go, but in the course of years it grows into a huge oak tree, and eagles build nests in it."

33 Another story. "God's kingdom is like yeast that a woman works into the dough for dozens of loaves of barley bread—and waits while the dough rises."

34-35 All Jesus did that day was tell stories—a long storytelling afternoon. His storytelling fulfilled the prophecy:

I will open my mouth and tell stories;
I will bring out into the open
things hidden since the world's
first day.

THE CURTAIN OF HISTORY

36 Jesus dismissed the congregation and went into the house. His disciples came in and said, "Explain to us that story of the thistles in the field."

37-39 So he explained. "The farmer who sows the pure seed is the Son of Man. The field is the world, the pure seeds are subjects of the kingdom, the thistles are subjects of the Devil, and the enemy who sows them is the Devil. The harvest is the end of the age, the curtain of history. The harvest hands are angels.

40-43 "The picture of thistles pulled up and burned is a scene from the final act. The Son of Man will send his angels, weed out the thistles from his kingdom, pitch them in the trash, and be done with them. They are going to complain to high heaven, but nobody is going to listen. At the same time, ripe, holy lives will mature and adorn the kingdom of their Father.

"Are you listening to this? Really listening?

44 "God's kingdom is like a treasure hidden in a field for years and then accidentally found by a trespasser. The finder is ecstatic—what a find!—and proceeds to sell everything he owns to raise money and buy that field.

45-46 "Or, God's kingdom is like a jewel merchant on the hunt for exquisite pearls. Finding one that is flawless, he immediately sells everything and buys it.

47-50 "Or, God's kingdom is like a fishnet cast into the sea, catching all kinds of fish. When it is full, it is hauled onto the beach. The good fish are picked out and put in a tub; those unfit to eat are thrown away. That's how it will be when the curtain comes down on history. The angels will come and cull the bad fish and throw them in the garbage. There will be a lot of desperate complaining, but it won't do any good."

51 Jesus asked, "Are you starting to get a handle on all this?"

They answered, "Yes."

52 He said, "Then you see how every student well-trained in God's kingdom is like the owner of a general store who can put his hands on anything you need, old or new, exactly when you need it."

53-57 When Jesus finished telling these stories, he left there, returned to his hometown, and gave a lecture in the meetinghouse. He stole the show, impressing everyone. "We had no idea he was this good!" they said. "How did he get so wise, get such ability?" But in the next breath they were cutting him down: "We've known him since he was a kid; he's the carpenter's son. We know his mother, Mary. We know his brothers James and Joseph, Simon and Judas. All his sisters live here. Who does he think he is?" They got all bent out of shape.

58 But Jesus said, "A prophet is taken for granted in his hometown and his family." He didn't do many miracles there because of their hostile indifference.

THE DEATH OF JOHN

14 1-2 At about this time, Herod, the regional ruler, heard what was being said about Jesus. He said to his servants, "This has to be John the Baptizer come back from the dead. That's why he's able to work miracles!"

3-5 Herod had arrested John, put him in chains, and sent him to prison to placate Herodias, his brother Philip's wife. John had provoked Herod by naming his relationship with Herodias "adultery." Herod wanted to kill him, but he was afraid because so many people revered John as a prophet of God.

6-12 But at his birthday celebration, he got his chance. Herodias's daughter provided the entertainment, dancing for the guests. She swept Herod away. In his drunken enthusiasm, he promised her on oath anything she wanted. Already coached by her mother, she was ready: "Give me, served up on a platter, the head of John the Baptizer." That sobered the king up fast. Unwilling to lose face with his guests, he did it—ordered John's head cut off and presented to the girl on a platter. She in turn gave it to her mother. Later, John's disciples got the body, gave it a reverent burial, and reported to Jesus.

SUPPER FOR FIVE THOUSAND

13-14 When Jesus got the news, he slipped away by boat to an out-of-the-way place by himself. But unsuccessfully—someone saw him and the word got around. Soon a lot of people from the nearby villages walked around the lake to where he was. When he saw them coming, he was overcome with pity and healed their sick.

15 Toward evening the disciples approached him. "We're out in the country and it's getting late. Dismiss the people so they can go to the villages and get some supper."

16 But Jesus said, "There is no need to dismiss them. You give them supper."

17 "All we have are five loaves of bread and two fish," they said.

18-21 Jesus said, "Bring them here." Then he had the people sit on the grass. He took the five loaves and two fish, lifted his face to heaven in prayer, blessed, broke, and gave the bread to the disciples. The disciples then gave the food to the congregation. They all ate their fill. They gathered twelve baskets of leftovers. About five thousand were fed.

WALKING ON THE WATER

22-23 As soon as the meal was finished, he insisted that the disciples get in the boat and go on ahead to the other side while he dismissed the people. With the crowd dispersed, he climbed the mountain so he could be by himself and pray. He stayed there alone, late into the night.

24-26 Meanwhile, the boat was far out to sea when the wind came up against them and they were battered by the waves. At about four o'clock in the morning, Jesus came toward them walking on the water. They were scared to death. "A ghost!" they said, crying out in terror.

27 But Jesus was quick to comfort them. "Courage, it's me. Don't be afraid."

28 Peter, suddenly bold, said, "Master, if it's really you, call me to come to you on the water."

29-30 He said, "Come ahead."

Jumping out of the boat, Peter walked on the water to Jesus. But when he looked down at the waves churning beneath his feet, he lost his nerve and started to sink. He cried, "Master, save me!"

31 Jesus didn't hesitate. He reached down and grabbed his hand. Then he said, "Faint-heart, what got into you?"

32-33 The two of them climbed into the boat, and the wind died down. The disciples in the boat, having watched the whole thing, worshiped Jesus, saying, "This is it! You are God's Son for sure!"

34-36 On return, they beached the boat at Gennesaret. When the people got wind that he was back, they sent out word through the neighborhood and rounded up all the sick, who asked for permission to touch the edge of his coat. And whoever touched him was healed.

WHAT POLLUTES YOUR LIFE

15 1-2 After that, Pharisees and religion scholars came to Jesus all the way from Jerusalem, criticizing, "Why do your disciples play fast and loose with the rules?"

3-9 But Jesus put it right back on them. "Why do you use your rules to play fast and loose with God's commands? God clearly says, 'Respect your father and mother,' and, 'Anyone denouncing father or mother should be killed.' But you weasel around that by saying, 'Whoever wants to, can say to father and mother, What I owed to you I've given to God.' That can hardly be called respecting a parent. You cancel God's command by your rules. Frauds! Isaiah's prophecy of you hit the bull's-eye:

These people make a big show of saying
the right thing,
but their heart isn't in it.
They act like they're worshiping me,
but they don't mean it.
They just use me as a cover
for teaching whatever suits their fancy."

10-11 He then called the crowd together and said, "Listen, and take this to heart. It's not what you swallow that pollutes your life, but what you vomit up."

12 Later his disciples came and told him, "Did you know how upset the Pharisees were when they heard what you said?"

13-14 Jesus shrugged it off. "Every tree that wasn't planted by my Father in heaven will be pulled up by its roots. Forget them. They are blind men leading blind men. When a blind man leads a blind man, they both end up in the ditch."

15 Peter said, "I don't get it. Put it in plain language."

16-20 Jesus replied, "You, too? Are you being willfully stupid? Don't you know that anything that is swallowed works its way through the intestines and is finally defecated? But what comes out of the mouth gets its start in the heart. It's from the heart that we vomit up evil arguments, murders, adulteries, fornications, thefts, lies, and cussing. That's what pollutes. Eating or not eating certain foods, washing or not washing your hands—that's neither here nor there."

HEALING THE PEOPLE

21-22 From there Jesus took a trip to Tyre and Sidon. They had hardly arrived when a Canaanite woman came down from the hills and pleaded, "Mercy, Master, Son of David! My daughter is cruelly afflicted by an evil spirit."

23 Jesus ignored her. The disciples came and complained, "Now she's bothering us. Would you please take care of her? She's driving us crazy."

24 Jesus refused, telling them, "I've got my hands full dealing with the lost sheep of Israel."

25 Then the woman came back to Jesus, dropped to her knees, and begged. "Master, help me."

26 He said, "It's not right to take bread out of children's mouths and throw it to dogs."

27 She was quick: "You're right, Master, but beggar dogs do get scraps from the master's table."

28 Jesus gave in. "Oh, woman, your faith is something else. What you want is what you get!" Right then her daughter became well.

29-31 After Jesus returned, he walked along Lake Galilee and then climbed a mountain and took his place, ready to receive visitors. They came, tons of them, bringing along the paraplegic, the blind, the maimed, the mute—all sorts of people in need—and more or less threw them down at Jesus' feet to see what he would do with them. He healed them. When the people saw the mutes speaking, the maimed healthy, the paraplegics walking around, the blind looking around, they were astonished and let everyone know that God was blazingly alive among them.

▲ ▲ ▲

32 But Jesus wasn't finished with them. He called his disciples and said, "I hurt for these people. For three days now they've been with me, and now they have nothing to eat. I can't send them away without a meal—they'd probably collapse on the road."

33 His disciples said, "But where in this deserted place are you going to dig up enough food for a meal?"

34-39 Jesus asked, "How much bread do you have?"

"Seven loaves," they said, "plus a few fish." At that, Jesus directed the people to sit down. He took the seven loaves and the fish. After giving thanks, he divided it up and gave it to the people. Everyone ate. They had all they wanted. It took seven large baskets to collect the leftovers. Over four thousand people ate their fill at that meal. After Jesus sent them away, he climbed in the boat and crossed over to the Magadan hills.

SOME BAD YEAST

16 1-4 Some Pharisees and Sadducees badgered him again, pressing him to prove himself to them. He told them, "You have a saying that goes, 'Red sky at night, sailor's delight; red sky at morning, sailors take warning.' You find it easy enough to forecast the weather—why can't you read the signs of the times? An evil and wanton generation is always wanting signs

and wonders. The only sign you'll get is the Jonah sign." Then he spun around and walked away.

5-6 On their way to the other side of the lake, the disciples discovered they had forgotten to bring along bread. In the meantime, Jesus said to them, "Keep a sharp eye out for Pharisee-Sadducee yeast."

7-12 Thinking he was scolding them for forgetting bread, they discussed in whispers what to do. Jesus knew what they were doing and said, "Why all these worried whispers about forgetting the bread? Baby believers! Haven't you caught on yet? Don't you remember the five loaves of bread and the five thousand people, and how many baskets of fragments you picked up? Or the seven loaves that fed four thousand, and how many baskets of leftovers you collected? Haven't you realized yet that bread isn't the problem? The problem is yeast, Pharisee-Sadducee yeast." Then they got it: that he wasn't concerned about eating, but teaching—the Pharisee-Sadducee kind of teaching.

SON OF MAN, SON OF GOD

13 When Jesus arrived in the villages of Caesarea Philippi, he asked his disciples, "What are people saying about who the Son of Man is?"

14 They replied, "Some think he is John the Baptizer, some say Elijah, some Jeremiah or one of the other prophets."

15 He pressed them, "And how about you? Who do you say I am?"

16 Simon Peter said, "You're the Christ, the Messiah, the Son of the living God."

17-18 Jesus came back, "God bless you, Simon, son of Jonah! You didn't get that answer out of books or from teachers. My Father in heaven, God himself, let you in on this secret of who I really am. And now I'm going to tell you who you are, *really* are. You are Peter, a rock. This is the rock on which I will put together my church, a church so expansive with energy that not even the gates of hell will be able to keep it out.

19 "And that's not all. You will have complete and free access to God's kingdom, keys to open any and every door: no more barriers between heaven and earth, earth and heaven. A yes on earth is yes in heaven. A no on earth is no in heaven."

20 He swore the disciples to secrecy. He made them promise they would tell no one that he was the Messiah.

YOU'RE NOT IN THE DRIVER'S SEAT

21-22 Then Jesus made it clear to his disciples that it was now necessary for him to go to Jerusalem, submit to an ordeal of suffering at the hands of the religious leaders, be killed, and then on the third day be raised up alive. Peter took him in hand, protesting, "Impossible, Master! That can never be!"

23 But Jesus didn't swerve. "Peter, get out of my way. Satan, get lost. You have no idea how God works."

24-26 Then Jesus went to work on his disciples. "Anyone who intends to come with me has to let me lead. You're not in the driver's seat; *I* am. Don't run from suffering; embrace it. Follow me and I'll show you how. Self-help is no help at all. Self-sacrifice is the way, my way, to finding yourself, your true self. What kind of deal is it to get everything you want but lose yourself? What could you ever trade your soul for?

27-28 "Don't be in such a hurry to go into business for yourself. Before you know it the Son of Man will arrive with all the splendor of his Father, accompanied by an army of angels. You'll get everything you have coming to you, a personal gift. This isn't pie in the sky by and by. Some of you standing here are going to see it take place, see the Son of Man in kingdom glory."

SUNLIGHT POURED FROM HIS FACE

17 1-3 Six days later, three of them saw that glory. Jesus took Peter and the brothers, James and John, and led them up a high mountain. His appearance changed from the inside out, right before their eyes. Sunlight poured from his face. His clothes were filled with light. Then they realized that Moses and Elijah were also there in deep conversation with him.

4 Peter broke in, "Master, this is a great moment! What would you think if I built three memorials here on the mountain—one for you, one for Moses, one for Elijah?"

5 While he was going on like this, babbling, a light-radiant cloud enveloped them, and sounding from deep in the cloud a voice: "This is my Son, marked by my love, focus of my delight. Listen to him."

6-8 When the disciples heard it, they fell flat on their faces, scared to death. But Jesus came over and touched them. "Don't be afraid." When they opened their eyes and looked around all they saw was Jesus, only Jesus.

9 Coming down the mountain, Jesus swore

them to secrecy. "Don't breathe a word of what you've seen. After the Son of Man is raised from the dead, you are free to talk."

10 The disciples, meanwhile, were asking questions. "Why do the religion scholars say that Elijah has to come first?"

11-13 Jesus answered, "Elijah does come and get everything ready. I'm telling you, Elijah has already come but they didn't know him when they saw him. They treated him like dirt, the same way they are about to treat the Son of Man." That's when the disciples realized that all along he had been talking about John the Baptizer.

WITH A MERE KERNEL OF FAITH

14-16 At the bottom of the mountain, they were met by a crowd of waiting people. As they approached, a man came out of the crowd and fell to his knees begging, "Master, have mercy on my son. He goes out of his mind and suffers terribly, falling into seizures. Frequently he is pitched into the fire, other times into the river. I brought him to your disciples, but they could do nothing for him."

17-18 Jesus said, "What a generation! No sense of God! No focus to your lives! How many times do I have to go over these things? How much longer do I have to put up with this? Bring the boy here." He ordered the afflicting demon out—and it was out, gone. From that moment on the boy was well.

19 When the disciples had Jesus off to themselves, they asked, "Why couldn't we throw it out?"

20 "Because you're not yet taking *God* seriously," said Jesus. "The simple truth is that if you had a mere kernel of faith, a poppy seed, say, you would tell this mountain, 'Move!' and it would move. There is nothing you wouldn't be able to tackle."

22-23 As they were regrouping in Galilee, Jesus told them, "The Son of Man is about to be betrayed to some people who want nothing to do with God. They will murder him—and three days later he will be raised alive." The disciples felt scared to death.

▲ ▲ ▲

24 When they arrived at Capernaum, the tax men came to Peter and asked, "Does your teacher pay taxes?"

25 Peter said, "Of course."

But as soon as they were in the house, Jesus confronted him. "Simon, what do you think? When a king levies taxes, who pays—his children or his subjects?"

26-27 He answered, "His subjects."

Jesus said, "Then the children get off free, right? But so we don't upset them needlessly, go down to the lake, cast a hook, and pull in the first fish that bites. Open its mouth and you'll find a coin. Take it and give it to the tax men. It will be enough for both of us."

WHOEVER BECOMES SIMPLE AGAIN

18

1 At about the same time, the disciples came to Jesus asking, "Who gets the highest rank in God's kingdom?"

2-5 For an answer Jesus called over a child, whom he stood in the middle of the room, and said, "I'm telling you, once and for all, that unless you return to square one and start over like children, you're not even going to get a look at the kingdom, let alone get in. Whoever becomes simple and elemental again, like this child, will rank high in God's kingdom. What's more, when you receive the childlike on my account, it's the same as receiving me.

6-7 "But if you give them a hard time, bullying or taking advantage of their simple trust, you'll soon wish you hadn't. You'd be better off dropped in the middle of the lake with a millstone around your neck. Doom to the world for giving these God-believing children a hard time! Hard times are inevitable, but you don't have to make it worse—and it's doomsday to you if you do.

8-9 "If your hand or your foot gets in the way of God, chop it off and throw it away. You're better off maimed or lame and alive than the proud owners of two hands and two feet, godless in a furnace of eternal fire. And if your eye distracts you from God, pull it out and throw it away. You're better off one-eyed and alive than exercising your twenty-twenty vision from inside the fire of hell.

10 "Watch that you don't treat a single one of these childlike believers arrogantly. You realize, don't you, that their personal angels are constantly in touch with my Father in heaven?

WORK IT OUT BETWEEN YOU

12-14 "Look at it this way. If someone has a hundred sheep and one of them wanders off, doesn't he leave the ninety-nine and go after the one? And if he finds it, doesn't he make far more over it than over the ninety-nine who stay put? Your Father in heaven feels the same way. He doesn't want to lose even one of these simple believers.

15-17 "If a fellow believer hurts you, go and tell him—work it out between the two of you. If he listens, you've made a friend. If he won't listen, take one or two others along so that the presence of witnesses will keep things honest, and try again. If he still won't listen, tell the church. If he won't listen to the church, you'll have to start over from scratch, confront him with the need for repentance, and offer again God's forgiving love.

18-20 "Take this most seriously: A yes on earth is yes in heaven; a no on earth is no in heaven. What you say to one another is eternal. I mean this. When two of you get together on anything at all on earth and make a prayer of it, my Father in heaven goes into action. And when two or three of you are together because of me, you can be sure that I'll be there."

A STORY ABOUT FORGIVENESS

21 At that point Peter got up the nerve to ask, "Master, how many times do I forgive a brother or sister who hurts me? Seven?"

22 Jesus replied, "Seven! Hardly. Try seventy times seven.

23-25 "The kingdom of God is like a king who decided to square accounts with his servants. As he got under way, one servant was brought before him who had run up a debt of a hundred thousand dollars. He couldn't pay up, so the king ordered the man, along with his wife, children, and goods, to be auctioned off at the slave market.

26-27 "The poor wretch threw himself at the king's feet and begged, 'Give me a chance and I'll pay it all back.' Touched by his plea, the king let him off, erasing the debt.

28 "The servant was no sooner out of the room when he came upon one of his fellow servants who owed him ten dollars. He seized him by the throat and demanded, 'Pay up. Now!'

29-31 "The poor wretch threw himself down and begged, 'Give me a chance and I'll pay it all back.' But he wouldn't do it. He had him arrested and put in jail until the debt was paid. When the other servants saw this going on, they were outraged and brought a detailed report to the king.

32-35 "The king summoned the man and said, 'You evil servant! I forgave your entire debt when you begged me for mercy. Shouldn't you be compelled to be merciful to your fellow servant who asked for mercy?' The king was furious and put the screws to the man until he paid back his entire debt. And that's exactly what my Father in heaven is going to do to each one of you who doesn't forgive unconditionally anyone who asks for mercy."

DIVORCE

19 1-2 When Jesus had completed these teachings, he left Galilee and crossed the region of Judea on the other side of the Jordan. Great crowds followed him there, and he healed them.

3 One day the Pharisees were badgering him: "Is it legal for a man to divorce his wife for any reason?"

4-6 He answered, "Haven't you read in your Bible that the Creator originally made man and woman for each other, male and female? And because of this, a man leaves father and mother and is firmly bonded to his wife, becoming one flesh—no longer two bodies but one. Because God created this organic union of the two sexes, no one should desecrate his art by cutting them apart."

7 They shot back in rebuttal, "If that's so, why did Moses give instructions for divorce papers and divorce procedures?"

8-9 Jesus said, "Moses provided for divorce as a concession to your hard heartedness, but it is not part of God's original plan. I'm holding you to the original plan, and holding you liable for adultery if you divorce your faithful wife and then marry someone else. I make an exception in cases where the spouse has committed adultery."

10 Jesus' disciples objected, "If those are the terms of marriage, we haven't got a chance. Why get married?"

11-12 But Jesus said, "Not everyone is mature enough to live a married life. It requires a certain aptitude and grace. Marriage isn't for everyone. Some, from birth seemingly, never give marriage a thought. Others never get asked—or accepted. And some decide not to get married for kingdom reasons. But if you're capable of growing into the largeness of marriage, do it."

TO ENTER GOD'S KINGDOM

13-15 One day children were brought to Jesus in the hope that he would lay hands on them and pray over them. The disciples shooed them off. But Jesus intervened: "Let the children alone, don't prevent them from coming to me. God's kingdom is made up of people like these." After laying hands on them, he left.

Embracing the Marginalized

Jesus didn't like divorce. However, he didn't merely suggest a new law (i.e., limiting divorce to cases of adultery) but a way to make marriages better.

Under the Mosaic law, only men could initiate divorce (see Deuteronomy 24:1-4). A woman in an abusive marriage was stuck, but if a man was displeased with his wife *for any reason* (burning the toast? sprouting a wrinkle?), he could simply throw her away. If he handed her the words "I divorce you" in writing, she could be sent away from her husband with no legal recourse to defend herself.

So limiting divorce to cases of adultery was a significant protection for women.

Jesus' ministry was never about making laws. With him, love trumps law. Jesus said that all the law hangs from only two commandments: love God with all your being and love others as well as you love yourself (Matthew 22:34-40). Instead of a new regulation, Jesus offered a radical alternative: *Love your spouse as you love your own body.*

This is what God has wanted from the beginning. The rule of love applies equally to both partners. This notion of equality was so radical that it made the disciples wonder whether marriage was worth the trouble (Matthew 19:10).

The Pharisees wanted to trap Jesus. If they could entice him to criticize the Mosaic law, they could silence him. They *expected* Jesus to stick up for disrespected women. After all:

- Jesus defended a sinful woman and forgave her for her sins while eating at a Pharisee's house (Luke 7:37-50).
- Jesus revealed that he was the Messiah to a Samaritan woman who had been divorced five times (John 4:1-30, 39-42).
- Jesus healed a hemorrhaging woman whom others wouldn't touch (Mark 5:25-34).
- Jesus saved a woman taken while she was committing adultery from being stoned (John 8:1-11).
- Jesus chose the formerly demon-possessed Mary Magdalene (Luke 8:2) to tell others that he'd risen from the dead (John 20:1-18).

In first-century Palestine, even "respectable" women were considered property, literally owned by men. Without a man to protect her, a divorced woman was helpless, homeless, and disgraced. She might have to sell her body to survive. Jesus said, "If you divorce your wife, *you're responsible* for making her an adulteress" (Matthew 5:32, emphasis added). Jesus didn't condemn such a woman; he blamed the husband and the system that supported her oppression.

Children were even more marginalized in this society. When the disciples tried to shoo them away, Jesus was indignant. "Let the children alone," he said. "Don't prevent them from coming to me" (Matthew 19:14). Another time (again over the disciples' grumbling), Jesus stopped to save a child's life (Mark 5:21-24, 35-43). I picture Jesus regularly doing things like swinging a child in the air or taking a toddler on his lap, asking their name, looking in their eyes, and enjoying a loving conversation with them. Jesus cited children as an example of how we should all approach God: with humility and with trust.

Jesus embraced women and children. Marginalized people matter to Jesus—and as his followers, we should make sure they matter to us.

16 Another day, a man stopped Jesus and asked, "Teacher, what good thing must I do to get eternal life?"

17 Jesus said, "Why do you question me about what's good? *God* is the One who is good. If you want to enter the life of God, just do what he tells you."

18-19 The man asked, "What in particular?"

Jesus said, "Don't murder, don't commit adultery, don't steal, don't lie, honor your father and mother, and love your neighbor as you do yourself."

20 The young man said, "I've done all that. What's left?"

21 "If you want to give it all you've got," Jesus replied, "go sell your possessions; give everything to the poor. All your wealth will then be in heaven. Then come follow me."

22 That was the last thing the young man expected to hear. And so, crestfallen, he walked away. He was holding on tight to a lot of things, and he couldn't bear to let go.

23-24 As he watched him go, Jesus told his disciples, "Do you have any idea how difficult it is for the rich to enter God's kingdom? Let me tell you, it's easier to gallop a camel through a needle's eye than for the rich to enter God's kingdom."

25 The disciples were staggered. "Then who has any chance at all?"

26 Jesus looked hard at them and said, "No chance at all if you think you can pull it off yourself. Every chance in the world if you trust God to do it."

27 Then Peter chimed in, "We left everything and followed you. What do we get out of it?"

28-30 Jesus replied, "Yes, you have followed me. In the re-creation of the world, when the Son of Man will rule gloriously, you who have followed me will also rule, starting with the twelve tribes of Israel. And not only you, but anyone who sacrifices home, family, fields—whatever—because of me will get it all back a hundred times over, not to mention the considerable bonus of eternal life. This is the Great Reversal: many of the first ending up last, and the last first."

A STORY ABOUT WORKERS

20 1-2 "God's kingdom is like an estate manager who went out early in the morning to hire workers for his vineyard. They agreed on a wage of a dollar a day, and went to work.

3-5 "Later, about nine o'clock, the manager saw some other men hanging around the town square unemployed. He told them to go to work in his vineyard and he would pay them a fair wage. They went.

5-6 "He did the same thing at noon, and again at three o'clock. At five o'clock he went back and found still others standing around. He said, 'Why are you standing around all day doing nothing?'

7 "They said, 'Because no one hired us.'

"He told them to go to work in his vineyard.

8 "When the day's work was over, the owner of the vineyard instructed his foreman, 'Call the workers in and pay them their wages. Start with the last hired and go on to the first.'

9-12 "Those hired at five o'clock came up and were each given a dollar. When those who were hired first saw that, they assumed they would get far more. But they got the same, each of them one dollar. Taking the dollar, they groused angrily to the manager, 'These last workers put in only one easy hour, and you just made them equal to us, who slaved all day under a scorching sun.'

13-15 "He replied to the one speaking for the rest, 'Friend, I haven't been unfair. We agreed on the wage of a dollar, didn't we? So take it and go. I decided to give to the one who came last the same as you. Can't I do what I want with my own money? Are you going to get stingy because I am generous?'

16 "Here it is again, the Great Reversal: many of the first ending up last, and the last first."

TO DRINK FROM THE CUP

17-19 Jesus, now well on the way up to Jerusalem, took the Twelve off to the side of the road and said, "Listen to me carefully. We are on our way up to Jerusalem. When we get there, the Son of Man will be betrayed to the religious leaders and scholars. They will sentence him to death. They will then hand him over to the Romans for mockery and torture and crucifixion. On the third day he will be raised up alive."

20 It was about that time that the mother of the Zebedee brothers came with her two sons and knelt before Jesus with a request.

21 "What do you want?" Jesus asked.

She said, "Give your word that these two sons of mine will be awarded the highest places of honor in your kingdom, one at your right hand, one at your left hand."

22 Jesus responded, "You have no idea what you're asking." And he said to James and John, "Are you capable of drinking the cup that I'm about to drink?"

They said, "Sure, why not?"

23 Jesus said, "Come to think of it, you *are* going to drink my cup. But as to awarding places of honor, that's not my business. My Father is taking care of that."

24-28 When the ten others heard about this, they lost their tempers, thoroughly disgusted with the two brothers. So Jesus got them together to settle things down. He said, "You've observed how godless rulers throw their weight around, how quickly a little power goes to their heads. It's not going to be that way with you. Whoever wants to be great must become a servant. Whoever wants to be first among you must be your slave. That is what the Son of Man has done: He came to serve, not be served—and then to give away his life in exchange for the many who are held hostage."

▲ ▲ ▲

29-31 As they were leaving Jericho, a huge crowd followed. Suddenly they came upon two blind men sitting alongside the road. When they heard it was Jesus passing, they cried out, "Master, have mercy on us! Mercy, Son of David!" The crowd tried to hush them up, but they got all the louder, crying, "Master, have mercy on us! Mercy, Son of David!"

32 Jesus stopped and called over, "What do you want from me?"

33 They said, "Master, we want our eyes opened. We want to see!"

34 Deeply moved, Jesus touched their eyes. They had their sight back that very instant, and joined the procession.

THE ROYAL WELCOME

21 1-3 When they neared Jerusalem, having arrived at Bethphage on Mount Olives, Jesus sent two disciples with these instructions: "Go over to the village across from you. You'll find a donkey tethered there, her colt with her. Untie her and bring them to me. If anyone asks what you're doing, say, 'The Master needs them!' He will send them with you."

4-5 This is the full story of what was sketched earlier by the prophet:

Tell Zion's daughter,
"Look, your king's on his way,
poised and ready, mounted
On a donkey, on a colt,
foal of a pack animal."

6-9 The disciples went and did exactly what Jesus told them to do. They led the donkey and colt out, laid some of their clothes on them, and Jesus mounted. Nearly all the people in the crowd threw their garments down on the road, giving him a royal welcome. Others cut branches from the trees and threw them down as a welcome mat. Crowds went ahead and crowds followed, all of them calling out, "Hosanna to David's son!" "Blessed is he who comes in God's name!" "Hosanna in highest heaven!"

10 As he made his entrance into Jerusalem, the whole city was shaken. Unnerved, people were asking, "What's going on here? Who is this?"

11 The parade crowd answered, "This is the prophet Jesus, the one from Nazareth in Galilee."

HE KICKED OVER THE TABLES

12-14 Jesus went straight to the Temple and threw out everyone who had set up shop, buying and selling. He kicked over the tables of loan sharks and the stalls of dove merchants. He quoted this text:

My house was designated a house
of prayer;
You have made it a hangout for thieves.

Now there was room for the blind and crippled to get in. They came to Jesus and he healed them.

15-16 When the religious leaders saw the outrageous things he was doing, and heard all the children running and shouting through the Temple, "Hosanna to David's Son!" they were up in arms and took him to task. "Do you hear what these children are saying?"

Jesus said, "Yes, I hear them. And haven't you read in God's Word, 'From the mouths of children and babies I'll furnish a place of praise'?"

17 Fed up, Jesus spun around and left the city for Bethany, where he spent the night.

THE WITHERED FIG TREE

18-20 Early the next morning Jesus was returning to the city. He was hungry. Seeing a lone fig tree alongside the road, he approached it anticipating a breakfast of figs. When he got to the tree, there was nothing but fig leaves. He said, "No more figs from this tree—ever!" The fig tree withered on the spot, a dry stick. The disciples saw it happen. They rubbed their eyes, saying, "Did we really see this? A leafy tree one minute, a dry stick the next?"

21-22 But Jesus was matter-of-fact: "Yes—and if you embrace this kingdom life and don't doubt God, you'll not only do minor feats like I did to the fig tree, but also triumph over huge obstacles. This mountain, for instance, you'll tell, 'Go jump in the lake,' and it will jump. Absolutely everything, ranging from small to large, as you make it a part of your believing prayer, gets included as you lay hold of God."

TRUE AUTHORITY

23 Then he was back in the Temple, teaching. The high priests and leaders of the people came up and demanded, "Show us your credentials. Who authorized you to teach here?"

24-25 Jesus responded, "First let me ask you a question. You answer my question and I'll answer yours. About the baptism of John—who authorized it: heaven or humans?"

25-27 They were on the spot and knew it. They pulled back into a huddle and whispered, "If we say 'heaven,' he'll ask us why we didn't believe him; if we say 'humans,' we're up against it with the people because they all hold John up as a prophet." They decided to concede that round to Jesus. "We don't know," they answered.

Jesus said, "Then neither will I answer your question.

THE STORY OF TWO SONS

28 "Tell me what you think of this story: A man had two sons. He went up to the first and said, 'Son, go out for the day and work in the vineyard.'

29 "The son answered, 'I don't want to.' Later on he thought better of it and went.

30 "The father gave the same command to the second son. He answered, 'Sure, glad to.' But he never went.

31-32 "Which of the two sons did what the father asked?"

They said, "The first."

Jesus said, "Yes, and I tell you that crooks and whores are going to precede you into God's kingdom. John came to you showing you the right road. You turned up your noses at him, but the crooks and whores believed him. Even when you saw their changed lives, you didn't care enough to change and believe him.

THE STORY OF THE GREEDY FARMHANDS

33-34 "Here's another story. Listen closely. There was once a man, a wealthy farmer, who planted a vineyard. He fenced it, dug a winepress, put up a watchtower, then turned it over to the farmhands and went off on a trip. When it was time to harvest the grapes, he sent his servants back to collect his profits.

35-37 "The farmhands grabbed the first servant and beat him up. The next one they murdered. They threw stones at the third but he got away. The owner tried again, sending more servants. They got the same treatment. The owner was at the end of his rope. He decided to send his son. 'Surely,' he thought, 'they will respect my son.'

38-39 "But when the farmhands saw the son arrive, they rubbed their hands in greed. 'This is the heir! Let's kill him and have it all for ourselves.' They grabbed him, threw him out, and killed him.

40 "Now, when the owner of the vineyard arrives home from his trip, what do you think he will do to the farmhands?"

41 "He'll kill them—a rotten bunch, and good riddance," they answered. "Then he'll assign the vineyard to farmhands who will hand over the profits when it's time."

42-44 Jesus said, "Right—and you can read it for yourselves in your Bibles:

> The stone the masons threw out
> is now the cornerstone.
> This is God's work;
> we rub our eyes, we can hardly
> believe it!

"This is the way it is with you. God's kingdom will be taken back from you and handed over to a people who will live out a kingdom life. Whoever stumbles on this Stone gets shattered; whoever the Stone falls on gets smashed."

45-46 When the religious leaders heard this story, they knew it was aimed at them. They wanted to arrest Jesus and put him in jail, but, intimidated by public opinion, they held back. Most people held him to be a prophet of God.

THE STORY OF THE WEDDING BANQUET

22 1-3 Jesus responded by telling still more stories. "God's kingdom," he said, "is like a king who threw a wedding

banquet for his son. He sent out servants to call in all the invited guests. And they wouldn't come!

4 "He sent out another round of servants, instructing them to tell the guests, 'Look, everything is on the table, the prime rib is ready for carving. Come to the feast!'

5-7 "They only shrugged their shoulders and went off, one to weed his garden, another to work in his shop. The rest, with nothing better to do, beat up on the messengers and then killed them. The king was outraged and sent his soldiers to destroy those thugs and level their city.

8-10 "Then he told his servants, 'We have a wedding banquet all prepared but no guests. The ones I invited weren't up to it. Go out into the busiest intersections in town and invite anyone you find to the banquet.' The servants went out on the streets and rounded up everyone they laid eyes on, good and bad, regardless. And so the banquet was on—every place filled.

11-13 "When the king entered and looked over the scene, he spotted a man who wasn't properly dressed. He said to him, 'Friend, how dare you come in here looking like that!' The man was speechless. Then the king told his servants, 'Get him out of here—fast. Tie him up and ship him to hell. And make sure he doesn't get back in.'

14 "That's what I mean when I say, 'Many get invited; only a few make it.'"

PAYING TAXES

15-17 That's when the Pharisees plotted a way to trap him into saying something damaging. They sent their disciples, with a few of Herod's followers mixed in, to ask, "Teacher, we know you have integrity, teach the way of God accurately, are indifferent to popular opinion, and don't pander to your students. So tell us honestly: Is it right to pay taxes to Caesar or not?"

18-19 Jesus knew they were up to no good. He said, "Why are you playing these games with me? Why are you trying to trap me? Do you have a coin? Let me see it." They handed him a silver piece.

20 "This engraving—who does it look like? And whose name is on it?"

21 They said, "Caesar."

"Then give Caesar what is his, and give God what is his."

22 The Pharisees were speechless. They went off shaking their heads.

MARRIAGE AND RESURRECTION

23-28 That same day, Sadducees approached him. This is the party that denies any possibility of resurrection. They asked, "Teacher, Moses said that if a man dies childless, his brother is obligated to marry his widow and father a child with her. Here's a case where there were seven brothers. The first brother married and died, leaving no child, and his wife passed to his brother. The second brother also left her childless, then the third—and on and on, all seven. Eventually the wife died. Now here's our question: At the resurrection, whose wife is she? She was a wife to each of them."

29-33 Jesus answered, "You're off base on two counts: You don't know what God said, and you don't know how God works. At the resurrection we're beyond marriage. As with the angels, all our ecstasies and intimacies then will be with God. And regarding your speculation on whether the dead are raised or not, don't you read your Bibles? The grammar is clear: God says, 'I am—not *was*—the God of Abraham, the God of Isaac, the God of Jacob.' The living God defines himself not as the God of dead men, but of the *living*." Hearing this exchange the crowd was much impressed.

THE MOST IMPORTANT COMMAND

34-36 When the Pharisees heard how he had bested the Sadducees, they gathered their forces for an assault. One of their religion scholars spoke for them, posing a question they hoped would show him up: "Teacher, which command in God's Law is the most important?"

37-40 Jesus said, "'Love the Lord your God with all your passion and prayer and intelligence.' This is the most important, the first on any list. But there is a second to set alongside it: 'Love others as well as you love yourself.' These two commands are pegs; everything in God's Law and the Prophets hangs from them."

DAVID'S SON AND MASTER

41-42 As the Pharisees were regrouping, Jesus caught them off balance with his own test question: "What do you think about the Christ? Whose son is he?" They said, "David's son."

43-45 Jesus replied, "Well, if the Christ is David's son, how do you explain that David, under inspiration, named Christ his 'Master'?

God said to my Master,
"Sit here at my right hand
until I make your enemies your
footstool."

"Now if David calls him 'Master,' how can he at the same time be his son?"

46 That stumped them, literalists that they were. Unwilling to risk losing face again in one of these public verbal exchanges, they quit asking questions for good.

RELIGIOUS FASHION SHOWS

23 1-3 Now Jesus turned to address his disciples, along with the crowd that had gathered with them. "The religion scholars and Pharisees are competent teachers in God's Law. You won't go wrong in following their teachings on Moses. But be careful about following *them*. They talk a good line, but they don't live it. They don't take it into their hearts and live it out in their behavior. It's all spit-and-polish veneer.

4-7 "Instead of giving you God's Law as food and drink by which you can banquet on God, they package it in bundles of rules, loading you down like pack animals. They seem to take pleasure in watching you stagger under these loads, and wouldn't think of lifting a finger to help. Their lives are perpetual fashion shows, embroidered prayer shawls one day and flowery prayers the next. They love to sit at the head table at church dinners, basking in the most prominent positions, preening in the radiance of public flattery, receiving honorary degrees, and getting called 'Doctor' and 'Reverend.'

8-10 "Don't let people do that to *you*, put you on a pedestal like that. You all have a single Teacher, and you are all classmates. Don't set people up as experts over your life, letting them tell you what to do. Save that authority for God; let *him* tell you what to do. No one else should carry the title of 'Father'; you have only one Father, and he's in heaven. And don't let people maneuver you into taking charge of them. There is only one Life-Leader for you and them—Christ.

11-12 "Do you want to stand out? Then step down. Be a servant. If you puff yourself up, you'll get the wind knocked out of you. But if you're content to simply be yourself, your life will count for plenty.

FRAUDS!

13 "I've had it with you! You're hopeless, you religion scholars, you Pharisees! Frauds! Your lives are roadblocks to God's kingdom. You refuse to enter, and won't let anyone else in either.

15 "You're hopeless, you religion scholars and Pharisees! Frauds! You go halfway around the world to make a convert, but once you get him you make him into a replica of yourselves, double-damned.

16-22 "You're hopeless! What arrogant stupidity! You say, 'If someone makes a promise with his fingers crossed, that's nothing; but if he swears with his hand on the Bible, that's serious.' What ignorance! Does the leather on the Bible carry more weight than the skin on your hands? And what about this piece of trivia: 'If you shake hands on a promise, that's nothing; but if you raise your hand that God is your witness, that's serious'? What ridiculous hairsplitting! What difference does it make whether you shake hands or raise hands? A promise is a promise. What difference does it make if you make your promise inside or outside a house of worship? A promise is a promise. God is present, watching and holding you to account regardless.

23-24 "You're hopeless, you religion scholars and Pharisees! Frauds! You keep meticulous account books, tithing on every nickel and dime you get, but on the meat of God's Law, things like fairness and compassion and commitment—the absolute basics!—you carelessly take it or leave it. Careful bookkeeping is commendable, but the basics are required. Do you have any idea how silly you look, writing a life story that's wrong from start to finish, nitpicking over commas and semicolons?

25-26 "You're hopeless, you religion scholars and Pharisees! Frauds! You buff the surface of your cups and bowls so they sparkle in the sun, while the insides are maggoty with your greed and gluttony. Stupid Pharisee! Scour the insides, and then the gleaming surface will mean something.

27-28 "You're hopeless, you religion scholars and Pharisees! Frauds! You're like manicured grave plots, grass clipped and the flowers bright, but six feet down it's all rotting bones and worm-eaten flesh. People look at you and think you're saints, but beneath the skin you're total frauds.

29-32 "You're hopeless, you religion scholars and Pharisees! Frauds! You build granite tombs for your prophets and marble monuments for your saints. And you say that if you had lived in the days of your ancestors, no blood would have been on your hands. You protest too much! You're cut from the same cloth as those murderers, and daily add to the death count.

33-34 "Snakes! Cold-blooded sneaks! Do you

think you can worm your way out of this? Never have to pay the piper? It's on account of people like you that I send prophets and wise guides and scholars generation after generation—and generation after generation you treat them like dirt, greeting them with lynch mobs, hounding them with abuse.

35-36 "You can't squirm out of this: Every drop of righteous blood ever spilled on this earth, beginning with the blood of that good man Abel right down to the blood of Zechariah, Barachiah's son, whom you murdered at his prayers, is on your head. All this, I'm telling you, is coming down on you, on your generation.

37-39 "Jerusalem! Jerusalem! Murderer of prophets! Killer of the ones who brought you God's news! How often I've ached to embrace your children, the way a hen gathers her chicks under her wings, and you wouldn't let me. And now you're so desolate, nothing but a ghost town. What is there left to say? Only this: I'm out of here soon. The next time you see me you'll say, 'Oh, God has blessed him! He's come, bringing God's rule!'"

ROUTINE HISTORY

24 1-2 Jesus then left the Temple. As he walked away, his disciples pointed out how very impressive the Temple architecture was. Jesus said, "You're not impressed by all this sheer *size*, are you? The truth of the matter is that there's not a stone in that building that is not going to end up in a pile of rubble."

3 Later as he was sitting on Mount Olives, his disciples approached and asked him, "Tell us, when are these things going to happen? What will be the sign of your coming, that the time's up?"

4-8 Jesus said, "Watch out for doomsday deceivers. Many leaders are going to show up with forged identities, claiming, 'I am Christ, the Messiah.' They will deceive a lot of people. When reports come in of wars and rumored wars, keep your head and don't panic. This is routine history; this is no sign of the end. Nation will fight nation and ruler fight ruler, over and over. Famines and earthquakes will occur in various places. This is nothing compared to what is coming.

9-10 "They are going to throw you to the wolves and kill you, everyone hating you because you carry my name. And then, going from bad to worse, it will be dog-eat-dog, everyone at each other's throat, everyone hating each other.

11-12 "In the confusion, lying preachers will come forward and deceive a lot of people. For many others, the overwhelming spread of evil will do them in—nothing left of their love but a mound of ashes.

13-14 "Staying with it—that's what God requires. Stay with it to the end. You won't be sorry, and you'll be saved. All during this time, the good news—the Message of the kingdom—will be preached all over the world, a witness staked out in every country. And then the end will come.

THE MONSTER OF DESECRATION

15-20 "But be ready to run for it when you see the monster of desecration set up in the Temple sanctuary. The prophet Daniel described this. If you've read Daniel, you'll know what I'm talking about. If you're living in Judea at the time, run for the hills; if you're working in the yard, don't return to the house to get anything; if you're out in the field, don't go back and get your coat. Pregnant and nursing mothers will have it especially hard. Hope and pray this won't happen during the winter or on a Sabbath.

21-22 "This is going to be trouble on a scale beyond what the world has ever seen, or will see again. If these days of trouble were left to run their course, nobody would make it. But on account of God's chosen people, the trouble will be cut short.

THE ARRIVAL OF THE SON OF MAN

23-25 "If anyone tries to flag you down, calling out, 'Here's the Messiah!' or points, 'There he is!' don't fall for it. Fake Messiahs and lying preachers are going to pop up everywhere. Their impressive credentials and bewitching performances will pull the wool over the eyes of even those who ought to know better. But I've given you fair warning.

26-28 "So if they say, 'Run to the country and see him arrive!' or, 'Quick, get downtown, see him come!' don't give them the time of day. The Arrival of the Son of Man isn't something you go to see. He comes like swift lightning to you! Whenever you see crowds gathering, think of carrion vultures circling, moving in, hovering over a rotting carcass. You can be quite sure that it's not the living Son of Man pulling in those crowds.

29 "Following those hard times,

Sun will fade out,
moon cloud over,

Stars fall out of the sky,
cosmic powers tremble.

30-31 "Then, the Arrival of the Son of Man! It will fill the skies—no one will miss it. Unready people all over the world, outsiders to the splendor and power, will raise a huge lament as they watch the Son of Man blazing out of heaven. At that same moment, he'll dispatch his angels with a trumpet-blast summons, pulling in God's chosen from the four winds, from pole to pole.

32-35 "Take a lesson from the fig tree. From the moment you notice its buds form, the merest hint of green, you know summer's just around the corner. So it is with you: When you see all these things, you'll know he's at the door. Don't take this lightly. I'm not just saying this for some future generation, but for all of you. This age continues until all these things take place. Sky and earth will wear out; my words won't wear out.

36 "But the exact day and hour? No one knows that, not even heaven's angels, not even the Son. Only the Father knows.

37-39 "The Arrival of the Son of Man will take place in times like Noah's. Before the great flood everyone was carrying on as usual, having a good time right up to the day Noah boarded the ark. They knew nothing—until the flood hit and swept everything away.

39-44 "The Son of Man's Arrival will be like that: Two men will be working in the field—one will be taken, one left behind; two women will be grinding at the mill—one will be taken, one left behind. So stay awake, alert. You have no idea what day your Master will show up. But you do know this: You know that if the homeowner had known what time of night the burglar would arrive, he would have been there with his dogs to prevent the break-in. Be vigilant just like that. You have no idea when the Son of Man is going to show up.

45-47 "Who here qualifies for the job of overseeing the kitchen? A person the Master can depend on to feed the workers on time each day. Someone the Master can drop in on unannounced and always find him doing his job. A God-blessed man or woman, I tell you. It won't be long before the Master will put this person in charge of the whole operation.

48-51 "But if that person only looks out for himself, and the minute the Master is away does what he pleases—abusing the help and throwing drunken parties for his friends—the Master is going to show up when he least expects it, and it won't be pretty. He'll end up in the dump with the hypocrites, out in the cold shivering, teeth chattering."

THE STORY OF THE VIRGINS

25 1-5 "God's kingdom is like ten young virgins who took oil lamps and went out to greet the bridegroom. Five were silly and five were smart. The silly virgins took lamps, but no extra oil. The smart virgins took jars of oil to feed their lamps. The bridegroom didn't show up when they expected him, and they all fell asleep.

6 "In the middle of the night someone yelled out, 'He's here! The bridegroom's here! Go out and greet him!'

7-8 "The ten virgins got up and got their lamps ready. The silly virgins said to the smart ones, 'Our lamps are going out; lend us some of your oil.'

9 "They answered, 'There might not be enough to go around; go buy your own.'

10 "They did, but while they were out buying oil, the bridegroom arrived. When everyone who was there to greet him had gone into the wedding feast, the door was locked.

11 "Much later, the other virgins, the silly ones, showed up and knocked on the door, saying, 'Master, we're here. Let us in.'

12 "He answered, 'Do I know you? I don't think I know you.'

13 "So stay alert. You have no idea when he might arrive.

THE STORY ABOUT INVESTMENT

14-18 "It's also like a man going off on an extended trip. He called his servants together and delegated responsibilities. To one he gave five thousand dollars, to another two thousand, to a third one thousand, depending on their abilities. Then he left. Right off, the first servant went to work and doubled his master's investment. The second did the same. But the man with the single thousand dug a hole and carefully buried his master's money.

19-21 "After a long absence, the master of those three servants came back and settled up with them. The one given five thousand dollars showed him how he had doubled his investment. His master commended him: 'Good work! You did your job well. From now on be my partner.'

22-23 "The servant with the two thousand showed how he also had doubled his master's

A Beacon of Caution

Silly. It's a word that stings a bit, perhaps even more than *foolish*, the word employed by many translations in reference to the ten virgins in Jesus' parable in Matthew 25:1-13. Most of us never want to be thought of as silly; we may fear the title more than we loathe actually *being* silly. In truth, this parable may take a few readings before we can move past the disparaging adjective and pay attention to what Jesus is teaching us.

All the virgins in Jesus' story were waiting for the bridegroom. But some of the virgins had paid attention when their scout troops had earned readiness badges. These women brought enough oil to cover the difference between the bridegroom's expected and actual time of arrival. The "silly" virgins didn't make this savvy calculation. They showed up (don't we wish there were points for showing up?), but they didn't consider what it would take to keep their lamps burning long enough to light up the pathway for the bridegroom whenever he happened to arrive.

When they realized he was arriving, they were stricken by their own failure, frantic to fix it. It seemed a small miracle that they could find an oil shop open at midnight. (I can imagine Jesus enjoying the details of his story, heightening the point that they were oh-so-close—but no cigar.) When they finally returned to the wedding party, it was too late. They were turned away at the door. *Silly girls.*

But this is a parable. These silly girls mean something. They are a beacon of caution to all of us, to the church. We worship the Christ who died, who is risen, who will come again. In the meantime, we wait. Not passively. Not halfheartedly. We wait with eager expectation and profound patience, recognizing that this wait is not on our time but God's time. We have no idea when he might arrive—and there is so much to do in the meantime.

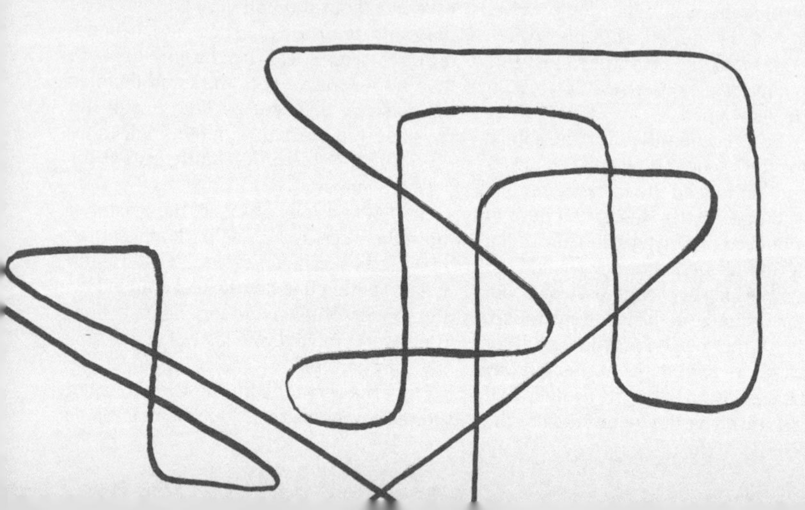

investment. His master commended him: 'Good work! You did your job well. From now on be my partner.'

24-25 "The servant given one thousand said, 'Master, I know you have high standards and hate careless ways, that you demand the best and make no allowances for error. I was afraid I might disappoint you, so I found a good hiding place and secured your money. Here it is, safe and sound down to the last cent.'

26-27 "The master was furious. 'That's a terrible way to live! It's criminal to live cautiously like that! If you knew I was after the best, why did you do less than the least? The least you could have done would have been to invest the sum with the bankers, where at least I would have gotten a little interest.

28-30 "'Take the thousand and give it to the one who risked the most. And get rid of this "play-it-safe" who won't go out on a limb. Throw him out into utter darkness.'

THE SHEEP AND THE GOATS

31-33 "When he finally arrives, blazing in beauty and all his angels with him, the Son of Man will take his place on his glorious throne. Then all the nations will be arranged before him and he will sort the people out, much as a shepherd sorts out sheep and goats, putting sheep to his right and goats to his left.

34-36 "Then the King will say to those on his right, 'Enter, you who are blessed by my Father! Take what's coming to you in this kingdom. It's been ready for you since the world's foundation. And here's why:

I was hungry and you fed me,
I was thirsty and you gave me a drink,
I was homeless and you gave me a room,
I was shivering and you gave me clothes,
I was sick and you stopped to visit,
I was in prison and you came to me.'

37-40 "Then those 'sheep' are going to say, 'Master, what are you talking about? When did we ever see you hungry and feed you, thirsty and give you a drink? And when did we ever see you sick or in prison and come to you?' Then the King will say, 'I'm telling the solemn truth: Whenever you did one of these things to someone overlooked or ignored, that was me—you did it to me.'

41-43 "Then he will turn to the 'goats,' the ones on his left, and say, 'Get out, worthless goats! You're good for nothing but the fires of hell. And why? Because—

I was hungry and you gave me no meal,
I was thirsty and you gave me no drink,
I was homeless and you gave me no bed,
I was shivering and you gave me no clothes,
Sick and in prison, and you never visited.'

44 "Then those 'goats' are going to say, 'Master, what are you talking about? When did we ever see you hungry or thirsty or homeless or shivering or sick or in prison and didn't help?'

45 "He will answer them, 'I'm telling the solemn truth: Whenever you failed to do one of these things to someone who was being overlooked or ignored, that was me—you failed to do it to me.'

46 "Then those 'goats' will be herded to their eternal doom, but the 'sheep' to their eternal reward."

ANOINTED FOR BURIAL

26 1-2 When Jesus finished saying these things, he told his disciples, "You know that Passover comes in two days. That's when the Son of Man will be betrayed and handed over for crucifixion."

3-5 At that very moment, the party of high priests and religious leaders was meeting in the chambers of the Chief Priest named Caiaphas, conspiring to seize Jesus by stealth and kill him. They agreed that it should not be done during Passover Week. "We don't want a riot on our hands," they said.

6-9 When Jesus was at Bethany, a guest of Simon the Leper, a woman came up to him as he was eating dinner and anointed him with a bottle of very expensive perfume. When the disciples saw what was happening, they were furious. "That's criminal! This could have been sold for a lot and the money handed out to the poor."

10-13 When Jesus realized what was going on, he intervened. "Why are you giving this woman a hard time? She has just done something wonderfully significant for me. You will have the poor with you every day for the rest of your lives, but not me. When she poured this perfume on my body, what she really did was anoint me for burial. You can be sure that wherever in the whole world the Message is preached, what she has just done is going to be remembered and admired."

14-16 That is when one of the Twelve, the one named Judas Iscariot, went to the cabal of high priests and said, "What will you give me if I hand him over to you?" They settled on thirty silver pieces. He began looking for just the right moment to hand him over.

THE TRAITOR

17 On the first of the Days of Unleavened Bread, the disciples came to Jesus and said, "Where do you want us to prepare your Passover meal?"

18-19 He said, "Enter the city. Go up to a certain man and say, 'The Teacher says, My time is near. I and my disciples plan to celebrate the Passover meal at your house.'" The disciples followed Jesus' instructions to the letter, and prepared the Passover meal.

20-21 After sunset, he and the Twelve were sitting around the table. During the meal, he said, "I have something hard but important to say to you: One of you is going to hand me over to the conspirators."

22 They were stunned, and then began to ask, one after another, "It isn't me, is it, Master?"

23-24 Jesus answered, "The one who hands me over is someone I eat with daily, one who passes me food at the table. In one sense the Son of Man is entering into a way of treachery well-marked by the Scriptures—no surprises here. In another sense that man who turns him in, turns traitor to the Son of Man—better never to have been born than do this!"

25 Then Judas, already turned traitor, said, "It isn't me, is it, Rabbi?"

Jesus said, "Don't play games with me, Judas."

THE BREAD AND THE CUP

26-29 During the meal, Jesus took and blessed the bread, broke it, and gave it to his disciples:

Take, eat.
This is my body.

Taking the cup and thanking God, he gave it to them:

Drink this, all of you.
This is my blood,
God's new covenant poured out for
many people
for the forgiveness of sins.

"I'll not be drinking wine from this cup again until that new day when I'll drink with you in the kingdom of my Father."

30 They sang a hymn and went directly to Mount Olives.

GETHSEMANE

31-32 Then Jesus told them, "Before the night's over, you're going to fall to pieces because of what happens to me. There is a Scripture that says,

I'll strike the shepherd;
dazed and confused, the sheep will
be scattered.

But after I am raised up, I, your Shepherd, will go ahead of you, leading the way to Galilee."

33 Peter broke in, "Even if everyone else falls to pieces on account of you, I won't."

34 "Don't be so sure," Jesus said. "This very night, before the rooster crows up the dawn, you will deny me three times."

35 Peter protested, "Even if I had to die with you, I would never deny you." All the others said the same thing.

36-38 Then Jesus went with them to a garden called Gethsemane and told his disciples, "Stay here while I go over there and pray." Taking along Peter and the two sons of Zebedee, he plunged into an agonizing sorrow. Then he said, "This sorrow is crushing my life out. Stay here and keep vigil with me."

39 Going a little ahead, he fell on his face, praying, "My Father, if there is any way, get me out of this. But please, not what I want. You, what do *you* want?"

40-41 When he came back to his disciples, he found them sound asleep. He said to Peter, "Can't you stick it out with me a single hour? Stay alert; be in prayer so you don't wander into temptation without even knowing you're in danger. There is a part of you that is eager, ready for anything in God. But there's another part that's as lazy as an old dog sleeping by the fire."

42 He then left them a second time. Again he prayed, "My Father, if there is no other way than this, drinking this cup to the dregs, I'm ready. Do it your way."

43-44 When he came back, he again found them sound asleep. They simply couldn't keep their eyes open. This time he let them sleep on, and went back a third time to pray, going over the same ground one last time.

45-46 When he came back the next time, he said, "Are you going to sleep on and make a night of it? My time is up, the Son of Man is about to be handed over to the hands of sinners. Get up! Let's get going! My betrayer is here."

THE WOMAN WHO ANOINTED JESUS

Each of the four Gospels tells a story of a woman entering a dinner party to anoint Jesus with perfume. But the timeline, place, method, and even the identity of the woman differ. Who exactly was she?

In Matthew 26:6-13, the woman is nameless. Mark and Luke do not name the woman in the episode they narrate either (Mark 14:3-9; Luke 7:36-50). In John's Gospel, Mary, the sister of Lazarus and Martha, anoints Jesus (John 12:1-8). Reading snippets from all four books, many of us mistakenly fuse multiple Marys into one person. We have fuzzy memories of there being a Mary who traveled with Jesus, a Mary at the cross, and another at the Resurrection. We may have vague notions of one Mary being some sort of sex worker, an impression reinforced in much of Christian history and many contemporary sermons (this despite no explicit textual reference in the Gospels to that effect). In any case, all we know of the woman from Matthew is that she anointed Jesus' feet with expensive perfume and she made Jesus' followers furious.

We may never know the true identity of this woman. But here's what we *do* know: She cared only for Jesus' opinion of her, ignoring the judgment of the others in the room. We know that she poured out everything to worship God in vulnerability, and this mundane dining room was transformed into a sacred temple by her simple act of faith. Smashing a year's worth of wages to anoint Jesus, this woman didn't equate sacrifice with waste.

What actions of ours might society label as wasteful? Lavish giving, opening our doors, or sharing our feasts perhaps? What plans or dreams have we "wasted" to follow God's lead in our lives? As this woman so vividly demonstrates, what the world considers wasteful God may consider worship.

WITH SWORDS AND CLUBS

47-49 The words were barely out of his mouth when Judas (the one from the Twelve) showed up, and with him a gang from the high priests and religious leaders brandishing swords and clubs. The betrayer had worked out a sign with them: "The one I kiss, that's the one—seize him." He went straight to Jesus, greeted him, "How are you, Rabbi?" and kissed him.

50-51 Jesus said, "Friend, why this charade?"

Then they came on him—grabbed him and roughed him up. One of those with Jesus pulled his sword and, taking a swing at the Chief Priest's servant, cut off his ear.

52-54 Jesus said, "Put your sword back where it belongs. All who use swords are destroyed by swords. Don't you realize that I am able right now to call to my Father, and twelve companies—more, if I want them—of fighting angels would be here, battle-ready? But if I did that, how would the Scriptures come true that say this is the way it has to be?"

55-56 Then Jesus addressed the mob: "What is this—coming out after me with swords and clubs as if I were a dangerous criminal? Day after day I have been sitting in the Temple teaching, and you never so much as lifted a hand against me. You've done it this way to confirm and fulfill the prophetic writings."

Then all the disciples cut and ran.

FALSE CHARGES

57-58 The gang that had seized Jesus led him before Caiaphas the Chief Priest, where the religion scholars and leaders had assembled. Peter followed at a safe distance until they got to the Chief Priest's courtyard. Then he slipped in and mingled with the servants, watching to see how things would turn out.

59-60 The high priests, conspiring with the Jewish Council, tried to cook up charges against Jesus in order to sentence him to death. But even though many stepped up, making up one false accusation after another, nothing was believable.

60-61 Finally two men came forward with this: "He said, 'I can tear down this Temple of God and after three days rebuild it.'"

62 The Chief Priest stood up and said, "What do you have to say to the accusation?"

63 Jesus kept silent.

Then the Chief Priest said, "I command you by the authority of the living God to say if you are the Messiah, the Son of God."

64 Jesus was curt: "You yourself said it. And that's not all. Soon you'll see it for yourself:

The Son of Man seated at the right hand
of the Mighty One,
Arriving on the clouds of heaven."

65-66 At that, the Chief Priest lost his temper, ripping his robes, yelling, "He blasphemed! Why do we need witnesses to accuse him? You all heard him blaspheme! Are you going to stand for such blasphemy?"

They all said, "Death! That seals his death sentence."

67-68 Then they were spitting in his face and knocking him around. They jeered as they slapped him: "Prophesy, Messiah: Who hit you that time?"

DENIAL IN THE COURTYARD

69 All this time, Peter was sitting out in the courtyard. One servant girl came up to him and said, "You were with Jesus the Galilean."

70 In front of everybody there, he denied it. "I don't know what you're talking about."

71 As he moved over toward the gate, someone else said to the people there, "This man was with Jesus the Nazarene."

72 Again he denied it, salting his denial with an oath: "I swear, I never laid eyes on the man."

73 Shortly after that, some bystanders approached Peter. "You've got to be one of them. Your accent gives you away."

74-75 Then he got really nervous and swore. "I don't know the man!"

Just then a rooster crowed. Peter remembered what Jesus had said: "Before the rooster crows, you will deny me three times." He went out and cried and cried and cried.

THIRTY SILVER COINS

27 1-2 In the first light of dawn, all the high priests and religious leaders met and put the finishing touches on their plot to kill Jesus. Then they tied him up and paraded him to Pilate, the governor.

3-4 Judas, the one who betrayed him, realized that Jesus was doomed. Overcome with remorse, he gave back the thirty silver coins to the high priests, saying, "I've sinned. I've betrayed an innocent man."

They said, "What do we care? That's *your* problem!"

5 Judas threw the silver coins into the Temple and left. Then he went out and hung himself.

6-10 The high priests picked up the silver pieces, but then didn't know what to do with them. "It wouldn't be right to give this—a payment for murder!—as an offering in the Temple." They decided to get rid of it by buying the "Potter's Field" and use it as a burial place for the homeless. That's how the field got called "Murder Meadow," a name that has stuck to this day. Then Jeremiah's words became history:

> They took the thirty silver pieces,
> The price of the one priced by some sons
> of Israel,
> And they purchased the potter's field.

And so they unwittingly followed the divine instructions to the letter.

PILATE

11 Jesus was placed before the governor, who questioned him: "Are you the 'King of the Jews'?"

Jesus said, "If you say so."

12-14 But when the accusations rained down hot and heavy from the high priests and religious leaders, he said nothing. Pilate asked him, "Do you hear that long list of accusations? Aren't you going to say something?" Jesus kept silence—not a word from his mouth. The governor was impressed, really impressed.

15-18 It was an old custom during the Feast for the governor to pardon a single prisoner named by the crowd. At the time, they had the infamous Jesus Barabbas in prison. With the crowd before him, Pilate said, "Which prisoner do you want me to pardon: Jesus Barabbas, or Jesus the so-called Christ?" He knew it was through sheer spite that they had turned Jesus over to him.

19 While court was still in session, Pilate's wife sent him a message: "Don't get mixed up in judging this noble man. I've just been through a long and troubled night because of a dream about him."

20 Meanwhile, the high priests and religious leaders had talked the crowd into asking for the pardon of Barabbas and the execution of Jesus.

21 The governor asked, "Which of the two do you want me to pardon?"

They said, "Barabbas!"

22 "Then what do I do with Jesus, the so-called Christ?"

They all shouted, "Nail him to a cross!"

23 He objected, "But for what crime?"

But they yelled all the louder, "Nail him to a cross!"

24 When Pilate saw that he was getting nowhere and that a riot was imminent, he took a basin of water and washed his hands in full sight of the crowd, saying, "I'm washing my hands of responsibility for this man's death. From now on, it's in your hands. You're judge and jury."

25 The crowd answered, "We'll take the blame, we and our children after us."

26 Then he pardoned Barabbas. But he had Jesus whipped, and then handed over for crucifixion.

THE CRUCIFIXION

27-31 The soldiers assigned to the governor took Jesus into the governor's palace and got the entire brigade together for some fun. They stripped him and dressed him in a red robe. They plaited a crown from branches of a thornbush and set it on his head. They put a stick in his right hand for a scepter. Then they knelt before him in mocking reverence: "Bravo, King of the Jews!" they said. "Bravo!" Then they spit on him and hit him on the head with the stick. When they had had their fun, they took off the robe and put his own clothes back on him. Then they proceeded out to the crucifixion.

32-34 Along the way they came on a man from Cyrene named Simon and made him carry Jesus' cross. Arriving at Golgotha, the place they call "Skull Hill," they offered him a mild painkiller (a mixture of wine and myrrh), but when he tasted it he wouldn't drink it.

35-40 After they had finished nailing him to the cross and were waiting for him to die, they killed time by throwing dice for his clothes. Above his head they had posted the criminal charge against him: THIS IS JESUS, THE KING OF THE JEWS. Along with him, they also crucified two criminals, one to his right, the other to his left. People passing along the road jeered, shaking their heads in mock lament: "You bragged that you could tear down the Temple and then rebuild it in three days—so show us your stuff! Save yourself! If you're really God's Son, come down from that cross!"

41-44 The high priests, along with the religion scholars and leaders, were right there mixing it up with the rest of them, having a great time poking fun at him: "He saved others—he can't save himself! King of Israel, is he? Then let him get down from that cross. We'll *all* become believers then! He was so sure of God—well, let him rescue his 'Son' now—if he wants him! He did claim to be

The Witness of Women

Jesus had brought Peter, James, and John with him to the garden of Gethsemane, where sweat had poured from his face like blood, so great was his agony as he contemplated his impending death. But hours later these disciples had fled. Jesus had been handed over to Pilate, sentenced to execution, mocked by Roman soldiers, and crucified between two criminals.

But several women stayed. Matthew notes that many of the women who had followed Jesus remained and watched Jesus' death, standing at a distance. They had walked somewhere between eighty and a hundred miles with Jesus, traveling from Galilee to Jerusalem. Matthew names Mary Magdalene, Mary the mother of James and Joseph, and the mother of the Zebedee brothers (Matthew 27:55-56). Later in the chapter, when Jesus is laid in the tomb, Mary Magdalene and "the other Mary" are there, too (Matthew 27:61).

These details can read like a few throwaway sentences, a backdrop to the main action happening on the cosmic stage: the crucifixion, burial, and resurrection of Jesus Christ.

Yet the presence of women at the Crucifixion and the empty tomb draws attention to the noticeable absence of Jesus' male disciples. These women stayed. They grieved. They kept vigil. They did not turn from the gruesome death. Their names are recorded in Scripture; they are among the ones to whom Jesus will say at the end of days, "Good work! You did your job well" (Matthew 25:23).

The witness of these women is notable too. They witnessed (saw) these events with their eyes and witnessed (reported) these events with their voices.

Socially and legally, women held little power in the world of the time. While two male individuals were enough to corroborate an eyewitness account, these soon-to-be witnesses of the empty tomb were women and would have therefore been considered incompetent to testify in Jewish legal courts. The fact that Matthew names these women—and that Jesus always honored and included them in his life and ministry—reminds us that Jesus' death and resurrection weren't only about atonement for our sinful choices. In his death, Jesus took on systemic sin as well as personal sin; he is the firstfruit of a new creation. In the new order of things, Jesus will restore what's been broken. No longer will men and women be at odds, no longer will the land bear thorns and thistles. No longer will power structures oppress the vulnerable. Through Jesus' death and resurrection, we—male and female alike—are welcomed into the family where all is being made new. We are restored to God, to purpose, and to each other.

These faithful, hopeful women were the first witnesses.

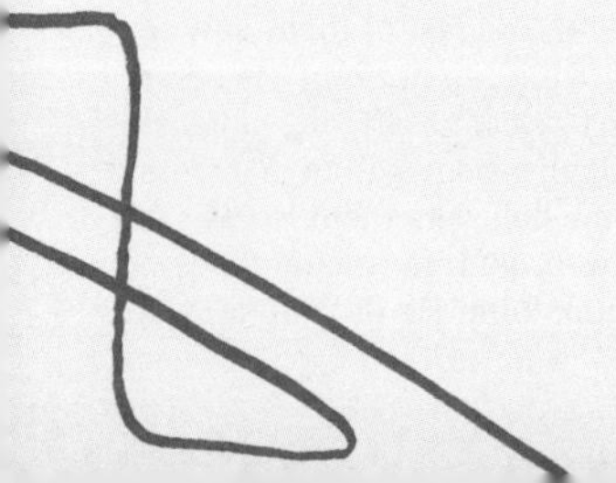

God's Son, didn't he?" Even the two criminals crucified next to him joined in the mockery.

45-46 From noon to three, the whole earth was dark. Around mid-afternoon Jesus groaned out of the depths, crying loudly, "*Eli, Eli, lama sabachthani?*" which means, "My God, my God, why have you abandoned me?"

47-49 Some bystanders who heard him said, "He's calling for Elijah." One of them ran and got a sponge soaked in sour wine and lifted it on a stick so he could drink. The others joked, "Don't be in such a hurry. Let's see if Elijah comes and saves him."

50 But Jesus, again crying out loudly, breathed his last.

51-53 At that moment, the Temple curtain was ripped in two, top to bottom. There was an earthquake, and rocks were split in pieces. What's more, tombs were opened up, and many bodies of believers asleep in their graves were raised. (After Jesus' resurrection, they left the tombs, entered the holy city, and appeared to many.)

54 The captain of the guard and those with him, when they saw the earthquake and everything else that was happening, were scared to death. They said, "This has to be the Son of God!"

55-56 There were also quite a few women watching from a distance, women who had followed Jesus from Galilee in order to serve him. Among them were Mary Magdalene, Mary the mother of James and Joseph, and the mother of the Zebedee brothers.

THE TOMB

57-61 Late in the afternoon a wealthy man from Arimathea, a disciple of Jesus, arrived. His name was Joseph. He went to Pilate and asked for Jesus' body. Pilate granted his request. Joseph took the body and wrapped it in clean linens, put it in his own tomb, a new tomb only recently cut into the rock, and rolled a large stone across the entrance. Then he went off. But Mary Magdalene and the other Mary stayed, sitting in plain view of the tomb.

62-64 After sundown, the high priests and Pharisees arranged a meeting with Pilate. They said, "Sir, we just remembered that that liar announced while he was still alive, 'After three days I will be raised.' We've got to get that tomb sealed until the third day. There's a good chance his disciples will come and steal the corpse and then go around saying, 'He's risen from the dead.' Then we'll be worse off than before, the final deceit surpassing the first."

65-66 Pilate told them, "You will have a guard. Go ahead and secure it the best you can." So they went out and secured the tomb, sealing the stone and posting guards.

RISEN FROM THE DEAD

28 1-4 After the Sabbath, as the first light of the new week dawned, Mary Magdalene and the other Mary came to keep vigil at the tomb. Suddenly the earth reeled and rocked under their feet as God's angel came down from heaven, came right up to where they were standing. He rolled back the stone and then sat on it. Shafts of lightning blazed from him. His garments shimmered snow-white. The guards at the tomb were scared to death. They were so frightened, they couldn't move.

5-6 The angel spoke to the women: "There is nothing to fear here. I know you're looking for Jesus, the One they nailed to the cross. He is not here. He was raised, just as he said. Come and look at the place where he was placed.

7 "Now, get on your way quickly and tell his disciples, 'He is risen from the dead. He is going on ahead of you to Galilee. You will see him there.' That's the message."

8-10 The women, deep in wonder and full of joy, lost no time in leaving the tomb. They ran to tell the disciples. Then Jesus met them, stopping them in their tracks. "Good morning!" he said. They fell to their knees, embraced his feet, and worshiped him. Jesus said, "You're holding on to me for dear life! Don't be frightened like that. Go tell my brothers that they are to go to Galilee, and that I'll meet them there."

11-15 Meanwhile, the guards had scattered, but a few of them went into the city and told the high priests everything that had happened. They called a meeting of the religious leaders and came up with a plan: They took a large sum of money and gave it to the soldiers, bribing them to say, "His disciples came in the night and stole the body while we were sleeping." They assured them, "If the governor hears about your sleeping on duty, we will make sure you don't get blamed." The soldiers took the bribe and did as they were told. That story, cooked up in the Jewish High Council, is still going around.

▲ ▲ ▲

16-17 Meanwhile, the eleven disciples were on their way to Galilee, headed for the mountain

The Worship of Women

Early on the first day of the week, Mary Magdalene and "the other Mary" went to the tomb where Jesus' body lay. They went to give Jesus one last ministration, one final duty of devotion: anointing his body with spices and perfumes (Mark 16:1). This would be their final faithful act of worship, caring for their Lord's body even after death.

Mary Magdalene, who had once been delivered from demons, had always been at her teacher's side. She, along with other women, had provided financially for Jesus. Even here, in death, she remained steadfast. She was ever faithful—so much so that, as commentator Frederick Dale Bruner observes in his commentary on Matthew, "it is as if she will never ever leave him, even when he has had to leave her."

But her care for Christ's body became more than just a sign of her love, gratitude, or faithfulness. In light of Jesus' resurrection, Mary's sadness and fear turned to adoration and worship. The Resurrection demonstrated that Jesus was more than a beloved healer and teacher. It showed him to be the Son of God, her Savior and Lord, who had conquered death through death.

Worship moves outward. Worship is not only a personal or small-group act of devotion. Worship is proclamation, communal. Worship involves bearing witness to the resurrected Christ, who comes to meet us in our distress, as he did Mary. Jesus commissioned Mary to be the evangelist to the core group of disciples. She ran to tell of Christ's resurrection with simple words: "I saw the Master!" (John 20:18).

Women were the first witnesses to the Resurrection. Mary was the first evangelist. Called to be an apostle to the apostles, Mary was charged with bringing resurrection news to the rest of the disciples. The teacher she'd followed was now the Lord she worshiped.

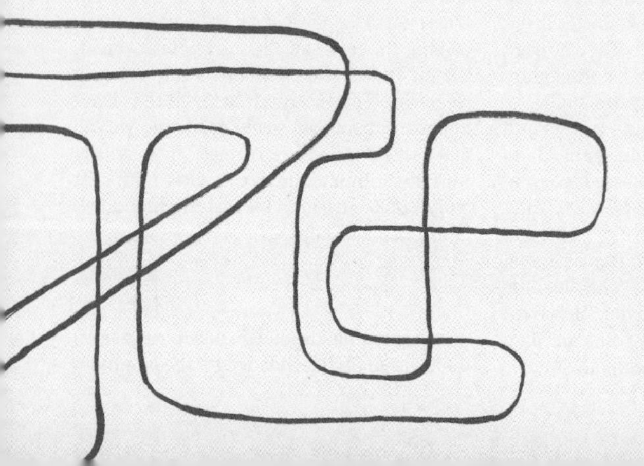

Jesus had set for their reunion. The moment they saw him they worshiped him. Some, though, held back, not sure about *worship*, about risking themselves totally.

18-20 Jesus, undeterred, went right ahead and gave his charge: "God authorized and commanded me to commission you: Go out and train everyone you meet, far and near, in this way of life, marking them by baptism in the threefold name: Father, Son, and Holy Spirit. Then instruct them in the practice of all I have commanded you. I'll be with you as you do this, day after day after day, right up to the end of the age."

Mark

GOD IS PASSIONATE TO SAVE US

Mark wastes no time in getting down to business—a single-sentence introduction ("The good news of Jesus Christ—the Message!—begins here"), and not a digression to be found from beginning to end. An event has taken place that radically changes the way we look at and experience the world, and he can't wait to tell us about it. There's an air of breathless excitement in nearly every sentence he writes. The sooner we get the message, the better off we'll be, for the message is good, incredibly good: God is here, and he's on our side. Mark says he even calls us "family."

> He was surrounded by the crowd when he was given the message, "Your mother and brothers and sisters are outside looking for you."
>
> Jesus responded, "Who do you think are my mother and brothers?" Looking around, taking in everyone seated around him, he said, "Right here, right in front of you—my mother and my brothers. Obedience is thicker than blood. The person who obeys God's will is my brother and sister and mother."
>
> MARK 3:32-35

The bare announcement that God exists doesn't particularly qualify as news. Most people in most centuries have believed in the existence of God or gods. It may well be, in fact, that human beings in aggregate and through the centuries have given more attention and concern to divinity than to all their other concerns put together—food, housing, clothing, pleasure, work, family, whatever.

But that God is here right now, and on our side, actively seeking to help us in the way we most need help—*this* qualifies as news. For, common as belief in God is, there is also an enormous amount of guesswork and gossip surrounding the subject, which results in runaway superstition, anxiety, and exploitation. So Mark, understandably, is in a hurry to tell us what happened in the birth, life, death, and resurrection of Jesus—the Event that reveals the truth of God to us, so that we can live in reality and not illusion. He doesn't want us to waste a minute of these precious lives of ours ignorant of this most practical of all matters—that God is passionate to save us.

JOHN THE BAPTIZER

1 1-3 The good news of Jesus Christ—the Message!—begins here, following to the letter the scroll of the prophet Isaiah.

> Watch closely: I'm sending my preacher
> ahead of you;
> He'll make the road smooth for you.
> Thunder in the desert!
> Prepare for God's arrival!
> Make the road smooth and straight!

4-6 John the Baptizer appeared in the wild, preaching a baptism of life-change that leads to forgiveness of sins. People thronged to him from Judea and Jerusalem and, as they confessed their sins, were baptized by him in the Jordan River into a changed life. John wore a camel-hair habit, tied at the waist with a leather belt. He ate locusts and wild field honey.

7-8 As he preached he said, "The real action comes next: The star in this drama, to whom I'm a mere stagehand, will change your life. I'm baptizing you here in the river, turning your old life in for a kingdom life. His baptism—a holy baptism by the Holy Spirit—will change you from the inside out."

9-11 At this time, Jesus came from Nazareth in Galilee and was baptized by John in the Jordan. The moment he came out of the water, he saw the sky split open and God's Spirit, looking like a dove, come down on him. Along with the Spirit, a voice: "You are my Son, chosen and marked by my love, pride of my life."

GOD'S KINGDOM IS HERE

12-13 At once, this same Spirit pushed Jesus out into the wild. For forty wilderness days and nights he was tested by Satan. Wild animals were his companions, and angels took care of him.

14-15 After John was arrested, Jesus went to Galilee preaching the Message of God: "Time's up! God's kingdom is here. Change your life and believe the Message."

16-18 Passing along the beach of Lake Galilee, he saw Simon and his brother Andrew net-fishing. Fishing was their regular work. Jesus said to them, "Come with me. I'll make a new kind of fisherman out of you. I'll show you how to catch men and women instead of perch and bass." They didn't ask questions. They dropped their nets and followed.

19-20 A dozen yards or so down the beach, he saw the brothers James and John, Zebedee's sons. They were in the boat, mending their fishnets. Right off, he made the same offer. Immediately, they left their father Zebedee, the boat, and the hired hands, and followed.

CONFIDENT TEACHING

21-22 Then they entered Capernaum. When the Sabbath arrived, Jesus lost no time in getting to the meeting place. He spent the day there teaching. They were surprised at his teaching—so forthright, so confident—not quibbling and quoting like the religion scholars.

23-24 Suddenly, while still in the meeting place, he was interrupted by a man who was deeply disturbed and yelling out, "What business do you have here with us, Jesus? Nazarene! I know what you're up to! You're the Holy One of God, and you've come to destroy us!"

25-26 Jesus shut him up: "Quiet! Get out of him!" The afflicting spirit threw the man into spasms, protesting loudly—and got out.

27-28 Everyone there was spellbound, buzzing with curiosity. "What's going on here? A new teaching that does what it says? He shuts up defiling, demonic spirits and tells them to get lost!" News of this traveled fast and was soon all over Galilee.

29-31 Directly on leaving the meeting place, they came to Simon and Andrew's house, accompanied by James and John. Simon's mother-in-law was sick in bed, burning up with fever. They told Jesus. He went to her, took her hand, and raised her up. No sooner had the fever left than she was up fixing dinner for them.

32-34 That evening, after the sun was down, they brought sick and evil-afflicted people to him, the whole city lined up at his door! He cured their sick bodies and tormented spirits. Because the demons knew his true identity, he didn't let them say a word.

THE LEPER

35-37 While it was still night, way before dawn, he got up and went out to a secluded spot and prayed. Simon and those with him went looking for him. They found him and said, "Everybody's looking for you."

38-39 Jesus said, "Let's go to the rest of the villages so I can preach there also. This is why I've come." He went to their meeting places all through Galilee, preaching and throwing out the demons.

40 A leper came to him, begging on his knees, "If you want to, you can cleanse me."

Jesus the Healer

She lay in bed, clothes damp from the fever wracking her body. Voices reached her ears through the fog as she sensed someone coming close.

A cool hand touched hers, fingers gently yet firmly pulling her to a sitting position. She felt the fever slip away as healing drew near.

We don't need to look far these days to see people in desperate need of healing. From cancer to arthritis to anxiety and depression, people's bodies and minds succumb to disease and despair that threaten to destroy their souls.

Perhaps you, too, lie in bed longing for relief from the pain wracking your body or mind. Maybe you struggle as you watch a loved one battle to survive.

The truth is that we are all in need of healing. That's why Jesus came. "God went for the jugular when he sent his own Son. He didn't deal with the problem as something remote and unimportant. In his Son, Jesus, he personally took on the human condition, entered the disordered mess of struggling humanity in order to set it right once and for all" (Romans 8:3).

With this backdrop of disordered mess, Mark 1 opens by declaring why Jesus entered this world and what he intended to do: "As [John the Baptizer] preached he said, 'The real action comes next: The star in this drama, to whom I'm a mere stagehand, will change your life'" (Mark 1:7).

Jesus came to change lives and rid this world of suffering and sin. Preaching a new type of kingdom, he revealed the depth of God's love. Jesus, the Son of God and true star of this drama, declared that it wasn't the healthy who needed a doctor—who needed him—but the sick (Matthew 9:12-13).

The drama of sickness and suffering is exactly where Jesus stepped in—in the life of Simon's mother-in-law, whom he healed of her fever; in the life of a leper who dared approach him and beg for healing.

Did Jesus recoil from the leper? No, Jesus reached out and touched him, breaking rules people had followed for centuries. Jesus, the healer, drew near.

Do you need Jesus' healing touch? Maybe for your body? Maybe for your soul? Through Jesus we witness the demonstration of the name Immanuel, "God-With-Us" (see Isaiah 7:14). Through Jesus, God is never separate from creation. God draws near to us in our suffering and sickness. And it is through Jesus that we experience true healing, which changes us from the inside out.

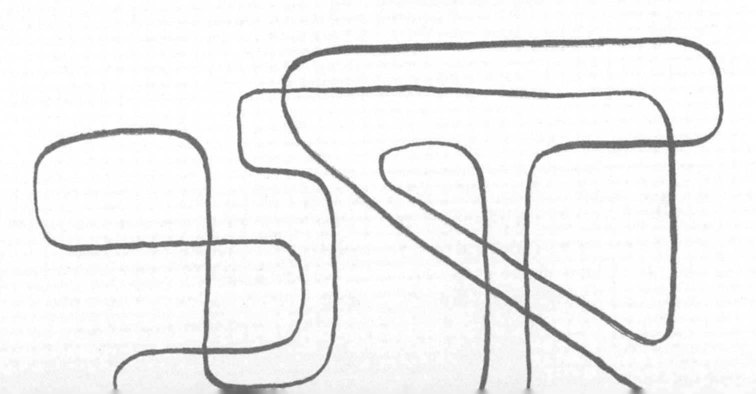

41-45 Deeply moved, Jesus put out his hand, touched him, and said, "I want to. Be clean." Then and there the leprosy was gone, his skin smooth and healthy. Jesus dismissed him with strict orders: "Say nothing to anyone. Take the offering for cleansing that Moses prescribed and present yourself to the priest. This will validate your healing to the people." But as soon as the man was out of earshot, he told everyone he met what had happened, spreading the news all over town. So Jesus kept to out-of-the-way places, no longer able to move freely in and out of the city. But people found him, and came from all over.

A PARAPLEGIC

2 1-5 After a few days, Jesus returned to Capernaum, and word got around that he was back home. A crowd gathered, jamming the entrance so no one could get in or out. He was teaching the Word. They brought a paraplegic to him, carried by four men. When they weren't able to get in because of the crowd, they removed part of the roof and lowered the paraplegic on his stretcher. Impressed by their bold belief, Jesus said to the paraplegic, "Son, I forgive your sins."

6-7 Some religion scholars sitting there started whispering among themselves, "He can't talk that way! That's blasphemy! God and only God can forgive sins."

8-12 Jesus knew right away what they were thinking, and said, "Why are you so skeptical? Which is simpler: to say to the paraplegic, 'I forgive your sins,' or say, 'Get up, take your stretcher, and start walking'? Well, just so it's clear that I'm the Son of Man and authorized to do either, or both . . ." (he looked now at the paraplegic), "Get up. Pick up your stretcher and go home." And the man did it—got up, grabbed his stretcher, and walked out, with everyone there watching him. They rubbed their eyes, stunned—and then praised God, saying, "We've never seen anything like this!"

THE TAX COLLECTOR

13-14 Then Jesus went again to walk alongside the lake. Again a crowd came to him, and he taught them. Strolling along, he saw Levi, son of Alphaeus, at his work collecting taxes. Jesus said, "Come along with me." He came.

15-16 Later Jesus and his disciples were at home having supper with a collection of disreputable guests. Unlikely as it seems, more than a few of them had become followers. The religion scholars and Pharisees saw him keeping this kind of company and lit into his disciples: "What kind of example is this, acting cozy with the misfits?"

17 Jesus, overhearing, shot back, "Who needs a doctor: the healthy or the sick? I'm here inviting the sin-sick, not the spiritually-fit."

FEASTING OR FASTING?

18 The disciples of John and the disciples of the Pharisees made a practice of fasting. Some people confronted Jesus: "Why do the followers of John and the Pharisees take on the discipline of fasting, but your followers don't?"

19-20 Jesus said, "When you're celebrating a wedding, you don't skimp on the cake and wine. You feast. Later you may need to pull in your belt, but not now. As long as the bride and groom are with you, you have a good time. No one throws cold water on a friendly bonfire. This is Kingdom Come!"

21-22 He went on, "No one cuts up a fine silk scarf to patch old work clothes; you want fabrics that match. And you don't put your wine in cracked bottles."

23-24 One Sabbath day he was walking through a field of ripe grain. As his disciples made a path, they pulled off heads of grain. The Pharisees told on them to Jesus: "Look, your disciples are breaking Sabbath rules!"

25-28 Jesus said, "Really? Haven't you ever read what David did when he was hungry, along with those who were with him? How he entered the sanctuary and ate fresh bread off the altar, with the Chief Priest Abiathar right there watching—holy bread that no one but priests were allowed to eat—and handed it out to his companions?" Then Jesus said, "The Sabbath was made to serve us; we weren't made to serve the Sabbath. The Son of Man is no yes-man to the Sabbath. He's in charge!"

DOING GOOD ON THE SABBATH

3 1-3 Then he went back in the meeting place where he found a man with a crippled hand. The Pharisees had their eyes on Jesus to see if he would heal him, hoping to catch him in a Sabbath violation. He said to the man with the crippled hand, "Stand here where we can see you."

4 Then he spoke to the people: "What kind of action suits the Sabbath best? Doing good or doing evil? Helping people or leaving them helpless?" No one said a word.

5-6 He looked them in the eye, one after another, angry now, furious at their hard-nosed religion. He said to the man, "Hold out your hand." He held it out—it was as good as new! The Pharisees got out as fast as they could, sputtering about how they would join forces with Herod's followers and ruin him.

THE TWELVE APOSTLES

7-10 Jesus went off with his disciples to the sea to get away. But a huge crowd from Galilee trailed after them—also from Judea, Jerusalem, Idumea, across the Jordan, and around Tyre and Sidon—swarms of people who had heard the reports and had come to see for themselves. He told his disciples to get a boat ready so he wouldn't be trampled by the crowd. He had healed many people, and now everyone who had something wrong was pushing and shoving to get near and touch him.

11-12 Evil spirits, when they recognized him, fell down and cried out, "You are the Son of God!" But Jesus would have none of it. He shut them up, forbidding them to identify him in public.

13-19 He climbed a mountain and invited those he wanted with him. They climbed together. He settled on twelve, and designated them apostles. The plan was that they would be with him, and he would send them out to proclaim the Word and give them authority to banish demons. These are the Twelve:

Simon (Jesus later named him Peter,
meaning "Rock"),
James, son of Zebedee,
John, brother of James (Jesus nicknamed
the Zebedee brothers Boanerges,
meaning "Sons of Thunder"),
Andrew,
Philip,
Bartholomew,
Matthew,
Thomas,
James, son of Alphaeus,
Thaddaeus,
Simon the Canaanite,
Judas Iscariot (who betrayed him).

SATAN FIGHTING SATAN?

20-21 Jesus came home and, as usual, a crowd gathered—so many making demands on him that there wasn't even time to eat. His friends heard what was going on and went to rescue him, by force if necessary. They suspected he was believing his own press.

22-27 The religion scholars from Jerusalem came down spreading rumors that he was working black magic, using devil tricks to impress them with spiritual power. Jesus confronted their slander with a story: "Does it make sense to send a devil to catch a devil, to use Satan to get rid of Satan? A constantly squabbling family disintegrates. If Satan were fighting Satan, there soon wouldn't be any Satan left. Do you think it's possible in broad daylight to enter the house of an awake, able-bodied man, and walk off with his possessions unless you tie him up first? Tie him up, though, and you can clean him out.

28-30 "Listen to this carefully. I'm warning you. There's nothing done or said that can't be forgiven. But if you persist in your slanders against God's Holy Spirit, you are repudiating the very One who forgives, sawing off the branch on which you're sitting, severing by your own perversity all connection with the One who forgives." He gave this warning because they were accusing him of being in league with Evil.

JESUS' MOTHER AND BROTHERS

31-32 Just then his mother and brothers showed up. Standing outside, they relayed a message that they wanted a word with him. He was surrounded by the crowd when he was given the message, "Your mother and brothers and sisters are outside looking for you."

33-35 Jesus responded, "Who do you think are my mother and brothers?" Looking around, taking in everyone seated around him, he said, "Right here, right in front of you—my mother and my brothers. Obedience is thicker than blood. The person who obeys God's will is my brother and sister and mother."

THE STORY OF THE SCATTERED SEED

4 1-2 He went back to teaching by the sea. A crowd built up to such a great size that he had to get into an offshore boat, using the boat as a pulpit as the people pushed to the water's edge. He taught by using stories, many stories.

3-8 "Listen. What do you make of this? A farmer planted seed. As he scattered the seed, some of it fell on the road and birds ate it. Some fell in the gravel; it sprouted quickly but didn't put down roots, so when the sun came up it withered just as quickly. Some fell in the weeds; as it came up, it was strangled among the weeds and nothing came of it. Some fell on good earth and came up with a flourish, producing a harvest exceeding his wildest dreams.

9 "Are you listening to this? Really listening?"

10-12 When they were off by themselves,

those who were close to him, along with the Twelve, asked about the stories. He told them, "You've been given insight into God's kingdom—you know how it works. But to those who can't see it yet, everything comes in stories, creating readiness, nudging them toward a welcome awakening. These are people—

Whose eyes are open but don't see a thing,
Whose ears are open but don't
understand a word,
Who avoid making an about-face and
getting forgiven."

13 He continued, "Do you see how this story works? All my stories work this way.

14-15 "The farmer plants the Word. Some people are like the seed that falls on the hardened soil of the road. No sooner do they hear the Word than Satan snatches away what has been planted in them.

16-17 "And some are like the seed that lands in the gravel. When they first hear the Word, they respond with great enthusiasm. But there is such shallow soil of character that when the emotions wear off and some difficulty arrives, there is nothing to show for it.

18-19 "The seed cast in the weeds represents the ones who hear the kingdom news but are overwhelmed with worries about all the things they have to do and all the things they want to get. The stress strangles what they heard, and nothing comes of it.

20 "But the seed planted in the good earth represents those who hear the Word, embrace it, and produce a harvest beyond their wildest dreams."

GIVING, NOT GETTING

21-22 Jesus went on: "Does anyone bring a lamp home and put it under a bucket or beneath the bed? Don't you put it up on a table or on the mantel? We're not keeping secrets, we're telling them; we're not hiding things, we're bringing them out into the open.

23 "Are you listening to this? Really listening?

24-25 "Listen carefully to what I am saying—and be wary of the shrewd advice that tells you how to get ahead in the world on your own. Giving, not getting, is the way. Generosity begets generosity. Stinginess impoverishes."

NEVER WITHOUT A STORY

26-29 Then Jesus said, "God's kingdom is like seed thrown on a field by a man who then goes to bed and forgets about it. The seed sprouts and grows—he has no idea how it happens. The earth does it all without his help: first a green stem of grass, then a bud, then the ripened grain. When the grain is fully formed, he reaps—harvest time!

30-32 "How can we picture God's kingdom? What kind of story can we use? It's like an acorn. When it lands on the ground it is quite small as seeds go, yet once it is planted it grows into a huge oak tree with thick branches. Eagles nest in it."

33-34 With many stories like these, he presented his message to them, fitting the stories to their experience and maturity. He was never without a story when he spoke. When he was alone with his disciples, he went over everything, sorting out the tangles, untying the knots.

THE WIND RAN OUT OF BREATH

35-38 Late that day he said to them, "Let's go across to the other side." They took him in the boat as he was. Other boats came along. A huge storm came up. Waves poured into the boat, threatening to sink it. And Jesus was in the stern, head on a pillow, sleeping! They roused him, saying, "Teacher, is it nothing to you that we're going down?"

39-40 Awake now, he told the wind to pipe down and said to the sea, "Quiet! Settle down!" The wind ran out of breath; the sea became smooth as glass. Jesus reprimanded the disciples: "Why are you such cowards? Don't you have any faith at all?"

41 They were in absolute awe, staggered. "Who is this, anyway?" they asked. "Wind and sea at his beck and call!"

THE MADMAN

5 1-5 They arrived on the other side of the sea in the country of the Gerasenes. As Jesus got out of the boat, a madman from the cemetery came up to him. He lived there among the tombs and graves. No one could restrain him—he couldn't be chained, couldn't be tied down. He had been tied up many times with chains and ropes, but he broke the chains, snapped the ropes. No one was strong enough to tame him. Night and day he roamed through the graves and the hills, screaming out and slashing himself with sharp stones.

6-8 When he saw Jesus a long way off, he ran and bowed in worship before him—then howled in protest, "What business do you have, Jesus, Son of the High God, messing with me? I swear to God, don't give me

Jesus the Dignifier

The demon-possessed man, the hemorrhaging woman, and the dead girl had one thing in common: In their ailments, isolation, and fear, Jesus met them and restored them to wholeness.

For this man and woman and girl specifically, life was marked by isolation, shame, and torment. The demon-possessed man spent his life among tombs—dark, impure places in his culture—unable to experience peace or even the joy of community. Held captive by unclean spirits, he was dehumanized, left to spend his nights crying out in agony and acting out in self-harm. As for the bleeding woman, for more than a decade she'd been considered impure by her neighbors, dubbed an outcast, and reduced to a life of loneliness and poverty. She was covered in shame. And the young girl, seemingly lost forever, was about to bring her family a bout of grief from which they might never recover.

Then they met Jesus.

Just as God spoke the world into existence—bringing life to nothingness and order to chaos—Jesus opened his mouth and spoke aloud the same divine word-to-action power. Jesus transformed these lives from chaos to order, from shame to honor, and from death to life.

In each of these stories, Jesus healed the body while simultaneously restoring the humanity and dignity of the person. In delivering them from harm, Jesus invited them to return to community, to family, to belonging—to a flourishing life.

In other words, where illness threatened to destroy their personhood, Jesus restored their honor and dignity. Jesus made them whole in every sense of the word.

It's worth noting that in each circumstance Jesus asked a question or called for a response.

To the evil spirit: "Tell me your name" (Mark 5:9).

To the crowd around the bleeding woman: "Who touched my robe?" (Mark 5:30).

To the young girl's grieving family: "Why all this busybody grief and gossip?" (Mark 5:39).

These, of course, are rhetorical. Jesus already knew the answers to the queries he posed. Yet by asking, he implied a bigger question for the person needing help, a question relevant to us as well: *Do you believe that I can heal you?*

What Jesus says next applies to all of us: "Just trust me" (Mark 5:36).

To those of us who are tormented, hurting, lonely, or covered in shame or sorrow: Jesus sees our pain. He is inviting us to trust his ability to bring God's shalom—order, peace, and wholeness—to our chaos.

This is what true healing in God's kingdom looks like. Jesus calls us, lifts us up, and replaces our shame with dignity.

No matter the dishonor, loneliness, ongoing pain, or weariness that threatens to keep you isolated and ashamed, you can trust Jesus, who has the power to restore your dignity.

a hard time!" (Jesus had just commanded the tormenting evil spirit, "Out! Get out of the man!")

9-10 Jesus asked him, "Tell me your name."

He replied, "My name is Mob. I'm a rioting mob." Then he desperately begged Jesus not to banish them from the country.

11-13 A large herd of pigs was grazing and rooting on a nearby hill. The demons begged him, "Send us to the pigs so we can live in them." Jesus gave the order. But it was even worse for the pigs than for the man. Crazed, they stampeded over a cliff into the sea and drowned.

14-15 Those tending the pigs, scared to death, bolted and told their story in town and country. Everyone wanted to see what had happened. They came up to Jesus and saw the madman sitting there wearing decent clothes and making sense, no longer a walking madhouse of a man.

16-17 Those who had seen it told the others what had happened to the demon-possessed man and the pigs. At first they were in awe—and then they were upset, upset over the drowned pigs. They demanded that Jesus leave and not come back.

18-20 As Jesus was getting into the boat, the demon-delivered man begged to go along, but he wouldn't let him. Jesus said, "Go home to your own people. Tell them your story—what the Master did, how he had mercy on you." The man went back and began to preach in the Ten Towns area about what Jesus had done for him. He was the talk of the town.

A RISK OF FAITH

21-24 After Jesus crossed over by boat, a large crowd met him at the seaside. One of the meeting-place leaders named Jairus came. When he saw Jesus, he fell to his knees, beside himself as he begged, "My dear daughter is at death's door. Come and lay hands on her so she will get well and live." Jesus went with him, the whole crowd tagging along, pushing and jostling him.

25-29 A woman who had suffered a condition of hemorrhaging for twelve years—a long succession of physicians had treated her, and treated her badly, taking all her money and leaving her worse off than before—had heard about Jesus. She slipped in from behind and touched his robe. She was thinking to herself, "If I can put a finger on his robe, I can get well." The moment she did it, the flow of blood dried up. She could feel the change and knew her plague was over and done with.

30 At the same moment, Jesus felt energy discharging from him. He turned around to the crowd and asked, "Who touched my robe?"

31 His disciples said, "What are you talking about? With this crowd pushing and jostling you, you're asking, 'Who touched me?' Dozens have touched you!"

32-33 But he went on asking, looking around to see who had done it. The woman, knowing what had happened, knowing she was the one, stepped up in fear and trembling, knelt before him, and gave him the whole story.

34 Jesus said to her, "Daughter, you took a risk of faith, and now you're healed and whole. Live well, live blessed! Be healed of your plague."

▲ ▲ ▲

35 While he was still talking, some people came from the leader's house and told him, "Your daughter is dead. Why bother the Teacher any more?"

36 Jesus overheard what they were talking about and said to the leader, "Don't listen to them; just trust me."

37-40 He permitted no one to go in with him except Peter, James, and John. They entered the leader's house and pushed their way through the gossips looking for a story and neighbors bringing in casseroles. Jesus was abrupt: "Why all this busybody grief and gossip? This child isn't dead; she's sleeping." Provoked to sarcasm, they told him he didn't know what he was talking about.

40-43 But when he had sent them all out, he took the child's father and mother, along with his companions, and entered the child's room. He clasped the girl's hand and said, "*Talitha koum*," which means, "Little girl, get up." At that, she was up and walking around! This girl was twelve years of age. They, of course, were all beside themselves with joy. He gave them strict orders that no one was to know what had taken place in that room. Then he said, "Give her something to eat."

JUST A CARPENTER

6 1-2 He left there and returned to his hometown. His disciples came along. On the Sabbath, he gave a lecture in the meeting place. He stole the show, impressing

everyone. "We had no idea he was this good!" they said. "How did he get so wise all of a sudden, get such ability?"

3 But in the next breath they were cutting him down: "He's just a carpenter—Mary's boy. We've known him since he was a kid. We know his brothers, James, Justus, Jude, and Simon, and his sisters. Who does he think he is?" They tripped over what little they knew about him and fell, sprawling. And they never got any further.

4-6 Jesus told them, "A prophet has little honor in his hometown, among his relatives, on the streets he played in as a child." Jesus wasn't able to do much of anything there—he laid hands on a few sick people and healed them, that's all. He couldn't get over their stubbornness. He left and made a circuit of the other villages, teaching.

THE TWELVE

7-8 Jesus called the Twelve to him, and sent them out in pairs. He gave them authority and power to deal with the evil opposition. He sent them off with these instructions:

8-9 "Don't think you need a lot of extra equipment for this. *You* are the equipment. No special appeals for funds. Keep it simple.

10 "And no luxury inns. Get a modest place and be content there until you leave.

11 "If you're not welcomed, not listened to, quietly withdraw. Don't make a scene. Shrug your shoulders and be on your way."

12-13 Then they were on the road. They preached with joyful urgency that life can be radically different; right and left they sent the demons packing; they brought wellness to the sick, anointing their bodies, healing their spirits.

THE DEATH OF JOHN

14 King Herod heard of all this, for by this time the name of Jesus was on everyone's lips. He said, "This has to be John the Baptizer come back from the dead—that's why he's able to work miracles!"

15 Others said, "No, it's Elijah."

Others said, "He's a prophet, just like one of the old-time prophets."

16 But Herod wouldn't budge: "It's John, sure enough. I cut off his head, and now he's back, alive."

17-20 Herod was the one who had ordered the arrest of John, put him in chains, and sent him to prison at the nagging of Herodias, his brother Philip's wife. For John had provoked Herod by naming his relationship with Herodias "adultery." Herodias, smoldering with hate, wanted to kill him, but didn't dare because Herod was in awe of John. Convinced that he was a holy man, he gave him special treatment. Whenever he listened to him he was miserable with guilt—and yet he couldn't stay away. Something in John kept pulling him back.

21-22 But a portentous day arrived when Herod threw a birthday party, inviting all the brass and bluebloods in Galilee. Herodias's daughter entered the banquet hall and danced for the guests. She charmed Herod and the guests.

22-23 The king said to the girl, "Ask me anything. I'll give you anything you want." Carried away, he kept on, "I swear, I'll split my kingdom with you if you say so!"

24 She went back to her mother and said, "What should I ask for?"

"Ask for the head of John the Baptizer."

25 Excited, she ran back to the king and said, "I want the head of John the Baptizer served up on a platter. And I want it now!"

26-29 That sobered the king up fast. But unwilling to lose face with his guests, he caved in and let her have her wish. The king sent the executioner off to the prison with orders to bring back John's head. He went, cut off John's head, brought it back on a platter, and presented it to the girl, who gave it to her mother. When John's disciples heard about this, they came and got the body and gave it a decent burial.

SUPPER FOR FIVE THOUSAND

30-31 The apostles then rendezvoused with Jesus and reported on all that they had done and taught. Jesus said, "Come off by yourselves; let's take a break and get a little rest." For there was constant coming and going. They didn't even have time to eat.

32-34 So they got in the boat and went off to a remote place by themselves. Someone saw them going and the word got around. From the surrounding towns people went out on foot, running, and got there ahead of them. When Jesus arrived, he saw this huge crowd. At the sight of them, his heart broke—like sheep with no shepherd they were. He went right to work teaching them.

35-36 When his disciples thought this had gone on long enough—it was now quite late in the day—they interrupted: "We are a long way out in the country, and it's very late.

Pronounce a benediction and send these folks off so they can get some supper."

37 Jesus said, "You do it. Fix supper for them."

They replied, "Are you serious? You want us to go spend a fortune on food for their supper?"

38 But he was quite serious. "How many loaves of bread do you have? Take an inventory."

That didn't take long. "Five," they said, "plus two fish."

39-44 Jesus got them all to sit down in groups of fifty or a hundred—they looked like a patchwork quilt of wildflowers spread out on the green grass! He took the five loaves and two fish, lifted his face to heaven in prayer, blessed, broke, and gave the bread to the disciples, and the disciples in turn gave it to the people. He did the same with the fish. They all ate their fill. The disciples gathered twelve baskets of leftovers. More than five thousand were at the supper.

WALKING ON THE SEA

45-46 As soon as the meal was finished, Jesus insisted that the disciples get in the boat and go on ahead across to Bethsaida while he dismissed the congregation. After sending them off, he climbed a mountain to pray.

47-49 Late at night, the boat was far out at sea; Jesus was still by himself on land. He could see his men struggling with the oars, the wind having come up against them. At about four o'clock in the morning, Jesus came toward them, walking on the sea. He intended to go right by them. But when they saw him walking on the sea, they thought it was a ghost and screamed, scared to death.

50-52 Jesus was quick to comfort them: "Courage! It's me. Don't be afraid." As soon as he climbed into the boat, the wind died down. They were stunned, shaking their heads, wondering what was going on. They didn't understand what he had done at the supper. None of this had yet penetrated their hearts.

53-56 They beached the boat at Gennesaret and tied up at the landing. As soon as they got out of the boat, word got around fast. People ran this way and that, bringing their sick on stretchers to where they heard he was. Wherever he went, village or town or country crossroads, they brought their sick to the marketplace and begged him to let them touch the edge of his coat—that's all. And whoever touched him became well.

THE SOURCE OF YOUR POLLUTION

7 1-4 The Pharisees, along with some religion scholars who had come from Jerusalem, gathered around him. They noticed that some of his disciples weren't being careful with ritual washings before meals. The Pharisees—Jews in general, in fact—would never eat a meal without going through the motions of a ritual hand-washing, with an especially vigorous scrubbing if they had just come from the market (to say nothing of the scourings they'd give jugs and pots and pans).

5 The Pharisees and religion scholars asked, "Why do your disciples brush off the rules, showing up at meals without washing their hands?"

6-8 Jesus answered, "Isaiah was right about frauds like you, hit the bull's-eye in fact:

These people make a big show of saying
the right thing,
but their heart isn't in it.
They act like they are worshiping me,
but they don't mean it.
They just use me as a cover
for teaching whatever suits their fancy,
Ditching God's command
and taking up the latest fads."

9-13 He went on, "Well, good for you. You get rid of God's command so you won't be inconvenienced in following the religious fashions! Moses said, 'Respect your father and mother,' and, 'Anyone denouncing father or mother should be killed.' But you weasel out of that by saying that it's perfectly acceptable to say to father or mother, 'Gift! What I owed you I've given as a gift to God,' thus relieving yourselves of obligation to father or mother. You scratch out God's Word and scrawl a whim in its place. You do a lot of things like this."

14-15 Jesus called the crowd together again and said, "Listen now, all of you—take this to heart. It's not what you swallow that pollutes your life; it's what you vomit—that's the real pollution."

17 When he was back home after being with the crowd, his disciples said, "We don't get it. Put it in plain language."

18-19 Jesus said, "Are you being willfully stupid? Don't you see that what you swallow can't contaminate you? It doesn't enter your heart but your stomach, works its way through the intestines, and is finally flushed." (That took care of dietary quibbling; Jesus was saying that *all* foods are fit to eat.)

Jesus, Dirt, and Dogs

Is your home a "please remove your shoes" or a "keep your shoes on" household? What we do with our shoes reflects something of what we believe about dirt. My Japanese friend Emily's family members remove their shoes before entering a home, keeping the dirt outside since they eat and sleep on tatami rugs and futons. In other words, they live much closer to the ground than my Western family members, who eat and sleep on high surfaces far away from the dirty ground (and our dirty shoes, which we wear indoors).

In Mark 7, Jesus confronts some deeply held beliefs about where dirt comes from. The Jews of Jesus' day "would never eat a meal without going through the motions of a ritual hand-washing" (Mark 7:3) and certainly would not share a meal with a Greek woman from Phoenicia. As both a Gentile and a woman, she was the epitome of an unclean outsider, holding the same status as a dog in a Jewish household.

But Jesus was ready to draw new lines in the dirt. We cannot become clean by going through the motions of any religious ceremony, because an outer washing can't cleanse our inner being—which is where the true dirt comes from. It's not what we eat or where we live that contaminates us; it's what comes out of our sinful hearts that pollutes the world: obscenity, lust, theft, adultery, greed, deception, even mean looks. Jesus has no interest in polishing apples that are rotten to the core.

But how can our inner selves be healed and cleansed? On our own, they cannot. Like the Syro-Phoenician woman whose daughter needed a cure, we come to Jesus, kneeling before him in humility and begging for any scraps of help he might offer. And Jesus, who acknowledged and honored this woman who was regarded as an outsider and a "dog" by engaging in theological wordplay with her, meets us with kindness.

Jesus is not impressed with religious posturing. But when we approach him in faith, there is nothing he is not willing to cleanse or heal. And like the man healed from the inside out at the end of this chapter, we may find ourselves bearing witness that "he's done it all and done it well" (Mark 7:37).

20-23 He went on: "It's what comes out of a person that pollutes: obscenities, lusts, thefts, murders, adulteries, greed, depravity, deceptive dealings, carousing, mean looks, slander, arrogance, foolishness—all these are vomit from the heart. *There* is the source of your pollution."

▲ ▲ ▲

24-26 From there Jesus set out for the vicinity of Tyre. He entered a house there where he didn't think he would be found, but he couldn't escape notice. He was barely inside when a woman who had a disturbed daughter heard where he was. She came and knelt at his feet, begging for help. The woman was Greek, Syro-Phoenician by birth. She asked him to cure her daughter.

27 He said, "Stand in line and take your turn. The children get fed first. If there's any left over, the dogs get it."

28 She said, "Of course, Master. But don't dogs under the table get scraps dropped by the children?"

29-30 Jesus was impressed. "You're right! On your way! Your daughter is no longer disturbed. The demonic affliction is gone." She went home and found her daughter relaxed on the bed, the torment gone for good.

31-35 Then he left the region of Tyre, went through Sidon back to Galilee Lake and over to the district of the Ten Towns. Some people brought a man who could neither hear nor speak and asked Jesus to lay a healing hand on him. He took the man off by himself, put his fingers in the man's ears and some spit on the man's tongue. Then Jesus looked up in prayer, groaned mightily, and commanded, "*Ephphatha!*—Open up!" And it happened. The man's hearing was clear and his speech plain—just like that.

36-37 Jesus urged them to keep it quiet, but they talked it up all the more, beside themselves with excitement. "He's done it all and done it well. He gives hearing to the deaf, speech to the speechless."

A MEAL FOR FOUR THOUSAND

8 1-3 At about this same time he again found himself with a hungry crowd on his hands. He called his disciples together and said, "This crowd is breaking my heart. They have stuck with me for three days, and now they have nothing to eat. If I send them home hungry, they'll faint along the way—some of them have come a long distance."

4 His disciples responded, "What do you expect us to do about it? Buy food out here in the desert?"

5 He asked, "How much bread do you have?"

"Seven loaves," they said.

6-10 So Jesus told the crowd to sit down on the ground. After giving thanks, he took the seven bread loaves, broke them into pieces, and gave them to his disciples so they could hand them out to the crowd. They also had a few fish. He pronounced a blessing over the fish and told his disciples to hand them out as well. The crowd ate its fill. Seven sacks of leftovers were collected. There were well over four thousand at the meal. Then he sent them home. He himself went straight to the boat with his disciples and set out for Dalmanoutha.

11-12 When they arrived, the Pharisees came out and started in on him, badgering him to prove himself, pushing him up against the wall. Provoked, he said, "Why does this generation clamor for miraculous guarantees? If I have anything to say about it, you'll not get so much as a hint of a guarantee."

CONTAMINATING YEAST

13-15 He then left them, got back in the boat, and headed for the other side. But the disciples forgot to pack a lunch. Except for a single loaf of bread, there wasn't a crumb in the boat. Jesus warned, "Be very careful. Keep a sharp eye out for the contaminating yeast of Pharisees and the followers of Herod."

16-19 Meanwhile, the disciples were finding fault with each other because they had forgotten to bring bread. Jesus overheard and said, "Why are you fussing because you forgot bread? Don't you see the point of all this? Don't you get it at all? Remember the five loaves I broke for the five thousand? How many baskets of leftovers did you pick up?"

They said, "Twelve."

20 "And the seven loaves for the four thousand—how many bags full of leftovers did you get?"

"Seven."

21 He said, "Do you still not get it?"

22-23 They arrived at Bethsaida. Some people brought a sightless man and begged Jesus to give him a healing touch. Taking him by the hand, he led him out of the village. He put spit in the man's eyes, laid hands on him, and asked, "Do you see anything?"

24-26 He looked up. "I see men. They look

THE SYRO-PHOENICIAN WOMAN

The Syro-Phoenician woman's story begins like so many others': A loved one is suffering, and Jesus is their last hope. She went looking and found him hiding, hoping for a moment's peace. Jesus—fully God *and* fully human—was apparently having that sort of day.

But she was undeterred by his need and pleaded for help. That's when the story takes a turn. Rather than remarking on her faith or being moved by compassion, Jesus told her, quite abruptly it seems, to "stand in line. . . . The children get fed first. If there's any left over, the dogs get it" (Mark 7:27).

Some commentators are quick to explain away Jesus' seemingly curt response in case he might be viewed as being racist or "hangry" perhaps. He was, it's often suggested, merely teasing, testing, setting up an object lesson on inclusion for his disciples. Whatever Jesus was doing, the woman wasn't surprised by his response to her request. Neither was she deterred. She seemed to have her response at the ready.

Turning Jesus' words upside down, she used wit and an excellent turn of phrase to reverse his logic and open a loophole to her advantage. "Of course, Master. But don't dogs under the table get scraps dropped by the children?" (Mark 7:28).

I have mad respect for this woman, who didn't miss a beat before going toe to toe with a powerful and respected miracle worker—on his day off, no less—to advocate for her daughter with playful, intelligent banter.

She earned Jesus' respect too, it seems. He didn't put her in her place or warn her against pushing limits. I can imagine him chuckling at her courageous turn of phrase. "Jesus was impressed" is how Mark puts it. "You're right!" Jesus replied (Mark 7:29).

This woman used her words—and got what she wanted. Returning home, she found her daughter completely healed.

like walking trees." So Jesus laid hands on his eyes again. The man looked hard and realized that he had recovered perfect sight, saw everything in bright, twenty-twenty focus. Jesus sent him straight home, telling him, "Don't enter the village."

THE MESSIAH

27 Jesus and his disciples headed out for the villages around Caesarea Philippi. As they walked, he asked, "Who do the people say I am?"

28 "Some say 'John the Baptizer,'" they said. "Others say 'Elijah.' Still others say 'one of the prophets.'"

29 He then asked, "And you—what are you saying about me? Who am I?"

Peter gave the answer: "You are the Christ, the Messiah."

30-32 Jesus warned them to keep it quiet, not to breathe a word of it to anyone. He then began explaining things to them: "It is necessary that the Son of Man proceed to an ordeal of suffering, be tried and found guilty by the elders, high priests, and religion scholars, be killed, and after three days rise up alive." He said this simply and clearly so they couldn't miss it.

32-33 But Peter grabbed him in protest. Turning and seeing his disciples wavering, wondering what to believe, Jesus confronted Peter. "Peter, get out of my way! Satan, get lost! You have no idea how God works."

34-37 Calling the crowd to join his disciples, he said, "Anyone who intends to come with me has to let me lead. You're not in the driver's seat; *I* am. Don't run from suffering; embrace it. Follow me and I'll show you how. Self-help is no help at all. Self-sacrifice is the way, my way, to saving yourself, your true self. What good would it do to get everything you want and lose you, the real you? What could you ever trade your soul for?

38 "If any of you are embarrassed over me and the way I'm leading you when you get around your fickle and unfocused friends, know that you'll be an even greater embarrassment to the Son of Man when he arrives in all the splendor of God, his Father, with an army of the holy angels."

9 1 Then he drove it home by saying, "This isn't pie in the sky by and by. Some of you who are standing here are going to see it happen, see the kingdom of God arrive in full force."

IN A LIGHT-RADIANT CLOUD

2-4 Six days later, three of them *did* see it. Jesus took Peter, James, and John and led them up a high mountain. His appearance changed from the inside out, right before their eyes. His clothes shimmered, glistening white, whiter than any bleach could make them. Elijah, along with Moses, came into view, in deep conversation with Jesus.

5-6 Peter interrupted, "Rabbi, this is a great moment! Let's build three memorials—one for you, one for Moses, one for Elijah." He blurted this out without thinking, stunned as they all were by what they were seeing.

7 Just then a light-radiant cloud enveloped them, and from deep in the cloud, a voice: "This is my Son, marked by my love. Listen to him."

8 The next minute the disciples were looking around, rubbing their eyes, seeing nothing but Jesus, only Jesus.

9-10 Coming down the mountain, Jesus swore them to secrecy. "Don't tell a soul what you saw. After the Son of Man rises from the dead, you're free to talk." They puzzled over that, wondering what on earth "rising from the dead" meant.

11 Meanwhile they were asking, "Why do the religion scholars say that Elijah has to come first?"

12-13 Jesus replied, "Elijah does come first and get everything ready for the coming of the Son of Man. They treated this Elijah like dirt, much like they will treat the Son of Man, who will, according to Scripture, suffer terribly and be kicked around contemptibly."

THERE ARE NO IFS

14-16 When they came back down the mountain to the other disciples, they saw a huge crowd around them, and the religion scholars cross-examining them. As soon as the people in the crowd saw Jesus, admiring excitement stirred them. They ran and greeted him. He asked, "What's going on? What's all the commotion?"

17-18 A man out of the crowd answered, "Teacher, I brought my mute son, made speechless by a demon, to you. Whenever it seizes him, it throws him to the ground. He foams at the mouth, grinds his teeth, and goes stiff as a board. I told your disciples, hoping they could deliver him, but they couldn't."

19-20 Jesus said, "What a generation! No sense of God! How many times do I have to go over these things? How much longer do I have to put up with this? Bring the boy here." They brought him. When the demon saw Jesus, it threw the boy into a seizure, causing him to writhe on the ground and foam at the mouth.

21-22 He asked the boy's father, "How long has this been going on?"

"Ever since he was a little boy. Many times it pitches him into fire or the river to do away with him. If you can do anything, do it. Have a heart and help us!"

23 Jesus said, "If? There are no 'ifs' among believers. Anything can happen."

24 No sooner were the words out of his mouth than the father cried, "Then I believe. Help me with my doubts!"

25-27 Seeing that the crowd was forming fast, Jesus gave the vile spirit its marching orders: "Dumb and deaf spirit, I command you—Out of him, and stay out!" Screaming, and with much thrashing about, it left. The boy was pale as a corpse, so people started saying, "He's dead." But Jesus, taking his hand, raised him. The boy stood up.

28 After arriving back home, his disciples cornered Jesus and asked, "Why couldn't we throw the demon out?"

29 He answered, "There is no way to get rid of this kind of demon except by prayer."

30-32 Leaving there, they went through Galilee. He didn't want anyone to know their whereabouts, for he wanted to teach his disciples. He told them, "The Son of Man is about to be betrayed to some people who want nothing to do with God. They will murder him. Three days after his murder, he will rise, alive." They didn't know what he was talking about, but were afraid to ask him about it.

SO YOU WANT FIRST PLACE?

33 They came to Capernaum. When he was safe at home, he asked them, "What were you discussing on the road?"

34 The silence was deafening—they had been arguing with one another over who among them was greatest.

35 He sat down and summoned the Twelve. "So you want first place? Then take the last place. Be the servant of all."

36-37 He put a child in the middle of the room. Then, cradling the little one in his arms, he said, "Whoever embraces one of these children as I do embraces me, and far more than me—God who sent me."

▲ ▲ ▲

38 John spoke up, "Teacher, we saw a man using your name to expel demons and we stopped him because he wasn't in our group."

39-41 Jesus wasn't pleased. "Don't stop him. No one can use my name to do something good and powerful, and in the next breath slam me. If he's not an enemy, he's an ally. Why, anyone by just giving you a cup of water in my name is on our side. Count on it that God will notice.

42 "On the other hand, if you give one of these simple, childlike believers a hard time, bullying or taking advantage of their simple trust, you'll soon wish you hadn't. You'd be better off dropped in the middle of the lake with a millstone around your neck.

43-48 "If your hand or your foot gets in God's way, chop it off and throw it away. You're better off maimed or lame and alive than the proud owner of two hands and two feet, godless in a furnace of eternal fire. And if your eye distracts you from God, pull it out and throw it away. You're better off one-eyed and alive than exercising your twenty-twenty vision from inside the fire of hell.

49-50 "Everyone's going through a refining fire sooner or later, but you'll be well-preserved, protected from the *eternal* flames. Be preservatives yourselves. Preserve the peace."

DIVORCE

10 1-2 From there he went to the area of Judea across the Jordan. A crowd of people, as was so often the case, went along, and he, as he so often did, taught them. Pharisees came up, intending to give him a hard time. They asked, "Is it legal for a man to divorce his wife?"

3 Jesus said, "What did Moses command?"

4 They answered, "Moses gave permission to fill out a certificate of dismissal and divorce her."

5-9 Jesus said, "Moses wrote this command only as a concession to your hardhearted ways. In the original creation, God made male and female to be together. Because of this, a man leaves father and mother, and in marriage he becomes one flesh with a woman—no longer two individuals, but forming a new unity. Because God created this organic union of the two sexes, no one should desecrate his art by cutting them apart."

10-12 When they were back home, the disciples brought it up again. Jesus gave it to them straight: "A man who divorces his wife so he can marry someone else commits adultery against her. And a woman who divorces her husband so she can marry someone else commits adultery."

▲ ▲ ▲

13-16 The people brought children to Jesus, hoping he might touch them. The disciples shooed them off. But Jesus was irate and let them know it: "Don't push these children away. Don't ever get between them and me. These children are at the very center of life in the kingdom. Mark this: Unless you accept God's kingdom in the simplicity of a child, you'll never get in." Then, gathering the children up in his arms, he laid his hands of blessing on them.

TO ENTER GOD'S KINGDOM

17 As he went out into the street, a man came running up, greeted him with great reverence, and asked, "Good Teacher, what must I do to get eternal life?"

18-19 Jesus said, "Why are you calling me good? No one is good, only God. You know the commandments: Don't murder, don't commit adultery, don't steal, don't lie, don't cheat, honor your father and mother."

20 He said, "Teacher, I have—from my youth—kept them all!"

21 Jesus looked him hard in the eye—and loved him! He said, "There's one thing left: Go sell whatever you own and give it to the poor. All your wealth will then be heavenly wealth. And come follow me."

22 The man's face clouded over. This was the last thing he expected to hear, and he walked off with a heavy heart. He was holding on tight to a lot of things, and not about to let go.

23-25 Looking at his disciples, Jesus said, "Do you have any idea how difficult it is for people who 'have it all' to enter God's kingdom?" The disciples couldn't believe what they were hearing, but Jesus kept on: "You can't imagine how difficult. I'd say it's easier for a camel to go through a needle's eye than for the rich to get into God's kingdom."

26 *That* got their attention. "Then who has any chance at all?" they asked.

27 Jesus was blunt: "No chance at all if you think you can pull it off by yourself. Every chance in the world if you let God do it."

28 Peter tried another angle: "We left everything and followed you."

29-31 Jesus said, "Mark my words, no one who sacrifices house, brothers, sisters, mother, father, children, land—whatever—because of me and the Message will lose out. They'll get it all back, but multiplied many times in homes, brothers, sisters, mothers, children, and land—but also in troubles. And then the bonus of eternal life! This is once again the Great Reversal: Many who are first will end up last, and the last first."

32-34 Back on the road, they set out for Jerusalem. Jesus had a head start on them, and they were following, puzzled and not just a little afraid. He took the Twelve and began again to go over what to expect next. "Listen to me carefully. We're on our way up to Jerusalem. When we get there, the Son of Man will be betrayed to the religious leaders and scholars. They will sentence him to death. Then they will hand him over to the Romans, who will mock and spit on him, give him the third degree, and kill him. After three days he will rise alive."

THE HIGHEST PLACES OF HONOR

35 James and John, Zebedee's sons, came up to him. "Teacher, we have something we want you to do for us."

36 "What is it? I'll see what I can do."

37 "Arrange it," they said, "so that we will be awarded the highest places of honor in your glory—one of us at your right, the other at your left."

38 Jesus said, "You have no idea what you're asking. Are you capable of drinking the cup I drink, of being baptized in the baptism I'm about to be plunged into?"

39-40 "Sure," they said. "Why not?"

Jesus said, "Come to think of it, you *will* drink the cup I drink, and be baptized in my baptism. But as to awarding places of honor, that's not my business. There are other arrangements for that."

41-45 When the other ten heard of this conversation, they lost their tempers with James and John. Jesus got them together to settle things down. "You've observed how godless rulers throw their weight around," he said, "and when people get a little power how quickly it goes to their heads. It's not going to be that way with you. Whoever wants to be great must become a servant. Whoever wants to be first among you must be your slave. That is what the Son of Man has done: He came to serve, not to be served—and then to give away his life in exchange for many who are held hostage."

▲ ▲ ▲

46-48 They spent some time in Jericho. As Jesus was leaving town, trailed by his disciples and a parade of people, a blind beggar by the name of Bartimaeus, son of Timaeus, was sitting alongside the road. When he heard that Jesus the Nazarene was passing by, he began to cry out, "Son of David, Jesus! Mercy, have mercy on me!" Many tried to hush him up, but he yelled all the louder, "Son of David! Mercy, have mercy on me!"

49-50 Jesus stopped in his tracks. "Call him over."

They called him. "It's your lucky day! Get up! He's calling you to come!" Throwing off his coat, he was on his feet at once and came to Jesus.

51 Jesus said, "What can I do for you?"

The blind man said, "Rabbi, I want to see."

52 "On your way," said Jesus. "Your faith has saved and healed you."

In that very instant he recovered his sight and followed Jesus down the road.

ENTERING JERUSALEM ON A COLT

11 1-3 When they were nearing Jerusalem, at Bethphage and Bethany on Mount Olives, he sent off two of the disciples with instructions: "Go to the village across from you. As soon as you enter, you'll find a colt tethered, one that has never yet been ridden. Untie it and bring it. If anyone asks, 'What are you doing?' say, 'The Master needs him, and will return him right away.'"

4-7 They went and found a colt tied to a door at the street corner and untied it. Some of those standing there said, "What are you doing untying that colt?" The disciples replied exactly as Jesus had instructed them, and the people let them alone. They brought the colt to Jesus, spread their coats on it, and he mounted.

8-10 The people gave him a wonderful welcome, some throwing their coats on the street, others spreading out rushes they had cut in the fields. Running ahead and following after, they were calling out,

Hosanna!
Blessed is he who comes in God's name!
Blessed the coming kingdom of our
father David!
Hosanna in highest heaven!

11 He entered Jerusalem, then entered the Temple. He looked around, taking it all in. But by now it was late, so he went back to Bethany with the Twelve.

THE CURSED FIG TREE

12-14 As they left Bethany the next day, he was hungry. Off in the distance he saw a fig tree in full leaf. He came up to it expecting to find something for breakfast, but found nothing but fig leaves. (It wasn't yet the season for figs.) He addressed the tree: "No one is going to eat fruit from you again—ever!" And his disciples overheard him.

15-17 They arrived at Jerusalem. Immediately on entering the Temple Jesus started throwing out everyone who had set up shop there, buying and selling. He kicked over the tables of the bankers and the stalls of the pigeon merchants. He didn't let anyone even carry a basket through the Temple. And then he taught them, quoting this text:

My house was designated a house of
prayer for the nations;
You've turned it into a hangout for
thieves.

18 The high priests and religion scholars heard what was going on and plotted how they might get rid of him. They panicked, for the entire crowd was carried away by his teaching.

19 At evening, Jesus and his disciples left the city.

20-21 In the morning, walking along the road, they saw the fig tree, shriveled to a dry stick. Peter, remembering what had happened the previous day, said to him, "Rabbi, look—the fig tree you cursed is shriveled up!"

22-25 Jesus was matter-of-fact: "Embrace this God-life. Really embrace it, and nothing will be too much for you. This mountain, for instance: Just say, 'Go jump in the lake'—no shuffling or hemming and hawing—and it's as good as done. That's why I urge you to pray for absolutely everything, ranging from small to large. Include everything as you embrace this God-life, and you'll get God's everything. And when you assume the posture of prayer, remember that it's not all *asking*. If you have anything against someone, *forgive*—only then will your heavenly Father be inclined to also wipe your slate clean of sins."

HIS CREDENTIALS

27-28 Then when they were back in Jerusalem once again, as they were walking through the

Temple, the high priests, religion scholars, and leaders came up and demanded, "Show us your credentials. Who authorized you to speak and act like this?"

29-30 Jesus responded, "First let me ask you a question. Answer my question and then I'll present my credentials. About the baptism of John—who authorized it: heaven or humans? Tell me."

31-33 They were on the spot, and knew it. They pulled back into a huddle and whispered, "If we say 'heaven,' he'll ask us why we didn't believe John; if we say 'humans,' we'll be up against it with the people because they all hold John up as a prophet." They decided to concede that round to Jesus. "We don't know," they said.

Jesus replied, "Then I won't answer your question either."

THE STORY ABOUT A VINEYARD

12 1-2 Then Jesus started telling them stories. "A man planted a vineyard. He fenced it, dug a winepress, erected a watchtower, turned it over to the farmhands, and went off on a trip. At the time for harvest, he sent a servant back to the farmhands to collect his profits.

3-5 "They grabbed him, beat him up, and sent him off empty-handed. So he sent another servant. That one they tarred and feathered. He sent another and that one they killed. And on and on, many others. Some they beat up, some they killed.

6 "Finally there was only one left: a beloved son. In a last-ditch effort, he sent him, thinking, 'Surely they will respect my son.'

7-8 "But those farmhands saw their chance. They rubbed their hands together in greed and said, 'This is the heir! Let's kill him and have it all for ourselves.' They grabbed him, killed him, and threw him over the fence.

9-11 "What do you think the owner of the vineyard will do? Right. He'll come and get rid of everyone. Then he'll assign the care of the vineyard to others. Read it for yourselves in Scripture:

> That stone the masons threw out
> is now the cornerstone!
> This is God's work;
> we rub our eyes—we can hardly
> believe it!"

12 They wanted to lynch him then and there but, intimidated by public opinion, held back. They knew the story was about them. They got away from there as fast as they could.

PAYING TAXES TO CAESAR

13-14 They sent some Pharisees and followers of Herod to bait him, hoping to catch him saying something incriminating. They came up and said, "Teacher, we know you have integrity, that you are indifferent to public opinion, don't pander to your students, and teach the way of God accurately. Tell us: Is it lawful to pay taxes to Caesar or not?"

15-16 He knew it was a trick question, and said, "Why are you playing these games with me? Bring me a coin and let me look at it." They handed him one.

"This engraving—who does it look like? And whose name is on it?"

"Caesar," they said.

17 Jesus said, "Give Caesar what is his, and give God what is his."

Their mouths hung open, speechless.

OUR INTIMACIES WILL BE WITH GOD

18-23 Some Sadducees, the party that denies any possibility of resurrection, came up and asked, "Teacher, Moses wrote that if a man dies and leaves a wife but no child, his brother is obligated to marry the widow and have children. Well, there once were seven brothers. The first took a wife. He died childless. The second married her. He died, and still no child. The same with the third. All seven took their turn, but no child. Finally the wife died. When they are raised at the resurrection, whose wife is she? All seven were her husband."

24-27 Jesus said, "You're way off base, and here's why: One, you don't know what God said; two, you don't know how God works. After the dead are raised up, we're past the marriage business. As it is with angels now, all our ecstasies and intimacies then will be with God. And regarding the dead, whether or not they are raised, don't you ever read the Bible? How God at the bush said to Moses, 'I am—not *was*—the God of Abraham, the God of Isaac, and the God of Jacob'? The living God is God of the *living*, not the dead. You're way, way off base."

THE MOST IMPORTANT COMMANDMENT

28 One of the religion scholars came up. Hearing the lively exchanges of question and answer and seeing how sharp Jesus was in his

answers, he put in his question: "Which is most important of all the commandments?"

29-31 Jesus said, "The first in importance is, 'Listen, Israel: The Lord your God is one; so love the Lord God with all your passion and prayer and intelligence and energy.' And here is the second: 'Love others as well as you love yourself.' There is no other commandment that ranks with these."

32-33 The religion scholar said, "A wonderful answer, Teacher! So clear-cut and accurate—that God is one and there is no other. And loving him with all passion and intelligence and energy, and loving others as well as you love yourself. Why, that's better than all offerings and sacrifices put together!"

34 When Jesus realized how insightful he was, he said, "You're almost there, right on the border of God's kingdom."

After that, no one else dared ask a question.

▲ ▲ ▲

35-37 While he was teaching in the Temple, Jesus asked, "How is it that the religion scholars say that the Messiah is David's 'son,' when we all know that David, inspired by the Holy Spirit, said,

God said to my Master,
"Sit here at my right hand
until I put your enemies under
your feet."

"David here designates the Messiah 'my Master'—so how can the Messiah also be his 'son'?"

The large crowd was delighted with what they heard.

38-40 He continued teaching. "Watch out for the religion scholars. They love to walk around in academic gowns, preening in the radiance of public flattery, basking in prominent positions, sitting at the head table at every church function. And all the time they are exploiting the weak and helpless. The longer their prayers, the worse they get. But they'll pay for it in the end."

41-44 Sitting across from the offering box, he was observing how the crowd tossed money in for the collection. Many of the rich were making large contributions. One poor widow came up and put in two small coins—a measly two cents. Jesus called his disciples over and said, "The truth is that this poor widow gave more to the collection than all the others put together. All the others gave what they'll never miss; she gave extravagantly what she couldn't afford—she gave her all."

DOOMSDAY DECEIVERS

13 1 As he walked away from the Temple, one of his disciples said, "Teacher, look at that stonework! Those buildings!"

2 Jesus said, "You're impressed by this grandiose architecture? There's not a stone in the whole works that is not going to end up in a heap of rubble."

3-4 Later, as he was sitting on Mount Olives in full view of the Temple, Peter, James, John, and Andrew got him off by himself and asked, "Tell us, when is this going to happen? What sign will we get that things are coming to a head?"

5-8 Jesus began, "Watch out for doomsday deceivers. Many leaders are going to show up with forged identities claiming, 'I'm the One.' They will deceive a lot of people. When you hear of wars and rumored wars, keep your head and don't panic. This is routine history, and no sign of the end. Nation will fight nation and ruler fight ruler, over and over. Earthquakes will occur in various places. There will be famines. But these things are nothing compared to what's coming.

9-10 "And watch out! They're going to drag you into court. And then it will go from bad to worse, dog-eat-dog, everyone at your throat because you carry my name. You're placed there as sentinels to truth. The Message has to be preached all across the world.

11 "When they bring you, betrayed, into court, don't worry about what you'll say. When the time comes, say what's on your heart—the Holy Spirit will make his witness in and through you.

12-13 "It's going to be brother killing brother, father killing child, children killing parents. There's no telling who will hate you because of me.

"Stay with it—that's what is required. Stay with it to the end. You won't be sorry; you'll be saved.

RUN FOR THE HILLS

14-18 "But be ready to run for it when you see the monster of desecration set up where it should *never* be. You who can read, make sure you understand what I'm talking about. If you're living in Judea at the time, run for the hills; if you're working in the yard, don't go

The Widow at the Temple

It was Hagar, way back in Genesis, who called God *El Roi*, "the God who sees" (Genesis 16:13). It was Jesus, in the crowded Temple, seated near the offering box, who saw one poor widow.

To grasp the fullness of this story, consider the context of the surrounding verses. What exactly did Jesus see?

Jesus saw the glory of the Temple, hearing one of his disciples remark on its beautiful stonework, its grandiose architecture (Mark 13:1-2).

Jesus saw the religious scholars, and with the people around him listening, said, "Watch out." Beware their academic gowns and the ways they demand respect . . . *while* they're devouring widows' houses (Mark 12:38-40).

Jesus saw a scholar approach him to discuss the most important commandment. They both agreed that loving God and loving others is better in God's eyes than all the offerings in the world. But then Jesus said, "You're almost there, right on the border of God's kingdom" (Mark 12:34), and no one dared ask him anything more.

Jesus saw the widow. When I envision this scene, time slows down. One by one, the people file by, tossing their obligations into the treasury. Slowly, deliberately, this woman takes her turn, dropping two very small copper coins into the box.

Calling his disciples over, Jesus told them what he saw.

"The truth is that this poor widow gave more to the collection than all the others put together. All the others gave what they'll never miss; she gave extravagantly what she couldn't afford—she gave her all" (Mark 12:43-44).

Within this context of watching and seeing, Jesus made his point, pointing out what we should see. A system where an impoverished, widowed woman is expected to give all she has while the rich won't even miss what they give—that system is broken. People who claim to love God but don't care for their neighbors—that so-called love is broken too. God sees injustice and wants us to see it too.

On the flip side of the same coin: See this woman, whom Jesus sees. Regardless of the broken system, she gave extravagantly from a heart that truly loved God. Did she hear Jesus' words on her behalf? As Jesus condemned those caught up in the riches of this world, did she hear Jesus' voice commending her faithfulness?

Lord, help us see.

back to the house to get anything; if you're out in the field, don't go back to get your coat. Pregnant and nursing mothers will have it especially hard. Hope and pray this won't happen in the middle of winter.

19-20 "These are going to be hard days—nothing like it from the time God made the world right up to the present. And there'll be nothing like it again. If he let the days of trouble run their course, nobody would make it. But because of God's chosen people, those he personally chose, he has already intervened.

NO ONE KNOWS THE DAY OR HOUR

21-23 "If anyone tries to flag you down, calling out, 'Here's the Messiah!' or points, 'There he is!' don't fall for it. Fake Messiahs and lying preachers are going to pop up everywhere. Their impressive credentials and bewitching performances will pull the wool over the eyes of even those who ought to know better. So watch out. I've given you fair warning.

24-25 "Following those hard times,

Sun will fade out,
  moon cloud over,
Stars fall out of the sky,
  cosmic powers tremble.

26-27 "And then they'll see the Son of Man enter in grand style, his Arrival filling the sky—no one will miss it! He'll dispatch the angels; they will pull in the chosen from the four winds, from pole to pole.

28-31 "Take a lesson from the fig tree. From the moment you notice its buds form, the merest hint of green, you know summer's just around the corner. And so it is with you. When you see all these things, you know he is at the door. Don't take this lightly. I'm not just saying this for some future generation, but for this one, too—these things will happen. Sky and earth will wear out; my words won't wear out.

32-37 "But the exact day and hour? No one knows that, not even heaven's angels, not even the Son. Only the Father. So keep a sharp lookout, for you don't know the timetable. It's like a man who takes a trip, leaving home and putting his servants in charge, each assigned a task, and commanding the gatekeeper to stand watch. So, stay at your post, watching. You have no idea when the homeowner is returning, whether evening, midnight, cockcrow, or morning. You don't want him showing up unannounced, with you asleep on the job. I say it to you, and I'm saying it to all: Stay at your post. Keep watch."

ANOINTING HIS HEAD

14 1-2 In only two days the eight-day Festival of Passover and the Feast of Unleavened Bread would begin. The high priests and religion scholars were looking for a way they could seize Jesus by stealth and kill him. They agreed that it should not be done during Passover Week. "We don't want the crowds up in arms," they said.

3-5 Jesus was at Bethany, a guest of Simon the Leper. While he was eating dinner, a woman came up carrying a bottle of very expensive perfume. Opening the bottle, she poured it on his head. Some of the guests became furious among themselves. "That's criminal! A sheer waste! This perfume could have been sold for well over a year's wages and handed out to the poor." They swelled up in anger, nearly bursting with indignation over her.

6-9 But Jesus said, "Let her alone. Why are you giving her a hard time? She has just done something wonderfully significant for me. You will have the poor with you every day for the rest of your lives. Whenever you feel like it, you can do something for them. Not so with me. She did what she could when she could—she pre-anointed my body for burial. And you can be sure that wherever in the whole world the Message is preached, what she just did is going to be talked about admiringly."

10-11 Judas Iscariot, one of the Twelve, went to the cabal of high priests, determined to betray him. They couldn't believe their ears, and promised to pay him well. He started looking for just the right moment to hand him over.

TRAITOR TO THE SON OF MAN

12 On the first of the Days of Unleavened Bread, the day they prepare the Passover sacrifice, his disciples asked him, "Where do you want us to go and make preparations so you can eat the Passover meal?"

13-15 He directed two of his disciples, "Go into the city. A man carrying a water jug will meet you. Follow him. Ask the owner of whichever house he enters, 'The Teacher wants to know, Where is my guest room where I can eat the Passover meal with my disciples?' He will show you a spacious second-story room, swept and ready. Prepare for us there."

Nameless but Remembered

Who was this woman who anointed Jesus? Ironically, Mark doesn't tell us her name, yet Jesus said that she would always be remembered. Rarely in the Gospels does Jesus offer such high praise.

We don't know her name. We don't know what her previous encounters with Jesus had been. But we know this: She knew Jesus' worth. She had experienced something great enough to ignore social decorum and personal security to be in his presence and honor him. Here at dinner with a friend who was willing to betray him for mere money, Jesus received the adoration of a woman willing to give up everything for him.

Our brave friend was out of place from the very beginning; there was likely no seat at the table for her. She interrupted Jesus' dinner with friends to anoint his head, honoring his kingship as much as preparing his body for burial. And while her eyes were fixed on Jesus, the disciples' were fixed on her—and they were horrified.

The perfume she used and even the jar itself may have been a family heirloom. It might have served as her dowry or as a retirement plan for herself and her children. In a world where economic options for women were limited, that jar was more than just a symbol. She cracked open her security and poured it out before Jesus. She knew that what she'd found in him was worth everything. In the presence of the giver of life, she had no need for insurance plans.

While Jesus received her gift with delight, his disciples missed the point. What the woman had to offer was unexpected. It didn't fit religious protocol. But she alone among them had discovered what following Jesus means—that he's not after our deeds as much as our hearts. So when the woman, out of place and out of line, fell into the irate disciples' line of fire, what did Jesus say?

He said, "Let her alone" (Mark 14:6).

Then he declared that she would be remembered everywhere the Message would be preached. Why? Because the good news tells us this: Jesus is worth everything. We can lay down our security *before* him because our security is found *in* him. And the gospel of Jesus includes women. It includes those without a formal seat at the table and those who don't always look right or act correctly. It includes those who face criticism and ostracism.

The Message is for anyone who sees Jesus' worth and is willing to find their security in him.

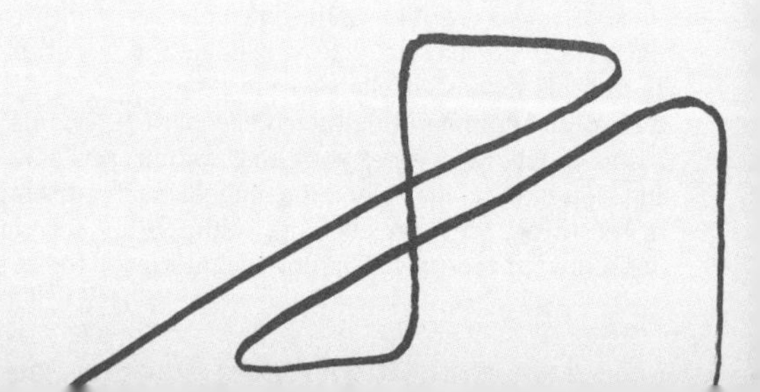

16 The disciples left, came to the city, found everything just as he had told them, and prepared the Passover meal.

17-18 After sunset he came with the Twelve. As they were at the supper table eating, Jesus said, "I have something hard but important to say to you: One of you is going to hand me over to the conspirators, one who at this moment is eating with me."

19 Stunned, they started asking, one after another, "It isn't me, is it?"

20-21 He said, "It's one of the Twelve, one who eats with me out of the same bowl. In one sense, it turns out that the Son of Man is entering into a way of treachery well-marked by the Scriptures—no surprises here. In another sense, the man who turns him in, turns traitor to the Son of Man—better never to have been born than do this!"

"THIS IS MY BODY"

22 In the course of their meal, having taken and blessed the bread, he broke it and gave it to them. Then he said,

Take, this is my body.

23-24 Taking the chalice, he gave it to them, thanking God, and they all drank from it. He said,

This is my blood,
God's new covenant,
Poured out for many people.

25 "I'll not be drinking wine again until the new day when I drink it in the kingdom of God."

26 They sang a hymn and then went directly to Mount Olives.

▲ ▲ ▲

27-28 Jesus told them, "You're all going to feel that your world is falling apart and that it's my fault. There's a Scripture that says,

I will strike the shepherd;
The sheep will scatter.

"But after I am raised up, I will go ahead of you, leading the way to Galilee."

29 Peter blurted out, "Even if everyone else is ashamed of you when things fall to pieces, I won't be."

30 Jesus said, "Don't be so sure. Today, this very night in fact, before the rooster crows twice, you will deny me three times."

31 He blustered in protest, "Even if I have to die with you, I will never deny you." All the others said the same thing.

GETHSEMANE

32-34 They came to an area called Gethsemane. Jesus told his disciples, "Sit here while I pray." He took Peter, James, and John with him. He sank into a pit of suffocating darkness. He told them, "I feel bad enough right now to die. Stay here and keep vigil with me."

35-36 Going a little ahead, he fell to the ground and prayed for a way out: "Papa, Father, you can—can't you?—get me out of this. Take this cup away from me. But please, not what I want—what do *you* want?"

37-38 He came back and found them sound asleep. He said to Peter, "Simon, you went to sleep on me? Can't you stick it out with me a single hour? Stay alert, be in prayer, so you don't enter the danger zone without even knowing it. Don't be naive. Part of you is eager, ready for anything in God; but another part is as lazy as an old dog sleeping by the fire."

39-40 He then went back and prayed the same prayer. Returning, he again found them sound asleep. They simply couldn't keep their eyes open, and they didn't have a plausible excuse.

41-42 He came back a third time and said, "Are you going to sleep all night? No—you've slept long enough. Time's up. The Son of Man is about to be betrayed into the hands of sinners. Get up. Let's get going. My betrayer has arrived."

A BUNCH OF THUGS

43-47 No sooner were the words out of his mouth when Judas, the one out of the Twelve, showed up, and with him a bunch of thugs, sent by the high priests, religion scholars, and leaders, brandishing swords and clubs. The betrayer had worked out a signal with them: "The one I kiss, that's the one—seize him. Make sure he doesn't get away." He went straight to Jesus and said, "Rabbi!" and kissed him. The others then grabbed him and roughed him up. One of the men standing there unsheathed his sword, swung, and came down on the Chief Priest's servant, lopping off the man's ear.

48-50 Jesus said to them, "What is this, coming after me with swords and clubs as if I were a dangerous criminal? Day after day I've been sitting in the Temple teaching, and you never so much as lifted a hand against me. What you in fact have done is confirm the prophetic writings." All the disciples bailed on him.

51-52 A young man was following along. All he had on was a bedsheet. Some of the men grabbed him but he got away, running off naked, leaving them holding the sheet.

CONDEMNED TO DEATH

53-54 They led Jesus to the Chief Priest, where the high priests, religious leaders, and scholars had gathered together. Peter followed at a safe distance until they got to the Chief Priest's courtyard, where he mingled with the servants and warmed himself at the fire.

55-59 The high priests conspiring with the Jewish Council looked high and low for evidence against Jesus by which they could sentence him to death. They found nothing. Plenty of people were willing to bring in false charges, but nothing added up, and they ended up canceling each other out. Then a few of them stood up and lied: "We heard him say, 'I am going to tear down this Temple, built by hard labor, and in three days build another without lifting a hand.'" But even they couldn't agree exactly.

60-61 In the middle of this, the Chief Priest stood up and asked Jesus, "What do you have to say to the accusation?" Jesus was silent. He said nothing.

The Chief Priest tried again, this time asking, "Are you the Messiah, the Son of the Blessed?"

62 Jesus said, "Yes, I am, and you'll see it yourself:

The Son of Man seated
At the right hand of the Mighty One,
Arriving on the clouds of heaven."

63-64 The Chief Priest lost his temper. Ripping his clothes, he yelled, "Did you hear that? After that do we need witnesses? You heard the blasphemy. Are you going to stand for it?"

They condemned him, one and all. The sentence: death.

65 Some of them started spitting at him. They blindfolded his eyes, then hit him, saying, "Who hit you? Prophesy!" The guards, punching and slapping, took him away.

THE ROOSTER CROWED

66-67 While all this was going on, Peter was down in the courtyard. One of the Chief Priest's servant girls came in and, seeing Peter warming himself there, looked hard at him and said, "You were with the Nazarene, Jesus."

68 He denied it: "I don't know what you're talking about." He went out on the porch. A rooster crowed.

69-70 The girl spotted him and began telling the people standing around, "He's one of them." He denied it again.

After a little while, the bystanders brought it up again. "You've *got* to be one of them. You've got 'Galilean' written all over you."

71-72 Now Peter got really nervous and swore, "I never laid eyes on this man you're talking about." Just then the rooster crowed a second time. Peter remembered how Jesus had said, "Before a rooster crows twice, you'll deny me three times." He collapsed in tears.

STANDING BEFORE PILATE

15 1 At dawn's first light, the high priests, with the religious leaders and scholars, arranged a conference with the entire Jewish Council. After tying Jesus securely, they took him out and presented him to Pilate.

2-3 Pilate asked him, "Are you the 'King of the Jews'?"

He answered, "If you say so." The high priests let loose a barrage of accusations.

4-5 Pilate asked again, "Aren't you going to answer anything? That's quite a list of accusations." Still, he said nothing. Pilate was impressed, really impressed.

6-10 It was a custom at the Feast to release a prisoner, anyone the people asked for. There was one prisoner called Barabbas, locked up with the insurrectionists who had committed murder during the uprising against Rome. As the crowd came up and began to present its petition for him to release a prisoner, Pilate anticipated them: "Do you want me to release the King of the Jews to you?" Pilate knew by this time that it was through sheer spite that the high priests had turned Jesus over to him.

11-12 But the high priests by then had worked up the crowd to ask for the release of Barabbas. Pilate came back, "So what do I do with this man you call King of the Jews?"

13 They yelled, "Nail him to a cross!"

14 Pilate objected, "But for what crime?"

But they yelled all the louder, "Nail him to a cross!"

15 Pilate gave the crowd what it wanted, set Barabbas free and turned Jesus over for whipping and crucifixion.

16-20 The soldiers took Jesus into the palace (called Praetorium) and called together the entire brigade. They dressed him up in purple and put a crown plaited from a thornbush on his head. Then they began their mockery: "Bravo, King of the Jews!" They banged on his head with a club, spit on him, and knelt down in mock worship. After they had had their fun, they took off the purple cape and put his own clothes back on him. Then they marched out to nail him to the cross.

THE CRUCIFIXION

21 There was a man walking by, coming from work, Simon from Cyrene, the father of Alexander and Rufus. They made him carry Jesus' cross.

22-24 The soldiers brought Jesus to Golgotha, meaning "Skull Hill." They offered him a mild painkiller (wine mixed with myrrh), but he wouldn't take it. And they nailed him to the cross. They divided up his clothes and threw dice to see who would get them.

25-30 They nailed him up at nine o'clock in the morning. The charge against him—THE KING OF THE JEWS—was scrawled across a sign. Along with him, they crucified two criminals, one to his right, the other to his left. People passing along the road jeered, shaking their heads in mock lament: "You bragged that you could tear down the Temple and then rebuild it in three days—so show us your stuff! Save yourself! If you're really God's Son, come down from that cross!"

31-32 The high priests, along with the religion scholars, were right there mixing it up with the rest of them, having a great time poking fun at him: "He saved others—but he can't save himself! Messiah, is he? King of Israel? Then let him climb down from that cross. We'll *all* become believers then!" Even the men crucified alongside him joined in the mockery.

33-34 At noon the sky became extremely dark. The darkness lasted three hours. At three o'clock, Jesus groaned out of the depths, crying loudly, "*Eloi, Eloi, lama sabachthani?*" which means, "My God, my God, why have you abandoned me?"

35-36 Some of the bystanders who heard him said, "Listen, he's calling for Elijah." Someone ran off, soaked a sponge in sour wine, put it on a stick, and gave it to him to drink, saying, "Let's see if Elijah comes to take him down."

37-39 But Jesus, with a loud cry, gave his last breath. At that moment the Temple curtain ripped right down the middle. When the Roman captain standing guard in front of him saw that he had quit breathing, he said, "This has to be the Son of God!"

TAKEN TO A TOMB

40-41 There were women watching from a distance, among them Mary Magdalene, Mary the mother of the younger James and Joses, and Salome. When Jesus was in Galilee, these women followed and served him, and had come up with him to Jerusalem.

42-45 Late in the afternoon, since it was the Day of Preparation (that is, Sabbath eve), Joseph of Arimathea, a highly respected member of the Jewish Council, came. He was one who lived expectantly, on the lookout for the kingdom of God. Working up his courage, he went to Pilate and asked for Jesus' body. Pilate questioned whether he could be dead that soon and called for the captain to verify that he was really dead. Assured by the captain, he gave Joseph the corpse.

46-47 Having already purchased a linen shroud, Joseph took him down, wrapped him in the shroud, placed him in a tomb that had been cut into the rock, and rolled a large stone across the opening. Mary Magdalene and Mary, mother of Joses, watched the burial.

THE RESURRECTION

16 1-3 When the Sabbath was over, Mary Magdalene, Mary the mother of James, and Salome bought spices so they could embalm him. Very early on Sunday morning, as the sun rose, they went to the tomb. They worried out loud to each other, "Who will roll back the stone from the tomb for us?"

4-5 Then they looked up, saw that it had been rolled back—it was a huge stone—and walked right in. They saw a young man sitting on the right side, dressed all in white. They were completely taken aback, astonished.

6-7 He said, "Don't be afraid. I know you're looking for Jesus the Nazarene, the One they nailed on the cross. He's been raised up; he's here no longer. You can see for yourselves that the place is empty. Now—on your way. Tell his disciples and Peter that he is going on ahead of you to Galilee. You'll see him there, exactly as he said."

8 They got out as fast as they could, beside themselves, their heads swimming. Stunned, they said nothing to anyone.

MARY MAGDALENE

Jesus freed a woman once bound by seven demons. In those days, the number seven was associated with completeness. It's reasonable to understand that those demons completely overpowered Mary Magdalene—until she met Jesus.

Though the Bible doesn't identify how Mary suffered, communities often banished those bound by demons. Regardless of her wealthy social status, she undoubtedly understood the pain of rejection, condemnation, and isolation. Her abundance of money couldn't save her or change her.

Forever described as the woman once bound by seven demons, Mary Magdalene was known by her past afflictions. Though that tag clung to her name, Jesus freed her completely. She responded to her freedom with selfless and sacrificial devotion to him.

Mary's life demonstrates the completeness of freedom in Christ. No demon is too strong for Jesus to banish. No person is too bound for Jesus to free. After Mary's encounter with Jesus, those unnamed demons no longer decided her value or had power over her. She moved forward as a freed woman, a healed woman. She was not a woman *in the process of* being freed, nor a work in progress still wrestling with her demons.

Proving the completeness of her freedom, Jesus honored her with the privilege of being the first to see him, the first to hear his voice, and the first entrusted with sharing the good news of the Resurrection. The woman who went from being completely shackled by sin to completely released from a life sentence was sent to the "disciples *and Peter*" to announce Jesus' resurrection (Mark 16:7, emphasis added). Who could be a better vessel than Mary to approach Peter with such an unbelievable message of redeeming love?

Mary Magdalene reminds us of Jesus' ability and willingness to use any of us, no matter what is in our pasts. In complete freedom, we're able to love both God and others.

9-11 [After rising from the dead, Jesus appeared early on Sunday morning to Mary Magdalene, whom he had delivered from seven demons. She went to his former companions, now weeping and carrying on, and told them. When they heard her report that she had seen him alive and well, they didn't believe her.

12-13 Later he appeared, but in a different form, to two of them out walking in the countryside. They went back and told the rest, but they weren't believed either.

14-16 Still later, as the Eleven were eating supper, he appeared and took them to task most severely for their stubborn unbelief, refusing to believe those who had seen him raised up. Then he said, "Go into the world. Go everywhere and announce the Message of God's good news to one and all. Whoever believes and is baptized is saved; whoever refuses to believe is damned.

17-18 "These are some of the signs that will accompany believers: They will throw out demons in my name, they will speak in new tongues, they will take snakes in their hands, they will drink poison and not be hurt, they will lay hands on the sick and make them well."

19-20 Then the Master Jesus, after briefing them, was taken up to heaven, and he sat down beside God in the place of honor. And the disciples went everywhere preaching, the Master working right with them, validating the Message with indisputable evidence.]

Note: Mark 16:9-20 [the portion in brackets] is not found in the earliest handwritten copies.

Luke

THERE ARE NO OUTSIDERS

Most of us, most of the time, feel left out—misfits. We don't belong. Others seem to be so confident, so sure of themselves, "insiders" who know the ropes, old hands in a club from which we are excluded.

One of the ways we have of responding to this is to form our own club, or join one that will have us. Here is at least one place where we are "in" and the others "out." The clubs range from informal to formal in gatherings that are variously political, social, cultural, and economic. But the one thing they have in common is the principle of exclusion. Identity or worth is achieved by excluding all but the chosen. The terrible price we pay for keeping all those other people out so that we can savor the sweetness of being insiders is a reduction of reality, a shrinkage of life.

Nowhere is this price more terrible than when it is paid in the cause of religion. But religion has a long history of doing just that, of reducing the huge mysteries of God to the respectability of club rules, of shrinking the vast human community to a "membership." But with God there are no outsiders. Jesus said, "The Son of Man came to find and restore the lost" (Luke 19:10).

Luke is a most vigorous champion of the outsider. An outsider himself, the only Gentile in an all-Jewish cast of New Testament writers, he shows how Jesus includes those who typically were treated as outsiders by the religious establishment of the day: women, common laborers (sheepherders), the racially different (Samaritans), the poor. He will not countenance religion as a club. As Luke tells the story, all of us who have found ourselves on the outside looking in on life with no hope of gaining entrance (and who of us hasn't felt it?) now find the doors wide open, found and welcomed by God in Jesus, who, in fact said, "Ask and you'll get; seek and you'll find; knock and the door will open" (Luke 11:9).

1 1-4 So many others have tried their hand at putting together a story of the wonderful harvest of Scripture and history that took place among us, using reports handed down by the original eyewitnesses who served this Word with their very lives. Since I have investigated all the reports in close detail, starting from the story's beginning, I decided to write it all out for you, most honorable Theophilus, so you can know beyond the shadow of a doubt the reliability of what you were taught.

A CHILDLESS COUPLE CONCEIVES

5-7 During the rule of Herod, King of Judea, there was a priest assigned service in the regiment of Abijah. His name was Zachariah. His wife was descended from the daughters of Aaron. Her name was Elizabeth. Together they lived honorably before God, careful in keeping to the ways of the commandments and enjoying a clear conscience before God. But they were childless because Elizabeth could never conceive, and now they were quite old.

8-12 It so happened that as Zachariah was carrying out his priestly duties before God, working the shift assigned to his regiment, it came his one turn in life to enter the sanctuary of God and burn incense. The congregation was gathered and praying outside the Temple at the hour of the incense offering. Unannounced, an angel of God appeared just to the right of the altar of incense. Zachariah was paralyzed in fear.

13-15 But the angel reassured him, "Don't fear, Zachariah. Your prayer has been heard. Elizabeth, your wife, will bear a son by you. You are to name him John. You're going to leap like a gazelle for joy, and not only you—many will delight in his birth. He'll achieve great stature with God.

15-17 "He'll drink neither wine nor beer. He'll be filled with the Holy Spirit from the moment he leaves his mother's womb. He will turn many sons and daughters of Israel back to their God. He will herald God's arrival in the style and strength of Elijah, soften the hearts of parents to children, and kindle devout understanding among hardened skeptics—he'll get the people ready for God."

18 Zachariah said to the angel, "Do you expect me to believe this? I'm an old man and my wife is an old woman."

19-20 But the angel said, "I am Gabriel, the sentinel of God, sent especially to bring you this glad news. But because you won't believe me, you'll be unable to say a word until the day of your son's birth. Every word I've spoken to you will come true on time—*God's* time."

21-22 Meanwhile, the congregation waiting for Zachariah was getting restless, wondering what was keeping him so long in the sanctuary. When he came out and couldn't speak, they knew he had seen a vision. He continued speechless and had to use sign language with the people.

23-25 When the course of his priestly assignment was completed, he went back home. It wasn't long before his wife, Elizabeth, conceived. She went off by herself for five months, relishing her pregnancy. "So, this is how God acts to remedy my unfortunate condition!" she said.

A VIRGIN CONCEIVES

26-28 In the sixth month of Elizabeth's pregnancy, God sent the angel Gabriel to the Galilean village of Nazareth to a virgin engaged to be married to a man descended from David. His name was Joseph, and the virgin's name, Mary. Upon entering, Gabriel greeted her:

Good morning!
You're beautiful with God's beauty,
Beautiful inside and out!
God be with you.

29-33 She was thoroughly shaken, wondering what was behind a greeting like that. But the angel assured her, "Mary, you have nothing to fear. God has a surprise for you: You will become pregnant and give birth to a son and call his name Jesus.

He will be great,
be called 'Son of the Highest.'
The Lord God will give him
the throne of his father David;
He will rule Jacob's house forever—
no end, ever, to his kingdom."

34 Mary said to the angel, "But how? I've never slept with a man."

35 The angel answered,

The Holy Spirit will come upon you,
the power of the Highest hover
over you;
Therefore, the child you bring to birth
will be called Holy, Son of God.

ELIZABETH

Tucked into the early pages of Luke's Gospel is Elizabeth. In a narrative saturated with fear, scandal, and imperial oppression, she is a prophetic deep breath making sure we do not write joy out of this story.

When Mary found herself pregnant, she went immediately to Elizabeth. I imagine that her journey was filled with fear and anxiety, her body aching, the nausea unbearable. Society made little room to accept this unmarried pregnant woman.

And then she met Elizabeth. They fell into one another's arms, and while I don't doubt that there were tears, we do know that there was joy—even Elizabeth's baby leaped for joy in her womb!

Elizabeth surely held Mary in her arms, called her by name, and saw the Spirit at work. This moment of love and joy prodded Mary's courage and dreams, calling forth a song with enough power to rock the foundation of society.

After the mighty words of the Magnificat, we're told that "Mary stayed with Elizabeth for three months" (Luke 1:56). Every time I read those words, I ache for more! I want all the boring details of how they spent those months with one another. I want to smell the cooking, hear the singing, feel the massaging, and listen to the dreaming they had for their children. I want to sit with them at the table.

Here in utero, John and Jesus were lulled to sleep by revolutionary lullabies and the sounds of shared labor. Even here they were being formed by visions of justice, gifts of hospitality, and the knowledge of what it means to be loved.

Elizabeth opened her heart and home—and bore witness to a new kingdom that would soon be coming. May we, too, testify against the fear, scandal, and oppression in our midst, trusting in community and the gifts of joy bursting from our bodies.

36-38 "And did you know that your cousin Elizabeth conceived a son, old as she is? Everyone called her barren, and here she is six months pregnant! Nothing, you see, is impossible with God."

And Mary said,

Yes, I see it all now:
I'm the Lord's maid, ready to serve.
Let it be with me
just as you say.

Then the angel left her.

BLESSED AMONG WOMEN

39-45 Mary didn't waste a minute. She got up and traveled to a town in Judah in the hill country, straight to Zachariah's house, and greeted Elizabeth. When Elizabeth heard Mary's greeting, the baby in her womb leaped. She was filled with the Holy Spirit, and sang out exuberantly,

You're so blessed among women,
and the babe in your womb,
also blessed!
And why am I so blessed that
the mother of my Lord visits me?
The moment the sound of your
greeting entered my ears,
The babe in my womb
skipped like a lamb for sheer joy.
Blessed woman, who believed what
God said,
believed every word would come true!

46-55 And Mary said,

I'm bursting with God-news;
I'm dancing the song of my Savior God.
God took one good look at me, and look
what happened—
I'm the most fortunate woman on earth!
What God has done for me will never
be forgotten,
the God whose very name is holy, set
apart from all others.
His mercy flows in wave after wave
on those who are in awe before him.
He bared his arm and showed his
strength,
scattered the bluffing braggarts.
He knocked tyrants off their high horses,
pulled victims out of the mud.
The starving poor sat down to a banquet;
the callous rich were left out in the cold.
He embraced his chosen child, Israel;
he remembered and piled on the
mercies, piled them high.
It's exactly what he promised,
beginning with Abraham and right
up to now.

56 Mary stayed with Elizabeth for three months and then went back to her own home.

THE BIRTH OF JOHN

57-58 When Elizabeth was full-term in her pregnancy, she gave birth to a son. Her neighbors and relatives, seeing that God had overwhelmed her with mercy, celebrated with her.

59-60 On the eighth day, they came to circumcise the child and were calling him Zachariah after his father. But his mother intervened: "No. He is to be called John."

61-62 "But," they said, "no one in your family is named that." They used sign language to ask Zachariah what he wanted him named.

63-64 Asking for a tablet, Zachariah wrote, "His name is to be John." That took everyone by surprise. Surprise followed surprise—Zachariah's mouth was now open, his tongue loose, and he was talking, praising God!

65-66 A deep, reverential fear settled over the neighborhood, and in all that Judean hill country people talked about nothing else. Everyone who heard about it took it to heart, wondering, "What will become of this child? Clearly, God has his hand in this."

67-79 Then Zachariah was filled with the Holy Spirit and prophesied,

Blessed be the Lord, the God of Israel;
he came and set his people free.
He set the power of salvation in the
center of our lives,
and in the very house of David his
servant,
Just as he promised long ago
through the preaching of his holy
prophets:
Deliverance from our enemies
and every hateful hand;
Mercy to our fathers,
as he remembers to do what he said
he'd do,
What he swore to our father Abraham—
a clean rescue from the enemy camp,
So we can worship him without a care in
the world,
made holy before him as long as
we live.

The Magnificat

Two women, two unlikely mothers. One was too old and barren, one was too young and unmarried. Both were chosen and blessed.

These women responded with praise when the angel proclaimed new life where there was none. Overjoyed, Elizabeth proclaimed, "You're so blessed among women . . . ! And why am I so blessed . . . ?" (Luke 1:42-43). In response to Elizabeth's greeting, Mary broke into a song of praise. Bursting with joy, singing with gratitude, Mary acknowledged the incredible strength and benevolent mercies of God.

This was not the path Mary had thought her life would take. It seemed too heavy a weight to carry. A child, a tiny human life, relies so much on his mother—during pregnancy, infancy, toddlerhood, and beyond. The added weight of knowing that this was not just a child but the Messiah, the long-awaited hope of countless men and women longing for justice and healing, was indescribably heavy. Mary was blessed with a burden and a gift, a fulfillment of what was, what is, and what will be. Rather than ask why, rather than complain of the burden, Mary recognized her place in God's story and how this unlikely miracle pregnancy aligned with the promises God had made to Abraham. Mary knew that God is a God of promises, mercy, strength, and power beyond all she could imagine. Mary knew this story was bigger than herself, bigger than her cousin Elizabeth, bigger than her family. She understood that the child she carried was at the center of a story that would change the whole world—and she burst into song.

Her prenatal song was not a nursery rhyme or lullaby. Rather, she sang of great and powerful things: tyrants toppled and victims saved, the poor offered a feast with the wealthy oppressors uninvited. She sang of all that God had done and all that God planned to do. Her soul song magnified and glorified and praised God for what God was doing right then and there—inside the body of a newly pregnant vulnerable young woman.

When our lives diverge from the paths we expect, from the paths that seem likely, it is hard to respond like Mary. It is hard to have the courage to recognize our place in God's story and, instead of worrying that our lives have gone off track, praise God for promises kept, mercy given, and enduring strength provided, expressing gratitude for including us in a story that is so much bigger than our lives. As we read Mary's song, may we each write our own song of praise for the unlikely as well as the known, a song that reaches back into a story as old as creation that continues its thread of redemption through our lives.

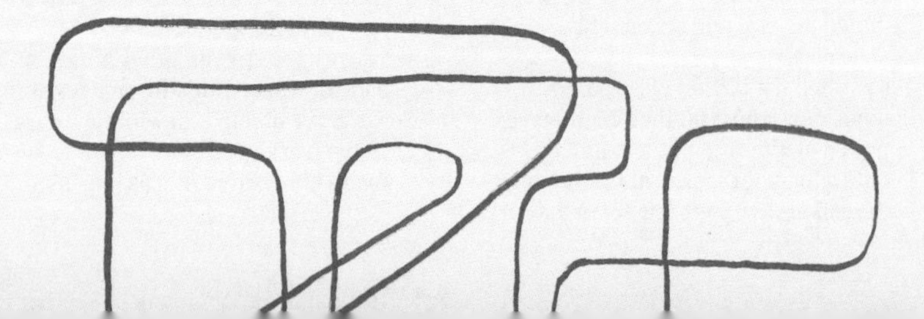

And you, my child, "Prophet of the Highest,"
will go ahead of the Master to prepare his ways,
Present the offer of salvation to his people,
the forgiveness of their sins.
Through the heartfelt mercies of our God,
God's Sunrise will break in upon us,
Shining on those in the darkness,
those sitting in the shadow of death,
Then showing us the way, one foot at a time,
down the path of peace.

80 The child grew up, healthy and spirited. He lived out in the desert until the day he made his prophetic debut in Israel.

THE BIRTH OF JESUS

2 1-5 About that time Caesar Augustus ordered a census to be taken throughout the Empire. This was the first census when Quirinius was governor of Syria. Everyone had to travel to his own ancestral hometown to be accounted for. So Joseph went from the Galilean town of Nazareth up to Bethlehem in Judah, David's town, for the census. As a descendant of David, he had to go there. He went with Mary, his fiancée, who was pregnant.

6-7 While they were there, the time came for her to give birth. She gave birth to a son, her firstborn. She wrapped him in a blanket and laid him in a manger, because there was no room in the hostel.

AN EVENT FOR EVERYONE

8-12 There were shepherds camping in the neighborhood. They had set night watches over their sheep. Suddenly, God's angel stood among them and God's glory blazed around them. They were terrified. The angel said, "Don't be afraid. I'm here to announce a great and joyful event that is meant for everybody, worldwide: A Savior has just been born in David's town, a Savior who is Messiah and Master. This is what you're to look for: a baby wrapped in a blanket and lying in a manger."

13-14 At once the angel was joined by a huge angelic choir singing God's praises:

Glory to God in the heavenly heights,
Peace to all men and women on earth who please him.

15-18 As the angel choir withdrew into heaven, the shepherds talked it over. "Let's get over to Bethlehem as fast as we can and see for ourselves what God has revealed to us." They left, running, and found Mary and Joseph, and the baby lying in the manger. Seeing was believing. They told everyone they met what the angels had said about this child. All who heard the shepherds were impressed.

19-20 Mary kept all these things to herself, holding them dear, deep within herself. The shepherds returned and let loose, glorifying and praising God for everything they had heard and seen. It turned out exactly the way they'd been told!

BLESSINGS

21 When the eighth day arrived, the day of circumcision, the child was named Jesus, the name given by the angel before he was conceived.

22-24 Then when the days stipulated by Moses for purification were complete, they took him up to Jerusalem to offer him to God as commanded in God's Law: "Every male who opens the womb shall be a holy offering to God," and also to sacrifice the "pair of doves or two young pigeons" prescribed in God's Law.

25-32 In Jerusalem at the time, there was a man, Simeon by name, a good man, a man who lived in the prayerful expectancy of help for Israel. And the Holy Spirit was on him. The Holy Spirit had shown him that he would see the Messiah of God before he died. Led by the Spirit, he entered the Temple. As the parents of the child Jesus brought him in to carry out the rituals of the Law, Simeon took him into his arms and blessed God:

God, you can now release your servant;
release me in peace as you promised.
With my own eyes I've seen your salvation;
it's now out in the open for everyone to see:
A God-revealing light to the non-Jewish nations,
and of glory for your people Israel.

33-35 Jesus' father and mother were speechless with surprise at these words. Simeon went on to bless them, and said to Mary his mother,

This child marks both the failure and
the recovery of many in Israel,

ANNA

Anna is one of the few women in the Bible explicitly identified as a prophet. We meet her during Mary's postpartum purification at the Temple. Anna herself was a childless widow, a perilous fate in that patriarchal ancient world. Interestingly, Luke identifies her not through her husband and his lineage but through her father, Phanuel, and his tribe, Asher.

Anna was a long way from her ancestral home. The tribe of Asher was located in the northwest corner of Israel, and Anna had spent most of her life in the southern city of Jerusalem. But she carried with her the spirit of her ancestor Asher (whose name means "happy"), named by his mother, Leah, with these words: "A happy day! The women will congratulate me in my happiness" (Genesis 30:13).

Indeed, though Anna had certainly known deep sorrow through the loss of her husband, she'd found deep happiness as a bride of God, giving her days to prayer, fasting, and Temple service while she waited with all Israel for the coming Messiah. It was out of that joy that she became one of the very first evangelists of the newborn Jesus. Upon seeing the baby, she "broke into an anthem of praise to God, and talked about the child to all who were waiting expectantly for the freeing of Jerusalem" (Luke 2:38).

From Anna and her ancestors, we learn the possibility of happiness that transcends our circumstances, a gift God gives us for the world.

A figure misunderstood and
contradicted—
the pain of a sword-thrust through
you—
But the rejection will force honesty,
as God reveals who they really are.

36-38 Anna the prophetess was also there, a daughter of Phanuel from the tribe of Asher. She was by now a very old woman. She had been married seven years and a widow for eighty-four. She never left the Temple area, worshiping night and day with her fastings and prayers. At the very time Simeon was praying, she showed up, broke into an anthem of praise to God, and talked about the child to all who were waiting expectantly for the freeing of Jerusalem.

39-40 When they finished everything required by God in the Law, they returned to Galilee and their own town, Nazareth. There the child grew strong in body and wise in spirit. And the grace of God was on him.

THEY FOUND HIM IN THE TEMPLE

41-45 Every year Jesus' parents traveled to Jerusalem for the Feast of Passover. When he was twelve years old, they went up as they always did for the Feast. When it was over and they left for home, the child Jesus stayed behind in Jerusalem, but his parents didn't know it. Thinking he was somewhere in the company of pilgrims, they journeyed for a whole day and then began looking for him among relatives and neighbors. When they didn't find him, they went back to Jerusalem looking for him.

46-48 The next day they found him in the Temple seated among the teachers, listening to them and asking questions. The teachers were all quite taken with him, impressed with the sharpness of his answers. But his parents were not impressed; they were upset and hurt.

His mother said, "Young man, why have you done this to us? Your father and I have been half out of our minds looking for you."

49-50 He said, "Why were you looking for me? Didn't you know that I had to be here, dealing with the things of my Father?" But they had no idea what he was talking about.

51-52 So he went back to Nazareth with them, and lived obediently with them. His mother held these things dearly, deep within herself. And Jesus matured, growing up in both body and spirit, blessed by both God and people.

A BAPTISM OF LIFE-CHANGE

3 1-6 In the fifteenth year of the rule of Caesar Tiberius—it was while Pontius Pilate was governor of Judea; Herod, ruler of Galilee; his brother Philip, ruler of Iturea and Trachonitis; Lysanias, ruler of Abilene; during the Chief-Priesthood of Annas and Caiaphas—John, Zachariah's son, out in the desert at the time, received a message from God. He went all through the country around the Jordan River preaching a baptism of life-change leading to forgiveness of sins, as described in the words of Isaiah the prophet:

Thunder in the desert!
"Prepare God's arrival!
Make the road smooth and straight!
Every ditch will be filled in,
Every bump smoothed out,
The detours straightened out,
All the ruts paved over.
Everyone will be there to see
The parade of God's salvation."

7-9 When crowds of people came out for baptism because it was the popular thing to do, John exploded: "Brood of snakes! What do you think you're doing slithering down here to the river? Do you think a little water on your snakeskins is going to deflect God's judgment? It's your *life* that must change, not your skin. And don't think you can pull rank by claiming Abraham as 'father.' Being a child of Abraham is neither here nor there—children of Abraham are a dime a dozen. God can make children from stones if he wants. What counts is your life. Is it green and flourishing? Because if it's deadwood, it goes on the fire."

10 The crowd asked him, "Then what are we supposed to do?"

11 "If you have two coats, give one away," he said. "Do the same with your food."

12 Tax men also came to be baptized and said, "Teacher, what should we do?"

13 He told them, "No more extortion—collect only what is required by law."

14 Soldiers asked him, "And what should we do?"

He told them, "No harassment, no blackmail—and be content with your rations."

15 The interest of the people by now was building. They were all beginning to wonder, "Could this John be the Messiah?"

16-17 But John intervened: "I'm baptizing you here in the river. The main character in this drama, to whom I'm a mere stagehand, will ignite the kingdom life, a fire, the Holy Spirit within you, changing you from the inside out. He's going to clean house—make a clean sweep of your lives. He'll place everything true in its proper place before God; everything false he'll put out with the trash to be burned."

18-20 There was a lot more of this—words that gave strength to the people, words that put heart in them. The Message! But Herod, the ruler, stung by John's rebuke in the matter of Herodias, his brother Philip's wife, capped his long string of evil deeds with this outrage: He put John in jail.

21-22 After all the people were baptized, Jesus was baptized. As he was praying, the sky opened up and the Holy Spirit, like a dove descending, came down on him. And along with the Spirit, a voice: "You are my Son, chosen and marked by my love, pride of my life."

SON OF ADAM, SON OF GOD

23-38 When Jesus entered public life he was about thirty years old, the son (in public perception) of Joseph, who was—

son of Heli,
son of Matthat,
son of Levi,
son of Melki,
son of Jannai,
son of Joseph,
son of Mattathias,
son of Amos,
son of Nahum,
son of Esli,
son of Naggai,
son of Maath,
son of Mattathias,
son of Semein,
son of Josech,
son of Joda,
son of Joanan,
son of Rhesa,
son of Zerubbabel,
son of Shealtiel,
son of Neri,
son of Melchi,
son of Addi,
son of Cosam,
son of Elmadam,
son of Er,
son of Joshua,
son of Eliezer,
son of Jorim,
son of Matthat,
son of Levi,
son of Simeon,
son of Judah,
son of Joseph,
son of Jonam,
son of Eliakim,
son of Melea,
son of Menna,
son of Mattatha,
son of Nathan,
son of David,
son of Jesse,
son of Obed,
son of Boaz,
son of Salmon,
son of Nahshon,
son of Amminadab,
son of Admin,
son of Arni,
son of Hezron,
son of Perez,
son of Judah,
son of Jacob,
son of Isaac,
son of Abraham,
son of Terah,
son of Nahor,
son of Serug,
son of Reu,
son of Peleg,
son of Eber,
son of Shelah,
son of Kenan,
son of Arphaxad,
son of Shem,
son of Noah,
son of Lamech,
son of Methuselah,
son of Enoch,
son of Jared,
son of Mahalaleel,
son of Kenan,
son of Enos,
son of Seth,
son of Adam,
son of God.

TESTED BY THE DEVIL

4 1-2 Now Jesus, full of the Holy Spirit, left the Jordan and was led by the Spirit into the wild. For forty wilderness days and nights he was tested by the Devil. He ate nothing during those days, and when the time was up he was hungry.

3 The Devil, playing on his hunger, gave the first test: "Since you're God's Son, command this stone to turn into a loaf of bread."

4 Jesus answered by quoting Deuteronomy: "It takes more than bread to really live."

5-7 For the second test he led him up and spread out all the kingdoms of the earth on display at once. Then the Devil said, "They're yours in all their splendor to serve your pleasure. I'm in charge of them all and can turn them over to whomever I wish. Worship me and they're yours, the whole works."

8 Jesus refused, again backing his refusal with Deuteronomy: "Worship the Lord your God and only the Lord your God. Serve him with absolute single-heartedness."

9-11 For the third test the Devil took him to Jerusalem and put him on top of the Temple. He said, "If you are God's Son, jump. It's written, isn't it, that 'he has placed you in the care of angels to protect you; they will catch you; you won't so much as stub your toe on a stone'?"

12 "Yes," said Jesus, "and it's also written, 'Don't you dare tempt the Lord your God.'"

13 That completed the testing. The Devil retreated temporarily, lying in wait for another opportunity.

TO SET THE BURDENED FREE

14-15 Jesus returned to Galilee powerful in the Spirit. News that he was back spread through the countryside. He taught in their meeting places to everyone's acclaim and pleasure.

16-21 He came to Nazareth where he had been raised. As he always did on the Sabbath, he went to the meeting place. When he stood up to read, he was handed the scroll of the prophet Isaiah. Unrolling the scroll, he found the place where it was written,

> God's Spirit is on me;
> he's chosen me to preach the Message
> of good news to the poor,
> Sent me to announce pardon to
> prisoners and
> recovery of sight to the blind,
> To set the burdened and battered free,
> to announce, "This is God's time
> to shine!"

He rolled up the scroll, handed it back to the assistant, and sat down. Every eye in the place was on him, intent. Then he started in, "You've just heard Scripture make history. It came true just now in this place."

22 All who were there, watching and listening, were surprised at how well he spoke. But they also said, "Isn't this Joseph's son, the one we've known since he was just a kid?"

23-27 He answered, "I suppose you're going to quote the proverb, 'Doctor, go heal yourself. Do here in your hometown what we heard you did in Capernaum.' Well, let me tell you something: No prophet is ever welcomed in his hometown. Isn't it a fact that there were many widows in Israel at the time of Elijah during that three and a half years of drought when famine devastated the land, but the only widow to whom Elijah was sent was in Sarepta in Sidon? And there were many lepers in Israel at the time of the prophet Elisha but the only one cleansed was Naaman the Syrian."

28-30 That set everyone in the meeting place seething with anger. They threw him out, banishing him from the village, then took him to a mountain cliff at the edge of the village to throw him to his doom, but he gave them the slip and was on his way.

31-32 He went down to Capernaum, a village in Galilee. He was teaching the people on the Sabbath. They were surprised and impressed—his teaching was so forthright, so confident, so authoritative, not the quibbling and quoting they were used to.

33-34 In the meeting place that day there was a man demonically disturbed. He screamed, "Stop! What business do you have here with us, Jesus? Nazarene! I know what you're up to. You're the Holy One of God and you've come to destroy us!"

35 Jesus shut him up: "Quiet! Get out of him!" The demonic spirit threw the man down in front of them all and left. The demon didn't hurt him.

36-37 That knocked the wind out of everyone and got them whispering and wondering, "What's going on here? Someone whose words make things happen? Someone who orders demonic spirits to get out and they go?" Jesus was the talk of the town.

HE HEALED THEM ALL

38-39 He left the meeting place and went to Simon's house. Simon's mother-in-law was running a high fever and they asked him to do something for her. He stood over her, told the fever to leave—and it left. Before they knew it, she was up getting dinner for them.

40-41 When the sun went down, everyone who had anyone sick with some ailment or other brought them to him. One by one he placed his hands on them and healed them. Demons left in droves, screaming, "Son of God! You're the Son of God!" But he shut them up, refusing to let them speak because they knew too much, knew him to be the Messiah.

42-44 He left the next day for open country. But the crowds went looking and, when they found him, clung to him so he couldn't go on. He told them, "Don't you realize that there are yet other villages where I have to tell the Message of God's kingdom, that this is the work God sent me to do?" Meanwhile he continued preaching in the meeting places of Galilee.

PUSH OUT INTO DEEP WATER

5 1-3 Once when he was standing on the shore of Lake Gennesaret, the crowd was pushing in on him to better hear the Word of God. He noticed two boats tied up. The fishermen had just left them and were out scrubbing their nets. He climbed into the boat that was Simon's and asked him to put out a little from the shore. Sitting there, using the boat for a pulpit, he taught the crowd.

4 When he finished teaching, he said to Simon, "Push out into deep water and let your nets out for a catch."

5-7 Simon said, "Master, we've been fishing hard all night and haven't caught even a minnow. But if you say so, I'll let out the nets." It was no sooner said than done—a huge haul of fish, straining the nets past capacity. They waved to their partners in the other boat to come help them. They filled both boats, nearly swamping them with the catch.

8-10 Simon Peter, when he saw it, fell to his knees before Jesus. "Master, leave. I'm a sinner and can't handle this holiness. Leave me to myself." When they pulled in that catch of fish, awe overwhelmed Simon and everyone with him. It was the same with James and John, Zebedee's sons, coworkers with Simon.

10-11 Jesus said to Simon, "There is nothing to fear. From now on you'll be fishing for men and women." They pulled their boats up on the beach, left them, nets and all, and followed him.

INVITATION TO A CHANGED LIFE

12 One day in one of the villages there was a man covered with leprosy. When he saw Jesus he fell down before him in prayer and said, "If you want to, you can cleanse me."

13 Jesus put out his hand, touched him, and said, "I want to. Be clean." Then and there his skin was smooth, the leprosy gone.

14-16 Jesus instructed him, "Don't talk about this all over town. Just quietly present your healed self to the priest, along with the offering ordered by Moses. Your cleansed and obedient life, not your words, will bear witness to what I have done." But the man couldn't keep it to himself, and the word got out. Soon a large crowd of people had gathered to listen and be healed of their sicknesses. As often as possible Jesus withdrew to out-of-the-way places for prayer.

17 One day as he was teaching, Pharisees and religion teachers were sitting around. They had come from nearly every village in Galilee and Judea, even as far away as Jerusalem, to be there. The healing power of God was on him.

18-20 Some men arrived carrying a paraplegic on a stretcher. They were looking for a way to get into the house and set him before Jesus. When they couldn't find a way in because of the crowd, they went up on the roof, removed some tiles, and let him down in the middle of everyone, right in front of Jesus. Impressed by their bold belief, he said, "Friend, I forgive your sins."

21 That set the religion scholars and Pharisees buzzing. "Who does he think he is? That's blasphemous talk! God and only God can forgive sins."

22-26 Jesus knew exactly what they were thinking and said, "Why all this gossipy whispering? Which is simpler: to say 'I forgive your sins,' or to say 'Get up and start walking'? Well, just so it's clear that I'm the Son of Man and authorized to do either, or both. . . ." He now spoke directly to the paraplegic: "Get up. Take your bedroll and go home." Without a moment's hesitation, he did it—got up, took his blanket, and left for home, giving glory to God all the way. The people rubbed their eyes, stunned—and then also gave glory to God. Awestruck, they said, "We've never seen anything like that!"

27-28 After this he went out and saw a man named Levi at his work collecting taxes. Jesus said, "Come along with me." And he did—walked away from everything and went with him.

29-30 Levi gave a large dinner at his home for Jesus. Everybody was there, tax men and other disreputable characters as guests at the dinner. The Pharisees and their religion scholars came to his disciples greatly offended. "What is he doing eating and drinking with misfits and 'sinners'?"

31-32 Jesus heard about it and spoke up, "Who needs a doctor: the healthy or the sick?

I'm here inviting outsiders, not insiders—an invitation to a changed life, changed inside and out."

33 They asked him, "John's disciples are well-known for keeping fasts and saying prayers. Also the Pharisees. But you seem to spend most of your time at parties. Why?"

34-35 Jesus said, "When you're celebrating a wedding, you don't skimp on the cake and wine. You feast. Later you may need to exercise moderation, but this isn't the time. As long as the bride and groom are with you, you have a good time. When the groom is gone, the fasting can begin. No one throws cold water on a friendly bonfire. This is Kingdom Come!

36-39 "No one cuts up a fine silk scarf to patch old work clothes; you want fabrics that match. And you don't put wine in old, cracked bottles; you get strong, clean bottles for your fresh vintage wine. And no one who has ever tasted fine aged wine prefers unaged wine."

IN CHARGE OF THE SABBATH

6 1-2 On a certain Sabbath Jesus was walking through a field of ripe grain. His disciples were pulling off heads of grain, rubbing them in their hands to get rid of the chaff, and eating them. Some Pharisees said, "Why are you doing that, breaking a Sabbath rule?"

3-4 But Jesus stood up for them. "Have you never read what David and those with him did when they were hungry? How he entered the sanctuary and ate fresh bread off the altar, bread that no one but priests were allowed to eat? He also handed it out to his companions."

5 Then he said, "The Son of Man is no slave to the Sabbath; he's in charge."

6-8 On another Sabbath he went to the meeting place and taught. There was a man there with a crippled right hand. The religion scholars and Pharisees had their eyes on Jesus to see if he would heal the man, hoping to catch him in a Sabbath violation. He knew what they were up to and spoke to the man with the crippled hand: "Get up and stand here before us." He did.

9 Then Jesus addressed them, "Let me ask you something: What kind of action suits the Sabbath best? Doing good or doing evil? Helping people or leaving them helpless?"

10-11 He looked around, looked each one in the eye. He said to the man, "Hold out your hand." He held it out—it was as good as new! They were beside themselves with anger, and started plotting how they might get even with him.

THE TWELVE APOSTLES

12-16 At about that same time he climbed a mountain to pray. He was there all night in prayer before God. The next day he summoned his disciples; from them he selected twelve he designated as apostles:

Simon, whom he named Peter,
Andrew, his brother,
James,
John,
Philip,
Bartholomew,
Matthew,
Thomas,
James, son of Alphaeus,
Simon, called the Zealot,
Judas, son of James,
Judas Iscariot, who betrayed him.

YOU'RE BLESSED

17-21 Coming down off the mountain with them, he stood on a plain surrounded by disciples, and was soon joined by a huge congregation from all over Judea and Jerusalem, even from the seaside towns of Tyre and Sidon. They had come both to hear him and to be cured of their diseases. Those disturbed by evil spirits were healed. Everyone was trying to touch him—so much energy surging from him, so many people healed! Then he spoke:

You're blessed when you've lost it all.
God's kingdom is there for the finding.

You're blessed when you're ravenously
hungry.
Then you're ready for the Messianic meal.

You're blessed when the tears flow freely.
Joy comes with the morning.

22-23 "Count yourself blessed every time someone cuts you down or throws you out, every time someone smears or blackens your name to discredit me. What it means is that the truth is too close for comfort and that that person is uncomfortable. You can be glad when that happens—skip like a lamb, if you like!—for even though they don't like it, I do . . . and all heaven applauds. And know that you are in good company; my preachers and witnesses have always been treated like this.

GIVE AWAY YOUR LIFE

24 But it's trouble ahead if you think you have it made.
What you have is all you'll ever get.

25 And it's trouble ahead if you're satisfied with yourself.
Your *self* will not satisfy you for long.

And it's trouble ahead if you think life's all fun and games.
There's suffering to be met, and you're going to meet it.

26 "There's trouble ahead when you live only for the approval of others, saying what flatters them, doing what indulges them. Popularity contests are not truth contests—look how many scoundrel preachers were approved by your ancestors! Your task is to be true, not popular.

27-30 "To you who are ready for the truth, I say this: Love your enemies. Let them bring out the best in you, not the worst. When someone gives you a hard time, respond with the supple moves of prayer for that person. If someone slaps you in the face, stand there and take it. If someone grabs your shirt, giftwrap your best coat and make a present of it. If someone takes unfair advantage of you, use the occasion to practice the servant life. No more payback. Live generously.

31-34 "Here is a simple rule of thumb for behavior: Ask yourself what you want people to do for you; then grab the initiative and do it for *them*! If you only love the lovable, do you expect a pat on the back? Run-of-the-mill sinners do that. If you only help those who help you, do you expect a medal? Garden-variety sinners do that. If you only give for what you hope to get out of it, do you think that's charity? The stingiest of pawnbrokers does that.

35-36 "I tell you, love your enemies. Help and give without expecting a return. You'll never—I promise—regret it. Live out this God-created identity the way our Father lives toward us, generously and graciously, even when we're at our worst. Our Father is kind; you be kind.

37-38 "Don't pick on people, jump on their failures, criticize their faults—unless, of course, you want the same treatment. Don't condemn those who are down; that hardness can boomerang. Be easy on people; you'll find life a lot easier. Give away your life; you'll find life given back, but not merely given back—given back with bonus and blessing. Giving, not getting, is the way. Generosity begets generosity."

39-40 He quoted a proverb: "'Can a blind man guide a blind man?' Wouldn't they both end up in the ditch? An apprentice doesn't lecture the master. The point is to be careful who you follow as your teacher.

41-42 "It's easy to see a smudge on your neighbor's face and be oblivious to the ugly sneer on your own. Do you have the nerve to say, 'Let me wash your face for you,' when your own face is distorted by contempt? It's this I-know-better-than-you mentality again, playing a holier-than-thou part instead of just living your own part. Wipe that ugly sneer off your own face and you might be fit to offer a washcloth to your neighbor.

WORK THE WORDS INTO YOUR LIFE

43-45 "You don't get wormy apples off a healthy tree, nor good apples off a diseased tree. The health of the apple tells the health of the tree. You must begin with your own life-giving lives. It's who you are, not what you say and do, that counts. Your true being brims over into true words and deeds.

46-47 "Why are you so polite with me, always saying 'Yes, sir,' and 'That's right, sir,' but never doing a thing I tell you? These words I speak to you are not mere additions to your life, homeowner improvements to your standard of living. They are foundation words, words to build a life on.

48-49 "If you work the words into your life, you are like a smart carpenter who dug deep and laid the foundation of his house on bedrock. When the river burst its banks and crashed against the house, nothing could shake it; it was built to last. But if you just use my words in Bible studies and don't work them into your life, you are like a dumb carpenter who built a house but skipped the foundation. When the swollen river came crashing in, it collapsed like a house of cards. It was a total loss."

A PLACE OF HOLY MYSTERY

7 1-5 When he finished speaking to the people, he entered Capernaum. A Roman captain there had a servant who was on his deathbed. He prized him highly and

didn't want to lose him. When he heard Jesus was back, he sent leaders from the Jewish community asking him to come and heal his servant. They came to Jesus and urged him to do it, saying, "He deserves this. He loves our people. He even built our meeting place."

6-8 Jesus went with them. When he was still quite far from the house, the captain sent friends to tell him, "Master, you don't have to go to all this trouble. I'm not that good a person, you know. I'd be embarrassed for you to come to my house, even embarrassed to come to you in person. Just give the order and my servant will get well. I'm a man under orders; I also give orders. I tell one soldier, 'Go,' and he goes; another, 'Come,' and he comes; my slave, 'Do this,' and he does it."

9-10 Taken aback, Jesus addressed the accompanying crowd: "I've yet to come across this kind of simple trust anywhere in Israel, the very people who are supposed to know about God and how he works." When the messengers got back home, they found the servant up and well.

11-15 Not long after that, Jesus went to the village Nain. His disciples were with him, along with quite a large crowd. As they approached the village gate, they met a funeral procession—a woman's only son was being carried out for burial. And the mother was a widow. When Jesus saw her, his heart broke. He said to her, "Don't cry." Then he went over and touched the coffin. The pallbearers stopped. He said, "Young man, I tell you: Get up." The dead son sat up and began talking. Jesus presented him to his mother.

16-17 They all realized they were in a place of holy mystery, that God was at work among them. They were quietly worshipful—and then noisily grateful, calling out among themselves, "God is back, looking to the needs of his people!" The news of Jesus spread all through the country.

IS THIS WHAT YOU WERE EXPECTING?

18-19 John's disciples reported back to him the news of all these events taking place. He sent two of them to the Master to ask the question, "Are you the One we've been expecting, or are we still waiting?"

20 The men showed up before Jesus and said, "John the Baptizer sent us to ask you, 'Are you the One we've been expecting, or are we still waiting?'"

21-23 In the next two or three hours Jesus healed many from diseases, distress, and evil spirits. To many of the blind he gave the gift of sight. Then he gave his answer: "Go back and tell John what you have just seen and heard:

The blind see,
The lame walk,
Lepers are cleansed,
The deaf hear,
The dead are raised,
The wretched of the earth
have God's salvation hospitality
extended to them.

"Is this what you were expecting? Then count yourselves fortunate!"

24-27 After John's messengers left to make their report, Jesus said more about John to the crowd of people. "What did you expect when you went out to see him in the wild? A weekend camper? Hardly. What then? A sheik in silk pajamas? Not in the wilderness, not by a long shot. What then? A messenger from God? That's right, a messenger! Probably the greatest messenger you'll ever hear. He is the messenger Malachi announced when he wrote,

I'm sending my messenger on ahead
To make the road smooth for you.

28-30 "Let me lay it out for you as plainly as I can: No one in history surpasses John the Baptizer, but in the kingdom he prepared you for, the lowliest person is ahead of him. The ordinary and disreputable people who heard John, by being baptized by him into the kingdom, are the clearest evidence; the Pharisees and religious officials would have nothing to do with such a baptism, wouldn't think of giving up their place in line to their inferiors.

31-35 "How can I account for the people of this generation? They're like spoiled children complaining to their parents, 'We wanted to skip rope and you were always too tired; we wanted to talk but you were always too busy.' John the Baptizer came fasting and you called him crazy. The Son of Man came feasting and you called him a boozer. Opinion polls don't count for much, do they? The proof of the pudding is in the eating."

ANOINTING HIS FEET

36-39 One of the Pharisees asked him over for a meal. He went to the Pharisee's house and sat down at the dinner table. Just then a woman of the village, the town harlot, having learned

The Forgiven Woman

She stepped into Jesus' presence, described only as "the town harlot" (Luke 7:37). Defined by what she'd done, perhaps accustomed to others battering her with judgment, this woman approached Jesus. Were her courage, gratitude, and hope laced with a few lingering strands of shame and guilt as she gathered her hair and washed Jesus' feet with her tears?

Bowing before Jesus placed her in a vulnerable position. Still, she offered him what she must have considered her most precious gift: a bottle filled with expensive perfume. The Pharisee who had invited Jesus into his home saw only a sinner crouched on the floor wasting something costly. Jesus, however, saw a repentant heart and an outpouring of sacrificial love and devotion as the woman wiped his feet with her crown of glory.

Jesus saw past her sin-stained reputation and proclaimed her redemption. Then, in a room filled with men who didn't recognize her worth as God's image bearer, Jesus said to her, "I forgive your sins" (Luke 7:48). Period. Jesus granted the woman freedom and hope for her future—and the future of all women who sin.

The mere hope of receiving that gift of forgiveness brought this woman to her knees. Were her hands trembling as she washed Jesus' feet? Did she fear rejection? Did she wonder if his love would be enough to redeem the sins that had kept her in bondage for so long?

As we consider our own résumés of sinfulness, we can rejoice over the connection between love and forgiveness in Christ. He loves us, so he forgives us. He forgives us, so we love him. With grateful praises, we can serve him and offer him our most priceless gift—every ounce of love tucked deep in our tender, scarred hearts—as we embrace God's redeeming love.

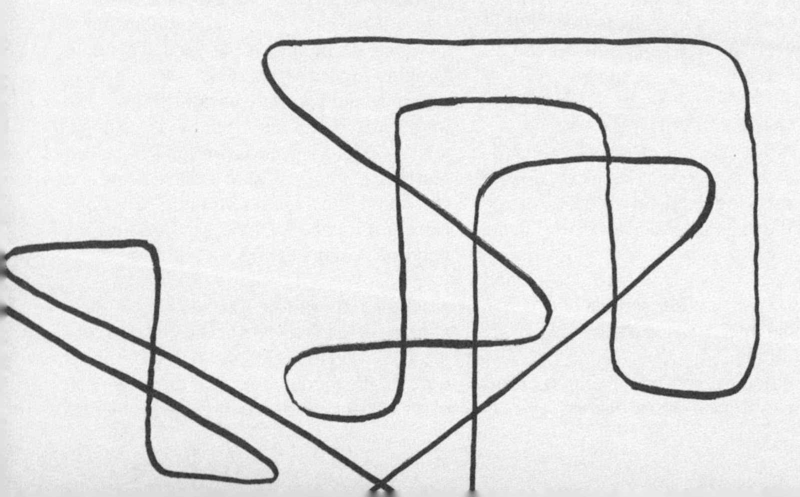

that Jesus was a guest in the home of the Pharisee, came with a bottle of very expensive perfume and stood at his feet, weeping, raining tears on his feet. Letting down her hair, she dried his feet, kissed them, and anointed them with the perfume. When the Pharisee who had invited him saw this, he said to himself, "If this man was the prophet I thought he was, he would have known what kind of woman this is who is falling all over him."

40 Jesus said to him, "Simon, I have something to tell you."

"Oh? Tell me."

41-42 "Two men were in debt to a banker. One owed five hundred silver pieces, the other fifty. Neither of them could pay up, and so the banker canceled both debts. Which of the two would be more grateful?"

43-47 Simon answered, "I suppose the one who was forgiven the most."

"That's right," said Jesus. Then turning to the woman, but speaking to Simon, he said, "Do you see this woman? I came to your home; you provided no water for my feet, but she rained tears on my feet and dried them with her hair. You gave me no greeting, but from the time I arrived she hasn't quit kissing my feet. You provided nothing for freshening up, but she has soothed my feet with perfume. Impressive, isn't it? She was forgiven many, many sins, and so she is very, very grateful. If the forgiveness is minimal, the gratitude is minimal."

48 Then he spoke to her: "I forgive your sins."

49 That set the dinner guests talking behind his back: "Who does he think he is, forgiving sins!"

50 He ignored them and said to the woman, "Your faith has saved you. Go in peace."

8

1-3 He continued according to plan, traveled to town after town, village after village, preaching God's kingdom, spreading the Message. The Twelve were with him. There were also some women in their company who had been healed of various evil afflictions and illnesses: Mary, the one called Magdalene, from whom seven demons had gone out; Joanna, wife of Chuza, Herod's manager; and Susanna—along with many others who used their considerable means to provide for the company.

THE STORY OF THE SEEDS

4-8 As they went from town to town, a lot of people joined in and traveled along. He addressed them, using this story: "A farmer went out to sow his seed. Some of it fell on the road; it was tramped down and the birds ate it. Other seed fell in the gravel; it sprouted, but withered because it didn't have good roots. Other seed fell in the weeds; the weeds grew with it and strangled it. Other seed fell in rich earth and produced a bumper crop.

"Are you listening to this? Really listening?"

9 His disciples asked, "Why did you tell this story?"

10 He said, "You've been given insight into God's kingdom—you know how it works. There are others who need stories. But even with stories some of them aren't going to get it:

> Their eyes are open but don't see a thing,
> Their ears are open but don't hear a thing.

11-12 "This story is about some of those people. The seed is the Word of God. The seeds on the road are those who hear the Word, but no sooner do they hear it than the Devil snatches it from them so they won't believe and be saved.

13 "The seeds in the gravel are those who hear with enthusiasm, but the enthusiasm doesn't go very deep. It's only another fad, and the moment there's trouble it's gone.

14 "And the seed that fell in the weeds—well, these are the ones who hear, but then the seed is crowded out and nothing comes of it as they go about their lives worrying about tomorrow, making money, and having fun.

15 "But the seed in the good earth—these are the good-hearts who seize the Word and hold on no matter what, sticking with it until there's a harvest.

MISERS OF WHAT YOU HEAR

16-18 "No one lights a lamp and then covers it with a washtub or shoves it under the bed. No, you set it up on a lamp stand so those who enter the room can see their way. We're not keeping secrets; we're telling them. We're not hiding things; we're bringing *everything* out into the open. So be careful that you don't become misers of what you hear. Generosity begets generosity. Stinginess impoverishes."

19-20 His mother and brothers showed up but couldn't get through to him because of the crowd. He was given the message, "Your mother and brothers are standing outside wanting to see you."

21 He replied, "My mother and brothers are the ones who hear and do God's Word. Obedience is thicker than blood."

22-24 One day he and his disciples got in a boat. "Let's cross the lake," he said. And off they went. It was smooth sailing, and he fell asleep. A terrific storm came up suddenly on the lake. Water poured in, and they were about to capsize. They woke Jesus: "Master, Master, we're going to drown!"

Getting to his feet, he told the wind, "Silence!" and the waves, "Quiet down!" They did it. The lake became smooth as glass.

25 Then he said to his disciples, "Why can't you trust me?"

They were in absolute awe, staggered and stammering, "Who is this, anyway? He calls out to the winds and sea, and they do what he tells them!"

THE MADMAN AND THE PIGS

26-29 They sailed on to the country of the Gerasenes, directly opposite Galilee. As he stepped out onto land, a madman from town met him; he was a victim of demons. He hadn't worn clothes for a long time, nor lived at home; he lived in the cemetery. When he saw Jesus he screamed, fell before him, and howled, "What business do you have messing with me? You're Jesus, Son of the High God, but don't give me a hard time!" (The man said this because Jesus had started to order the unclean spirit out of him.) Time after time the demon threw the man into convulsions. He had been placed under constant guard and tied with chains and shackles, but crazed and driven wild by the demon, he would shatter the bonds.

30-31 Jesus asked him, "What is your name?"

"Mob. My name is Mob," he said, because many demons afflicted him. And they begged Jesus desperately not to order them to the bottomless pit.

32-33 A large herd of pigs was grazing and rooting on a nearby hill. The demons begged Jesus to order them into the pigs. He gave the order. It was even worse for the pigs than for the man. Crazed, they stampeded over a cliff into the lake and drowned.

34-36 Those tending the pigs, scared to death, bolted and told their story in town and country. People went out to see what had happened. They came to Jesus and found the man from whom the demons had been sent, sitting there at Jesus' feet, wearing decent clothes and making sense. It was a holy moment, and for a short time they were more reverent than curious. Then those who had seen it happen told how the demoniac had been saved.

37-39 Later, a great many people from the Gerasene countryside got together and asked Jesus to leave—too much change, too fast, and they were scared. So Jesus got back in the boat and set off. The man whom he had delivered from the demons asked to go with him, but he sent him back, saying, "Go home and tell everything God did in you." So he went back and preached all over town everything Jesus had done in him.

HIS TOUCH

40-42 On his return, Jesus was welcomed by a crowd. They were all there expecting him. A man came up, Jairus by name. He was president of the meeting place. He fell at Jesus' feet and begged him to come to his home because his twelve-year-old daughter, his only child, was dying. Jesus went with him, making his way through the pushing, jostling crowd.

43-45 In the crowd that day there was a woman who for twelve years had been afflicted with hemorrhages. She had spent every penny she had on doctors but not one had been able to help her. She slipped in from behind and touched the edge of Jesus' robe. At that very moment her hemorrhaging stopped. Jesus said, "Who touched me?"

When no one stepped forward, Peter said, "But Master, we've got crowds of people on our hands. Dozens have touched you."

46 Jesus insisted, "Someone touched me. I felt power discharging from me."

47 When the woman realized that she couldn't remain hidden, she knelt trembling before him. In front of all the people, she blurted out her story—why she touched him and how at that same moment she was healed.

48 Jesus said, "Daughter, you took a risk trusting me, and now you're healed and whole. Live well, live blessed!"

49 While he was still talking, someone from the leader's house came up and told him, "Your daughter died. No need now to bother the Teacher."

50-51 Jesus overheard and said, "Don't be upset. Just trust me and everything will be all right." Going into the house, he wouldn't let anyone enter with him except Peter, John, James, and the child's parents.

52-53 Everyone was crying and carrying on over her. Jesus said, "Don't cry. She didn't die;

THE HEMORRHAGING WOMAN

We know her as the hemorrhaging woman. We aren't introduced to her family or daily activities or even given her name. She is defined by her chronic condition.

Along with having twelve years of bodily pain and exhaustion under her belt, she was living with the social stigma of being considered unclean. Not only was she held back from full participation in community, but anyone who touched her—or the furnishings she sat on—was temporarily considered unclean too (see Leviticus 15:25-30).

Those struggling with physical health, mental health, or disconnection in vital relationships can empathize with her desperation. Yet we can also be inspired by her boldness. She persistently invested in her healing, draining her savings to pay for potential cures. Even when nothing worked, she held on to a vision for wholeness. Her only chance now was to get near Jesus.

Unlike others needing help in Capernaum, this woman had no one to plead her cause. So she became her own advocate. She took great care to go undetected in the crowd; we witness her strategic yet self-protective manner. Her approach to Jesus held both audacity and anxiety.

When she touched Jesus' robe, her flow of blood stopped exactly as she'd hoped it would. But her plan unraveled when Jesus called her out before the crowd. As she knelt and nervously told her story, Jesus affirmed her faith and publicly declared her intrinsic worth. We may call her the hemorrhaging woman, but Jesus claimed her as "Daughter" (Luke 8:48). No longer defined or confined by her condition, the woman became known by her connection with Jesus. Her true healing included belonging.

Something shifts when our faith and self-advocacy meet Jesus' power and loving attention. Each of us is invited to be defined not by our condition but by Jesus' affirmation. He cares for our physical and mental needs—and for our social healing too.

she's sleeping." They laughed at him. They knew she was dead.

54-56 Then Jesus, gripping her hand, called, "My dear child, get up." She was up in an instant, up and breathing again! He told them to give her something to eat. Her parents were ecstatic, but Jesus warned them to keep quiet. "Don't tell a soul what happened in this room."

KEEP IT SIMPLE

9 1-5 Jesus now called the Twelve and gave them authority and power to deal with all the demons and cure diseases. He commissioned them to preach the news of God's kingdom and heal the sick. He said, "Don't load yourselves up with equipment. Keep it simple; *you* are the equipment. And no luxury inns—get a modest place and be content there until you leave. If you're not welcomed, leave town. Don't make a scene. Shrug your shoulders and move on."

6 Commissioned, they left. They traveled from town to town telling the latest news of God, the Message, and curing people everywhere they went.

7-9 Herod, the ruler, heard of these goings on and didn't know what to think. There were people saying John had come back from the dead, others that Elijah had appeared, still others that some prophet of long ago had shown up. Herod said, "But I killed John—took off his head. So who is this that I keep hearing about?" Curious, he looked for a chance to see him in action.

10-11 The apostles returned and reported on what they had done. Jesus took them away, off by themselves, near the town called Bethsaida. But the crowds got wind of it and followed. Jesus graciously welcomed them and talked to them about the kingdom of God. Those who needed healing, he healed.

BREAD AND FISH FOR FIVE THOUSAND

12 As the sun set, the Twelve said, "Dismiss the crowd so they can go to the farms or villages around here and get a room for the night and a bite to eat. We're out in the middle of nowhere."

13-14 "You feed them," Jesus said.

They said, "We couldn't scrape up more than five loaves of bread and a couple of fish—unless, of course, you want us to go to town ourselves and buy food for everybody." (There were more than five thousand people in the crowd.)

14-17 But he went ahead and directed his disciples, "Sit them down in groups of about fifty." They did what he said, and soon had everyone seated. He took the five loaves and two fish, lifted his face to heaven in prayer, blessed, broke, and gave the bread and fish to the disciples to hand out to the crowd. After the people had all eaten their fill, twelve baskets of leftovers were gathered up.

DON'T RUN FROM SUFFERING

18 One time when Jesus was off praying by himself, his disciples nearby, he asked them, "What are the crowds saying about me, about who I am?"

19 They said, "John the Baptizer. Others say Elijah. Still others say that one of the prophets from long ago has come back."

20-21 He then asked, "And you—what are you saying about me? Who am I?"

Peter answered, "The Messiah of God." Jesus then warned them to keep it quiet. They were to tell no one what Peter had said.

22 He went on, "It is necessary that the Son of Man proceed to an ordeal of suffering, be tried and found guilty by the religious leaders, high priests, and religion scholars, be killed, and on the third day be raised up alive."

23-27 Then he told them what they could expect for themselves: "Anyone who intends to come with me has to let me lead. You're not in the driver's seat—I am. Don't run from suffering; embrace it. Follow me and I'll show you how. Self-help is no help at all. Self-sacrifice is the way, *my* way, to finding yourself, your true self. What good would it do to get everything you want and lose you, the real you? If any of you is embarrassed with me and the way I'm leading you, know that the Son of Man will be far more embarrassed with you when he arrives in all his splendor in company with the Father and the holy angels. This isn't, you realize, pie in the sky by and by. Some who have taken their stand right here are going to see it happen, see with their own eyes the kingdom of God."

JESUS IN HIS GLORY

28-31 About eight days after saying this, he climbed the mountain to pray, taking Peter, John, and James along. While he was in prayer, the appearance of his face changed and his clothes became blinding white. At once two men were there talking with him. They turned out to be Moses and Elijah—and what a glorious appearance they made! They talked over his exodus, the one Jesus was about to complete in Jerusalem.

32-33 Meanwhile, Peter and those with him were slumped over in sleep. When they came to, rubbing their eyes, they saw Jesus in his glory and the two men standing with him. When Moses and Elijah had left, Peter said to Jesus, "Master, this is a great moment! Let's build three memorials: one for you, one for Moses, and one for Elijah." He blurted this out without thinking.

34-35 While he was babbling on like this, a light-radiant cloud enveloped them. As they found themselves buried in the cloud, they became deeply aware of God. Then there was a voice out of the cloud: "This is my Son, the Chosen! Listen to him."

36 When the sound of the voice died away, they saw Jesus there alone. They were speechless. And they continued speechless, said not one thing to anyone during those days of what they had seen.

▲ ▲ ▲

37-40 When they came down off the mountain the next day, a big crowd was there to meet them. A man called from out of the crowd, "Please, please, Teacher, take a look at my son. He's my only child. Often a spirit seizes him. Suddenly he's screaming, thrown into convulsions, his mouth foaming. And then it beats him black-and-blue before it leaves. I asked your disciples to deliver him but they couldn't."

41 Jesus said, "What a generation! No sense of God! No focus to your lives! How many times do I have to go over these things? How much longer do I have to put up with this? Bring your son here."

42-43 While he was coming, the demon slammed him to the ground and threw him into convulsions. Jesus stepped in, ordered the foul spirit gone, healed the boy, and handed him back to his father. They all shook their heads in wonder, astonished at God's greatness, God's majestic greatness.

YOUR BUSINESS IS LIFE

43-44 While they continued to stand around exclaiming over all the things he was doing, Jesus said to his disciples, "Treasure and ponder each of these next words: The Son of Man is about to be betrayed into human hands."

45 They didn't get what he was saying. It was like he was speaking a foreign language and they couldn't make heads or tails of it. But they were embarrassed to ask him what he meant.

46-48 They started arguing over which of them would be most famous. When Jesus realized how much this mattered to them, he brought a child to his side. "Whoever accepts this child as if the child were me, accepts me," he said. "And whoever accepts me, accepts the One who sent me. You become great by accepting, not asserting. Your spirit, not your size, makes the difference."

49 John spoke up, "Master, we saw a man using your name to expel demons and we stopped him because he wasn't of our group."

50 Jesus said, "Don't stop him. If he's not an enemy, he's an ally."

51-54 When it came close to the time for his Ascension, he gathered up his courage and steeled himself for the journey to Jerusalem. He sent messengers on ahead. They came to a Samaritan village to make arrangements for his hospitality. But when the Samaritans learned that his destination was Jerusalem, they refused hospitality. When the disciples James and John learned of it, they said, "Master, do you want us to call a bolt of lightning down out of the sky and incinerate them?"

55-56 Jesus turned on them: "Of course not!" And they traveled on to another village.

57 On the road someone asked if he could go along. "I'll go with you, wherever," he said.

58 Jesus was curt: "Are you ready to rough it? We're not staying in the best inns, you know."

Jesus said to another, "Follow me."

59 He said, "Certainly, but first excuse me for a couple of days, please. I have to make arrangements for my father's funeral."

60 Jesus refused. "First things first. Your business is life, not death. And life is urgent: Announce God's kingdom!"

61 Then another said, "I'm ready to follow you, Master, but first excuse me while I get things straightened out at home."

62 Jesus said, "No procrastination. No backward looks. You can't put God's kingdom off till tomorrow. Seize the day."

LAMBS IN A WOLF PACK

10 1-2 Later the Master selected seventy and sent them ahead of him in pairs to every town and place where he intended to go. He gave them this charge:

"What a huge harvest! And how few the

Work That Jesus Highly Regarded

As Jesus and the twelve disciples entered the village, they were welcomed by Martha, who opened up her home to them. Then, while Martha was pulled away by food prep in the kitchen, Mary sat at Jesus' feet with the other disciples, listening intently to his every word. A frazzled Martha eventually interrupted Jesus to complain that Mary should be helping her in the kitchen, demanding that Jesus command Mary to work with her. Jesus gently reprimanded Martha, countering that Mary had actually chosen the essential thing—"the main course" (Luke 10:42).

The lesson often gleaned from this popular story is that Martha was focused on material things while Mary was focused on spiritual things. Martha is painted as a busybody, and we are admonished to not be a Martha. However, reading this story in context provides a different perspective to consider.

Luke 10 opens with Jesus selecting seventy disciples; he sends them out in pairs to prepare towns and villages for his arrival. Prior to the groups heading out, Jesus gives them instructions on how to decide in which towns they should proclaim the gospel and heal the sick. They are to stay in the homes of families who welcome their greeting of "Peace." Jesus tells them to eat and drink whatever is offered to them in such homes and not go house hopping "looking for the best cook in town." Jesus ends his travel instructions by saying, "The one who listens to you, listens to me. The one who rejects you, rejects me. And rejecting me is the same as rejecting God, who sent me" (Luke 10:1-16).

Through this we see that Jesus places value on two things: (1) the act of actively listening to God and (2) acts of hospitality, such as welcoming messengers of God into one's home and offering them food and drink.

Jesus had told the seventy to eat whatever was set before them. He understood that while some homes could offer six-course meals, others might only be able to offer basic meals of grains, veggies, and fruit. Cheese and crackers, according to Jesus, would be hospitality enough; the Message would be the main course.

The Greek word used to describe Martha's actions is *diakonia*, which is used throughout the New Testament to describe ministry. Another form of this word (*diakonos*) is translated "servant" or "minister." With this new information in mind, we realize that both Martha and Mary were doing work that Jesus highly regarded as ministry in the kingdom.

So why was Martha reprimanded? Not for opening her home to Jesus. Not for offering him and his followers food and drink. These acts of thoughtfulness were acts of ministry. It was the thought that counted. But Mary's ministry counted too. It was a gift, and Martha was wrong to devalue it.

harvest hands. So on your knees; ask the God of the Harvest to send harvest hands.

3 "On your way! But be careful—this is hazardous work. You're like lambs in a wolf pack.

4 "Travel light. Comb and toothbrush and no extra luggage.

"Don't loiter and make small talk with everyone you meet along the way.

5-6 "When you enter a home, greet the family, 'Peace.' If your greeting is received, then it's a good place to stay. But if it's not received, take it back and get out. Don't impose yourself.

7 "Stay at one home, taking your meals there, for a worker deserves three square meals. Don't move from house to house, looking for the best cook in town.

8-9 "When you enter a town and are received, eat what they set before you, heal anyone who is sick, and tell them, 'God's kingdom is right on your doorstep!'

10-12 "When you enter a town and are not received, go out in the street and say, 'The only thing we got from you is the dirt on our feet, and we're giving it back. Did you have any idea that God's kingdom was right on your doorstep?' Sodom will have it better on Judgment Day than the town that rejects you.

13-14 "Doom, Chorazin! Doom, Bethsaida! If Tyre and Sidon had been given half the chances given you, they'd have been on their knees long ago, repenting and crying for mercy. Tyre and Sidon will have it easy on Judgment Day compared to you.

15 "And you, Capernaum! Do you think you're about to be promoted to heaven? Think again. You're on a fast track to hell.

16 "The one who listens to you, listens to me. The one who rejects you, rejects me. And rejecting me is the same as rejecting God, who sent me."

17 The seventy came back triumphant. "Master, even the demons danced to your tune!"

18-20 Jesus said, "I know. I saw Satan fall, a bolt of lightning out of the sky. See what I've given you? Safe passage as you walk on snakes and scorpions, and protection from every assault of the Enemy. No one can put a hand on you. All the same, the great triumph is not in your authority over evil, but in God's authority over you and presence with you. Not what you do for God but what God does for you—that's the agenda for rejoicing."

21 At that, Jesus rejoiced, exuberant in the Holy Spirit. "I thank you, Father, Master of heaven and earth, that you hid these things from the know-it-alls and showed them to these innocent newcomers. Yes, Father, it pleased you to do it this way.

22 "I've been given it all by my Father! Only the Father knows who the Son is and only the Son knows who the Father is. The Son can introduce the Father to anyone he wants to."

23-24 He then turned in a private aside to his disciples. "Fortunate the eyes that see what you're seeing! There are plenty of prophets and kings who would have given their right arm to see what you are seeing but never got so much as a glimpse, to hear what you are hearing but never got so much as a whisper."

DEFINING "NEIGHBOR"

25 Just then a religion scholar stood up with a question to test Jesus. "Teacher, what do I need to do to get eternal life?"

26 He answered, "What's written in God's Law? How do you interpret it?"

27 He said, "That you love the Lord your God with all your passion and prayer and muscle and intelligence—and that you love your neighbor as well as you do yourself."

28 "Good answer!" said Jesus. "Do it and you'll live."

29 Looking for a loophole, he asked, "And just how would you define 'neighbor'?"

30-32 Jesus answered by telling a story. "There was once a man traveling from Jerusalem to Jericho. On the way he was attacked by robbers. They took his clothes, beat him up, and went off leaving him half-dead. Luckily, a priest was on his way down the same road, but when he saw him he angled across to the other side. Then a Levite religious man showed up; he also avoided the injured man.

33-35 "A Samaritan traveling the road came on him. When he saw the man's condition, his heart went out to him. He gave him first aid, disinfecting and bandaging his wounds. Then he lifted him onto his donkey, led him to an inn, and made him comfortable. In the morning he took out two silver coins and gave them to the innkeeper, saying, 'Take good care of him. If it costs any more, put it on my bill—I'll pay you on my way back.'

36 "What do you think? Which of the three became a neighbor to the man attacked by robbers?"

37 "The one who treated him kindly," the religion scholar responded.

Jesus said, "Go and do the same."

MARY AND MARTHA

38-40 As they continued their travel, Jesus entered a village. A woman by the name of Martha welcomed him and made him feel quite at home. She had a sister, Mary, who sat before the Master, hanging on every word he said. But Martha was pulled away by all she had to do in the kitchen. Later, she stepped in, interrupting them. "Master, don't you care that my sister has abandoned the kitchen to me? Tell her to lend me a hand."

41-42 The Master said, "Martha, dear Martha, you're fussing far too much and getting yourself worked up over nothing. One thing only is essential, and Mary has chosen it—it's the main course, and won't be taken from her."

ASK FOR WHAT YOU NEED

11 1 One day he was praying in a certain place. When he finished, one of his disciples said, "Master, teach us to pray just as John taught his disciples."

2-4 So he said, "When you pray, say,

Father,
Reveal who you are.
Set the world right.
Keep us alive with three square meals.
Keep us forgiven with you and forgiving others.
Keep us safe from ourselves and the Devil."

5-6 Then he said, "Imagine what would happen if you went to a friend in the middle of the night and said, 'Friend, lend me three loaves of bread. An old friend traveling through just showed up, and I don't have a thing on hand.'

7 "The friend answers from his bed, 'Don't bother me. The door's locked; my children are all down for the night; I can't get up to give you anything.'

8 "But let me tell you, even if he won't get up because he's a friend, if you stand your ground, knocking and waking all the neighbors, he'll finally get up and get you whatever you need.

9 "Here's what I'm saying:

Ask and you'll get;
Seek and you'll find;
Knock and the door will open.

10-13 "Don't bargain with God. Be direct. Ask for what you need. This is not a cat-and-mouse, hide-and-seek game we're in. If your little boy asks for a serving of fish, do you scare him with a live snake on his plate? If your little girl asks for an egg, do you trick her with a spider? As bad as you are, you wouldn't think of such a thing—you're at least decent to your own children. And don't you think the Father who conceived you in love will give the Holy Spirit when you ask him?"

NO NEUTRAL GROUND

14-16 Jesus delivered a man from a demon that had kept him speechless. The demon gone, the man started talking a blue streak, taking the crowd by complete surprise. But some from the crowd were cynical. "Black magic," they said. "Some devil trick he's pulled from his sleeve." Others were skeptical, waiting around for him to prove himself with a spectacular miracle.

17-20 Jesus knew what they were thinking and said, "Any country in civil war for very long is wasted. A constantly squabbling family falls to pieces. If Satan cancels Satan, is there any Satan left? You accuse me of ganging up with the Devil, the prince of demons, to cast out demons, but if you're slinging devil mud at me, calling me a devil who kicks out devils, doesn't the same mud stick to your own exorcists? But if it's *God's* finger I'm pointing that sends the demons on their way, then God's kingdom is here for sure.

21-22 "When a strong man, armed to the teeth, stands guard in his front yard, his property is safe and sound. But what if a stronger man comes along with superior weapons? Then he's beaten at his own game, the arsenal that gave him such confidence hauled off, and his precious possessions plundered.

23 "This is war, and there is no neutral ground. If you're not on my side, you're the enemy; if you're not helping, you're making things worse.

24-26 "When a corrupting spirit is expelled from someone, it drifts along through the desert looking for an oasis, some unsuspecting soul it can bedevil. When it doesn't find anyone, it says, 'I'll go back to my old haunt.' On return, it finds the person swept and dusted, but vacant. It then runs out and rounds up seven other spirits dirtier than itself and they all move in, whooping it up. That person ends up far worse than if he'd never gotten cleaned up in the first place."

27 While he was saying these things, some woman lifted her voice above the murmur of

the crowd: "Blessed the womb that carried you, and the breasts at which you nursed!"

28 Jesus commented, "Even more blessed are those who hear God's Word and guard it with their lives!"

KEEP YOUR EYES OPEN

29-30 As the crowd swelled, he took a fresh tack: "The mood of this age is all wrong. Everybody's looking for proof, but you're looking for the wrong kind. All you're looking for is something to titillate your curiosity, satisfy your lust for miracles. But the only proof you're going to get is the Jonah-proof given to the Ninevites, which looks like no proof at all. What Jonah was to Nineveh, the Son of Man is to this age.

31-32 "On Judgment Day the Ninevites will stand up and give evidence that will condemn this generation, because when Jonah preached to them they changed their lives. A far greater preacher than Jonah is here, and you squabble about 'proofs.' On Judgment Day the Queen of Sheba will come forward and bring evidence that condemns this generation, because she traveled from a far corner of the earth to listen to wise Solomon. Wisdom far greater than Solomon's is right in front of you, and you quibble over 'evidence.'

33-36 "No one lights a lamp, then hides it in a drawer. It's put on a lamp stand so those entering the room have light to see where they're going. Your eye is a lamp, lighting up your whole body. If you live wide-eyed in wonder and belief, your body fills up with light. If you live squinty-eyed in greed and distrust, your body is a musty cellar. Keep your eyes open, your lamp burning, so you don't get musty and murky. Keep your life as well-lighted as your best-lighted room."

FRAUDS!

37-41 When he finished that talk, a Pharisee asked him to dinner. He entered his house and sat right down at the table. The Pharisee was shocked and somewhat offended when he saw that Jesus didn't wash up before the meal. But the Master said to him, "I know you Pharisees buff the surface of your cups and plates so they sparkle in the sun, but I also know your insides are maggoty with greed and secret evil. Stupid Pharisees! Didn't the One who made the outside also make the inside? Turn both your pockets and your hearts inside out and give generously to the poor; then your *lives* will be clean, not just your dishes and your hands.

42 "I've had it with you! You're hopeless, you Pharisees! Frauds! You keep meticulous account books, tithing on every nickel and dime you get, but manage to find loopholes for getting around basic matters of justice and God's love. Careful bookkeeping is commendable, but the basics are required.

43-44 "You're hopeless, you Pharisees! Frauds! You love sitting at the head table at church dinners, love preening yourselves in the radiance of public flattery. Frauds! You're just like unmarked graves: People walk over that nice, grassy surface, never suspecting the rot and corruption that is six feet under."

45 One of the religion scholars spoke up: "Teacher, do you realize that in saying these things you're insulting us?"

46 He said, "Yes, and I can be even more explicit. You're hopeless, you religion scholars! You load people down with rules and regulations, nearly breaking their backs, but never lift even a finger to help.

47-51 "You're hopeless! You build tombs for the prophets your ancestors killed. The tombs you build are monuments to your murdering ancestors more than to the murdered prophets. That accounts for God's Wisdom saying, 'I will send them prophets and apostles, but they'll kill them and run them off.' What it means is that every drop of righteous blood ever spilled from the time earth began until now, from the blood of Abel to the blood of Zechariah, who was struck down between altar and sanctuary, is on your heads. Yes, it's on the bill of this generation and this generation will pay.

52 "You're hopeless, you religion scholars! You took the key of knowledge, but instead of unlocking doors, you locked them. You won't go in yourself, and won't let anyone else in either."

53-54 As soon as Jesus left the table, the religion scholars and Pharisees went into a rage. They went over and over everything he said, plotting how they could trap him in something from his own mouth.

CAN'T HIDE BEHIND A RELIGIOUS MASK

12 1-3 By this time the crowd, unwieldy and stepping on each other's toes, numbered into the thousands. But Jesus' primary concern was his disciples. He said to them, "Watch yourselves carefully so you don't get contaminated with Pharisee yeast, Pharisee phoniness. You can't keep your true self hidden forever; before long you'll

Trust God and Pay Attention

Worry is a powerful distraction. The Pharisees and political figures of Jesus' day actively sought to entrap him and his disciples at nearly every turn. The disciples trusted Jesus enough to leave their livelihoods to follow him, but at the same time they were aware of the real concern that following Jesus put their lives in danger.

Following Jesus is risky. But in Luke 12, Jesus says a curious thing to his followers: "They can kill you, but *then* what can they do? There's nothing they can do to your soul, your core being. Save your fear for God, who holds your entire life—body and soul—in his hands" (Luke 12:4-5). At first, it sounds like Jesus was unconcerned about whatever physical harm might befall his followers, warning instead of the spiritual harm in failing to trust God. But then he demonstrated that he cares about the whole person.

Jesus told the disciples that God pays attention to people—"even numbering the hairs on your head!" (Luke 12:7). He comforted them by teaching that they needn't worry about what to say should they be confronted about following Jesus because "the Holy Spirit will give you the right words when the time comes" (Luke 12:12). God knew what these people were up against. God saw every detail of their lives, and the Spirit was ready to minister to them in the hour of trouble.

This good news wasn't only for them but is for us, too, as we fret and worry about how to speak up, how to follow Jesus in our own dangerous world. But the problem with spending energy on worry is that when we focus on fears and concerns we no longer focus on God. "What I'm trying to do here is get you to relax," Jesus says. The solution is to "steep yourself in God-reality, God-initiative, God-provisions. You'll find all your everyday human concerns will be met" (Luke 12:29, 31).

When we worry about what to eat or drink, where to live, who is talking about us or not talking about us, we stop paying attention to what God is doing. Worry distracts us from the truer things that are most important. When we are preoccupied with fear, we become "lazy and careless" toward spiritual things (see Luke 12:40).

"I've come to change everything," Jesus reminds us (Luke 12:50). We can trust his word. Undistracted by worry, we can begin to pay attention, looking for God's promised presence in our everyday lives.

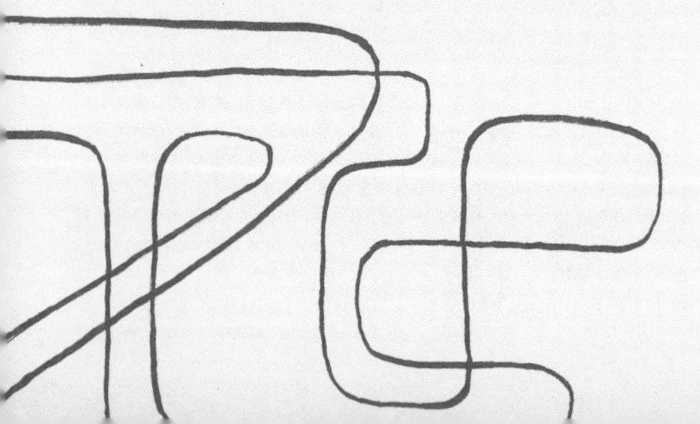

be exposed. You can't hide behind a religious mask forever; sooner or later the mask will slip and your true face will be known. You can't whisper one thing in private and preach the opposite in public; the day's coming when those whispers will be repeated all over town.

4-5 "I'm speaking to you as dear friends. Don't be bluffed into silence or insincerity by the threats of religious bullies. True, they can kill you, but *then* what can they do? There's nothing they can do to your soul, your core being. Save your fear for God, who holds your entire life—body and soul—in his hands.

6-7 "What's the price of two or three pet canaries? Some loose change, right? But God never overlooks a single one. And he pays even greater attention to you, down to the last detail—even numbering the hairs on your head! So don't be intimidated by all this bully talk. You're worth more than a million canaries.

8-9 "Stand up for me among the people you meet and the Son of Man will stand up for you before all God's angels. But if you pretend you don't know me, do you think I'll defend you before God's angels?

10 "If you bad-mouth the Son of Man out of misunderstanding or ignorance, that can be overlooked. But if you're knowingly attacking God himself, taking aim at the Holy Spirit, that won't be overlooked.

11-12 "When they drag you into their meeting places, or into police courts and before judges, don't worry about defending yourselves—what you'll say or how you'll say it. The right words will be there. The Holy Spirit will give you the right words when the time comes."

THE STORY OF THE GREEDY FARMER

13 Someone out of the crowd said, "Teacher, order my brother to give me a fair share of the family inheritance."

14 He replied, "Mister, what makes you think it's any of my business to be a judge or mediator for you?"

15 Speaking to the people, he went on, "Take care! Protect yourself against the least bit of greed. Life is not defined by what you have, even when you have a lot."

16-19 Then he told them this story: "The farm of a certain rich man produced a terrific crop. He talked to himself: 'What can I do? My barn isn't big enough for this harvest.' Then he said, 'Here's what I'll do: I'll tear down my barns and build bigger ones. Then I'll gather in all my grain and goods, and I'll say to myself, Self, you've done well! You've got it made and can now retire. Take it easy and have the time of your life!'

20 "Just then God showed up and said, 'Fool! Tonight you die. And your barnful of goods—who gets it?'

21 "That's what happens when you fill your barn with Self and not with God."

STEEP YOURSELF IN GOD-REALITY

22-24 He continued this subject with his disciples. "Don't fuss about what's on the table at mealtimes or if the clothes in your closet are in fashion. There is far more to your inner life than the food you put in your stomach, more to your outer appearance than the clothes you hang on your body. Look at the ravens, free and unfettered, not tied down to a job description, carefree in the care of God. And you count far more.

25-28 "Has anyone by fussing before the mirror ever gotten taller by so much as an inch? If fussing can't even do that, why fuss at all? Walk into the fields and look at the wildflowers. They don't fuss with their appearance—but have you ever seen color and design quite like it? The ten best-dressed men and women in the country look shabby alongside them. If God gives such attention to the wildflowers, most of them never even seen, don't you think he'll attend to you, take pride in you, do his best for you?

29-32 "What I'm trying to do here is get you to relax, not be so preoccupied with *getting* so you can respond to God's *giving*. People who don't know God and the way he works fuss over these things, but you know both God and how he works. Steep yourself in God-reality, God-initiative, God-provisions. You'll find all your everyday human concerns will be met. Don't be afraid of missing out. You're my dearest friends! The Father wants to give you the very kingdom itself.

33-34 "Be generous. Give to the poor. Get yourselves a bank that can't go bankrupt, a bank in heaven far from bankrobbers, safe from embezzlers, a bank you can bank on. It's obvious, isn't it? The place where your treasure is, is the place you will most want to be, and end up being.

WHEN THE MASTER SHOWS UP

35-38 "Keep your shirts on; keep the lights on! Be like house servants waiting for their master to come back from his honeymoon, awake and ready to open the door when he arrives and knocks. Lucky the servants whom the master finds on watch! He'll put on an apron, sit them at the table, and serve them a meal, sharing his wedding feast with them. It doesn't matter what time of the night he arrives; they're awake—and so blessed!

39-40 "You know that if the house owner had known what night the burglar was coming, he wouldn't have stayed out late and left the place unlocked. So don't you be lazy and careless. Just when you don't expect him, the Son of Man will show up."

41 Peter said, "Master, are you telling this story just for us? Or is it for everybody?"

42-46 The Master said, "Let me ask you: Who is the dependable manager, full of common sense, that the master puts in charge of his staff to feed them well and on time? He is a blessed man if when the master shows up he's doing his job. But if he says to himself, 'The master is certainly taking his time,' begins beating up on the servants and maids, throws parties for his friends, and gets drunk, the master will walk in when he least expects it, give him the thrashing of his life, and put him back in the kitchen peeling potatoes.

47-48 "The servant who knows what his master wants and ignores it, or insolently does whatever he pleases, will be thoroughly thrashed. But if he does a poor job through ignorance, he'll get off with a slap on the hand. Great gifts mean great responsibilities; greater gifts, greater responsibilities!

TO START A FIRE

49-53 "I've come to start a fire on this earth—how I wish it were blazing right now! I've come to change everything, turn everything rightside up—how I long for it to be finished! Do you think I came to smooth things over and make everything nice? Not so. I've come to disrupt and confront! From now on, when you find five in a house, it will be—

Three against two,
  and two against three;
Father against son,
  and son against father;
Mother against daughter,
  and daughter against mother;
Mother-in-law against bride,
  and bride against mother-in-law."

54-56 Then he turned to the crowd: "When you see clouds coming in from the west, you say, 'Storm's coming'—and you're right. And when the wind comes out of the south, you say, 'This'll be a hot one'—and you're right. Frauds! You know how to tell a change in the weather, so don't tell me you can't tell a change in the season, the God-season we're in right now.

57-59 "You don't have to be a genius to understand these things. Just use your common sense, the kind you'd use if, while being taken to court, you decided to settle up with your accuser on the way, knowing that if the case went to the judge you'd probably go to jail and pay every last penny of the fine. That's the kind of decision I'm asking you to make."

UNLESS YOU TURN TO GOD

13 1-5 About that time some people came up and told him about the Galileans Pilate had killed while they were at worship, mixing their blood with the blood of the sacrifices on the altar. Jesus responded, "Do you think those murdered Galileans were worse sinners than all other Galileans? Not at all. Unless you turn to God, you, too, will die. And those eighteen in Jerusalem the other day, the ones crushed and killed when the Tower of Siloam collapsed and fell on them, do you think they were worse citizens than all other Jerusalemites? Not at all. Unless you turn to God, you, too, will die."

6-7 Then he told them a story: "A man had an apple tree planted in his front yard. He came to it expecting to find apples, but there weren't any. He said to his gardener, 'What's going on here? For three years now I've come to this tree expecting apples and not one apple have I found. Chop it down! Why waste good ground with it any longer?'

8-9 "The gardener said, 'Let's give it another year. I'll dig around it and fertilize, and maybe it will produce next year; if it doesn't, then chop it down.'"

HEALING ON THE SABBATH

10-13 He was teaching in one of the meeting places on the Sabbath. There was a woman present, so twisted and bent over with arthritis that she couldn't even look up. She had been afflicted with this for eighteen years. When Jesus saw her, he called her over. "Woman, you're free!" He laid hands on her and suddenly she was standing straight and tall, giving glory to God.

14 The meeting-place president, furious because Jesus had healed on the Sabbath,

THE BENT-OVER WOMAN

What would cause a woman to have such bad arthritis that she'd remain permanently fixed in a bent-over position? Since our natural stance is upright, this woman may have been doing constant, backbreaking manual labor for years to solidify her frame in this position. Perhaps her job was pulling weeds, picking greens, or sorting grains. Jesus said that Satan had tied her to a stall for eighteen years in this position, indicating that the woman's state was not what God had intended but the result of evil, oppressive forces. Today we might compare this to economic systems that forbid workers the chance to rest from their labor and hold their heads high.

This bent-over woman managed to subvert Satan's intentions by showing up to one of Jesus' teaching sessions—and on the Sabbath, no less. She claimed for herself the benefit of the Sabbath, the day of rest and restoration intended for all God's creation. By putting her body—which bore witness to the oppression at work in the world—in one of the meeting places, a space intended to channel God's goodness, this woman showed God's people the incongruence between their present reality and God's desires. She knew that people would be discomfited by her twisted body, but she had the courage to show up anyway.

Jesus saw this woman's God-given dignity and freed her from the ties that bound her. Then "suddenly she was standing straight and tall, giving glory to God" (Luke 13:13).

How can we participate with Christ in his liberating work so that more women can have dignity, stand up straight and tall, and praise their creator?

said to the congregation, "Six days have been defined as work days. Come on one of the six if you want to be healed, but not on the seventh, the Sabbath."

15-16 But Jesus shot back, "You frauds! Each Sabbath every one of you regularly unties your cow or donkey from its stall, leads it out for water, and thinks nothing of it. So why isn't it all right for me to untie this daughter of Abraham and lead her from the stall where Satan has had her tied these eighteen years?"

17 When he put it that way, his critics were left looking quite silly and red-faced. The congregation was delighted and cheered him on.

THE WAY TO GOD

18-19 Then he said, "How can I picture God's kingdom for you? What kind of story can I use? It's like an acorn that a man plants in his front yard. It grows into a huge oak tree with thick branches, and eagles build nests in it."

20-21 He tried again. "How can I picture God's kingdom? It's like yeast that a woman works into enough dough for three loaves of bread—and waits while the dough rises."

22 He went on teaching from town to village, village to town, but keeping on a steady course toward Jerusalem.

23-25 A bystander said, "Master, will only a few be saved?"

He said, "Whether few or many is none of your business. Put your mind on your life with God. The way to life—to God!—is vigorous and requires your total attention. A lot of you are going to assume that you'll sit down to God's salvation banquet just because you've been hanging around the neighborhood all your lives. Well, one day you're going to be banging on the door, wanting to get in, but you'll find the door locked and the Master saying, 'Sorry, you're not on my guest list.'

26-27 "You'll protest, 'But we've known you all our lives!' only to be interrupted with his abrupt, 'Your kind of knowing can hardly be called knowing. You don't know the first thing about me.'

28-30 "That's when you'll find yourselves out in the cold, strangers to grace. You'll watch Abraham, Isaac, Jacob, and all the prophets march into God's kingdom. You'll watch outsiders stream in from east, west, north, and south and sit down at the table of God's kingdom. And all the time you'll be outside looking in—and wondering what happened. This is the Great Reversal: the last in line put at the head of the line, and the so-called first ending up last."

▲ ▲ ▲

31 Just then some Pharisees came up and said, "Run for your life! Herod's got your number. He's out to kill you!"

32-35 Jesus said, "Tell that fox that I've no time for him right now. Today and tomorrow I'm busy clearing out the demons and healing the sick; the third day I'm wrapping things up. Besides, it's not proper for a prophet to come to a bad end outside Jerusalem.

Jerusalem, Jerusalem, killer of prophets,
abuser of the messengers of God!
How often I've longed to gather your children,
gather your children like a hen,
Her brood safe under her wings—
but you refused and turned away!
And now it's too late: You won't see me again
until the day you say,
'Blessed is he
who comes in
the name of God.'"

14 1-3 One time when Jesus went for a Sabbath meal with one of the top leaders of the Pharisees, all the guests had their eyes on him, watching his every move. Right before him there was a man hugely swollen in his joints. So Jesus asked the religion scholars and Pharisees present, "Is it permitted to heal on the Sabbath? Yes or no?"

4-6 They were silent. So he took the man, healed him, and sent him on his way. Then he said, "Is there anyone here who, if a child or animal fell down a well, wouldn't rush to pull him out immediately, not asking whether or not it was the Sabbath?" They were stumped. There was nothing they could say to that.

INVITE THE MISFITS

7-9 He went on to tell a story to the guests around the table. Noticing how each had tried to elbow into the place of honor, he said, "When someone invites you to dinner, don't take the place of honor. Somebody more important than you might have been invited by the host. Then he'll come and call out in front of everybody, 'You're in the wrong place. The place of honor belongs to this man.'

Hospitality and Human Dignity

"Could your son wash his hands before coming in? He leaves fingerprints."

We'd barely walked in the door before our welcome ran out. Our family had just joined a church small group for the first time. Adults pored over Scripture, coffee in hand, while children played outside. Well, all except ours. Autistic and requiring constant supervision, our son, Jeremy, sat firmly wedged between his dad's hypervigilance and mine. But somehow Jeremy slipped away—and flooded the toilet of this spotless and freshly remodeled home.

No amount of apologizing or frantic mopping could erase the stain of my shame. I snatched our son's too-dirty hand and vowed never to return.

I assumed our exile was permanent, but several weeks later one of the group members called. "Please come back!" Alice blurted. "I'm sorry if this sounds selfish, but we need you. Jeremy is the first person we've met with autism. My kids have been asking important questions. Your family challenges us to work out our theology. Please don't take that blessing away!"

And so we, the outsiders, were invited. We were included in the community—messy hands and everything.

Misfits and outliers are easy to avoid until, one day, we become them. "That strange person" is *my* person, and we are now "those people." And our tendency to avoid "those people" stretches back thousands of years.

When Jesus went to a fancy dinner, he saw the posturing taking place under the guise of hospitality. A prominent person invited other prominent guests, everyone keenly aware of where they stood in the pecking order. But, Jesus said, this is not what God means by hospitality.

Instead of friends, family, and wealthy neighbors, Jesus suggested inviting misfits, people from the wrong side of the tracks. Bring in the homeless and those hard on their luck and have dinner with *them*. This is what hospitality looks like in the kingdom of God.

Looking at our social circles, churches, and guest lists today, it seems that our idea of hospitality still looks more like the fancy dinner Jesus attended than the chaotic dinner Jesus described. We put stock in our good food, decorated rooms, and engaging guest lists; we would never consider looking for misfits and homeless folks to be the guests of honor. That would be terribly awkward and inconvenient.

Yet Jesus taught that blessing comes in the chaos of real people coming together to care for each other. It may cost us our comfort and convenience—certainly a roll of paper towels and a series of awkward conversations—but it's worth it to give birth to blessing. We might even entertain angels unaware.

The next time you gather, don't just invite friends and family or people who look, live, love, believe, and behave just like you. Invite the messy, mysterious, and marginalized outliers—and feast in the kingdom of God.

Embarrassed, you'll have to make your way to the very last table, the only place left.

10-11 "When you're invited to dinner, go and sit at the last place. Then when the host comes he may very well say, 'Friend, come up to the front.' That will give the dinner guests something to talk about! What I'm saying is, If you walk around all high and mighty, you're going to end up flat on your face. But if you're content to be simply yourself, you will become more than yourself."

12-14 Then he turned to the host. "The next time you put on a dinner, don't just invite your friends and family and rich neighbors, the kind of people who will return the favor. Invite some people who never get invited out, the misfits from the wrong side of the tracks. You'll be—and experience—a blessing. They won't be able to return the favor, but the favor will be returned—oh, how it will be returned!—at the resurrection of God's people."

THE STORY OF THE DINNER PARTY

15 That triggered a response from one of the guests: "How fortunate the one who gets to eat dinner in God's kingdom!"

16-17 Jesus followed up. "Yes. For there was once a man who threw a great dinner party and invited many. When it was time for dinner, he sent out his servant to the invited guests, saying, 'Come on in; the food's on the table.'

18 "Then they all began to beg off, one after another making excuses. The first said, 'I bought a piece of property and need to look it over. Send my regrets.'

19 "Another said, 'I just bought five teams of oxen, and I really need to check them out. Send my regrets.'

20 "And yet another said, 'I just got married and need to get home to my wife.'

21 "The servant went back and told the master what had happened. He was outraged and told the servant, 'Quickly, get out into the city streets and alleys. Collect all who look like they need a square meal, all the misfits and homeless and down-and-out you can lay your hands on, and bring them here.'

22 "The servant reported back, 'Master, I did what you commanded—and there's still room.'

23-24 "The master said, 'Then go to the country roads. Whoever you find, drag them in. I want my house full! Let me tell you, not one of those originally invited is going to get so much as a bite at my dinner party.'"

FIGURE THE COST

25-27 One day when large groups of people were walking along with him, Jesus turned and told them, "Anyone who comes to me but refuses to let go of father, mother, spouse, children, brothers, sisters—yes, even one's own self!—can't be my disciple. Anyone who won't shoulder his own cross and follow behind me can't be my disciple.

28-30 "Is there anyone here who, planning to build a new house, doesn't first sit down and figure the cost so you'll know if you can complete it? If you only get the foundation laid and then run out of money, you're going to look pretty foolish. Everyone passing by will poke fun at you: 'He started something he couldn't finish.'

31-32 "Or can you imagine a king going into battle against another king without first deciding whether it is possible with his ten thousand troops to face the twenty thousand troops of the other? And if he decides he can't, won't he send an emissary and work out a truce?

33 "Simply put, if you're not willing to take what is dearest to you, whether plans or people, and kiss it good-bye, you can't be my disciple.

34-35 "Salt is excellent. But if the salt goes flat, it's useless, good for nothing.

"Are you listening to this? Really listening?"

THE STORY OF THE LOST SHEEP

15 1-3 By this time a lot of men and women of questionable reputation were hanging around Jesus, listening intently. The Pharisees and religion scholars were not pleased, not at all pleased. They growled, "He takes in sinners and eats meals with them, treating them like old friends." Their grumbling triggered this story.

4-7 "Suppose one of you had a hundred sheep and lost one. Wouldn't you leave the ninety-nine in the wilderness and go after the lost one until you found it? When found, you can be sure you would put it across your shoulders, rejoicing, and when you got home call in your friends and neighbors, saying, 'Celebrate with me! I've found my lost sheep!' Count on it—there's more joy in heaven over one sinner's rescued life than over ninety-nine good people in no need of rescue.

THE STORY OF THE LOST COIN

8-10 "Or imagine a woman who has ten coins and loses one. Won't she light a lamp and scour the house, looking in every nook and cranny until she finds it? And when she finds it you can be sure she'll call her friends and neighbors: 'Celebrate with me! I found my lost coin!' Count on it—that's the kind of party God's angels throw every time one lost soul turns to God."

THE STORY OF THE LOST SON

11-12 Then he said, "There was once a man who had two sons. The younger said to his father, 'Father, I want right now what's coming to me.'

12-16 "So the father divided the property between them. It wasn't long before the younger son packed his bags and left for a distant country. There, undisciplined and dissipated, he wasted everything he had. After he had gone through all his money, there was a bad famine all through that country and he began to feel it. He signed on with a citizen there who assigned him to his fields to slop the pigs. He was so hungry he would have eaten the corn-cobs in the pig slop, but no one would give him any.

17-20 "That brought him to his senses. He said, 'All those farmhands working for my father sit down to three meals a day, and here I am starving to death. I'm going back to my father. I'll say to him, Father, I've sinned against God, I've sinned before you; I don't deserve to be called your son. Take me on as a hired hand.' He got right up and went home to his father.

20-21 "When he was still a long way off, his father saw him. His heart pounding, he ran out, embraced him, and kissed him. The son started his speech: 'Father, I've sinned against God, I've sinned before you; I don't deserve to be called your son ever again.'

22-24 "But the father wasn't listening. He was calling to the servants, 'Quick. Bring a clean set of clothes and dress him. Put the family ring on his finger and sandals on his feet. Then get a prize-winning heifer and roast it. We're going to feast! We're going to have a wonderful time! My son is here—given up for dead and now alive! Given up for lost and now found!' And they began to have a wonderful time.

25-27 "All this time his older son was out in the field. When the day's work was done he came in. As he approached the house, he heard the music and dancing. Calling over one of the houseboys, he asked what was going on. He told him, 'Your brother came home. Your father has ordered a feast—barbecued beef!—because he has him home safe and sound.'

28-30 "The older brother stomped off in an angry sulk and refused to join in. His father came out and tried to talk to him, but he wouldn't listen. The son said, 'Look how many years I've stayed here serving you, never giving you one moment of grief, but have you ever thrown a party for me and my friends? Then this son of yours who has thrown away your money on whores shows up and you go all out with a feast!'

31-32 "His father said, 'Son, you don't understand. You're with me all the time, and everything that is mine is yours—but this is a wonderful time, and we had to celebrate. This brother of yours was dead, and he's alive! He was lost, and he's found!'"

THE STORY OF THE CROOKED MANAGER

16

1-2 Jesus said to his disciples, "There was once a rich man who had a manager. He got reports that the manager had been taking advantage of his position by running up huge personal expenses. So he called him in and said, 'What's this I hear about you? You're fired. And I want a complete audit of your books.'

3-4 "The manager said to himself, 'What am I going to do? I've lost my job as manager. I'm not strong enough for a laboring job, and I'm too proud to beg. . . . Ah, I've got a plan. Here's what I'll do . . . then when I'm turned out into the street, people will take me into their houses.'

5 "Then he went at it. One after another, he called in the people who were in debt to his master. He said to the first, 'How much do you owe my master?'

6 "He replied, 'A hundred jugs of olive oil.'

"The manager said, 'Here, take your bill, sit down here—quick now—write fifty.'

7 "To the next he said, 'And you, what do you owe?'

"He answered, 'A hundred sacks of wheat.'

"He said, 'Take your bill, write in eighty.'

8-9 "Now here's a surprise: The master praised the crooked manager! And why? Because he knew how to look after himself. Streetwise people are smarter in this regard than law-abiding citizens. They are on constant alert, looking for angles, surviving by their wits. I want you to be smart in the same way—but for what is *right*—using every adversity to stimulate you to creative survival, to concentrate your attention on the bare essentials, so you'll live, really live, and not complacently just get by on good behavior."

GOD SEES BEHIND APPEARANCES

10-13 Jesus went on to make these comments:

If you're honest in small things,
you'll be honest in big things;
If you're a crook in small things,
you'll be a crook in big things.
If you're not honest in small jobs,
who will put you in charge of the store?
No worker can serve two bosses:
He'll either hate the first and love
the second
Or adore the first and despise the second.
You can't serve both God and the Bank.

14-18 When the Pharisees, a money-obsessed bunch, heard him say these things, they rolled their eyes, dismissing him as hopelessly out of touch. So Jesus spoke to them: "You are masters at making yourselves look good in front of others, but God knows what's behind the appearance.

What society sees and calls monumental,
God sees through and calls monstrous.
God's Law and the Prophets climaxed
in John;
Now it's all kingdom of God—the glad
news
and compelling invitation to every
man and woman.
The sky will disintegrate and the earth
dissolve
before a single letter of God's Law
wears out.
Using the legalities of divorce
as a cover for lust is adultery;
Using the legalities of marriage
as a cover for lust is adultery.

THE RICH MAN AND LAZARUS

19-21 "There once was a rich man, expensively dressed in the latest fashions, wasting his days in conspicuous consumption. A poor man named Lazarus, covered with sores, had been dumped on his doorstep. All he lived for was to get a meal from scraps off the rich man's table. His best friends were the dogs who came and licked his sores.

22-24 "Then he died, this poor man, and was taken up by the angels to the lap of Abraham. The rich man also died and was buried. In hell and in torment, he looked up and saw Abraham in the distance and Lazarus in his lap. He called out, 'Father Abraham, mercy! Have mercy! Send Lazarus to dip his finger in water to cool my tongue. I'm in agony in this fire.'

25-26 "But Abraham said, 'Child, remember that in your lifetime you got the good things and Lazarus the bad things. It's not like that here. Here he's consoled and you're tormented. Besides, in all these matters there is a huge chasm set between us so that no one can go from us to you even if he wanted to, nor can anyone cross over from you to us.'

27-28 "The rich man said, 'Then let me ask you, Father: Send him to the house of my father where I have five brothers, so he can tell them the score and warn them so they won't end up here in this place of torment.'

29 "Abraham answered, 'They have Moses and the Prophets to tell them the score. Let them listen to them.'

30 "'I know, Father Abraham,' he said, 'but they're not listening. If someone came back to them from the dead, they would change their ways.'

31 "Abraham replied, 'If they won't listen to Moses and the Prophets, they're not going to be convinced by someone who rises from the dead.'"

A KERNEL OF FAITH

17 1-2 He said to his disciples, "Hard trials and temptations are bound to come, but too bad for whoever brings them on! Better to wear a concrete vest and take a swim with the fishes than give even one of these dear little ones a hard time!

3-4 "Be alert. If you see your friend going wrong, correct him. If he responds, forgive him. Even if it's personal against you and repeated seven times through the day, and seven times he says, 'I'm sorry, I won't do it again,' forgive him."

5 The apostles came up and said to the Master, "Give us more faith."

6 But the Master said, "You don't need *more* faith. There is no 'more' or 'less' in faith. If you have a bare kernel of faith, say the size of a poppy seed, you could say to this sycamore tree, 'Go jump in the lake,' and it would do it.

7-10 "Suppose one of you has a servant who comes in from plowing the field or tending the sheep. Would you take his coat, set the table, and say, 'Sit down and eat'? Wouldn't you be more likely to say, 'Prepare dinner; change your clothes and wait table for me until I've finished my coffee; then go to the kitchen and have your supper'? Does the servant get special thanks for doing what's expected of him? It's the same with you. When you've done everything expected of you, be matter-of-fact and say, 'The work is done. What we were told to do, we did.'"

11-13 It happened that as he made his way toward Jerusalem, he crossed over the border between Samaria and Galilee. As he entered a village, ten men, all lepers, met him. They kept their distance but raised their voices, calling out, "Jesus, Master, have mercy on us!"

14-16 Taking a good look at them, he said, "Go, show yourselves to the priests."

They went, and while still on their way, became clean. One of them, when he realized that he was healed, turned around and came back, shouting his gratitude, glorifying God. He kneeled at Jesus' feet, so grateful. He couldn't thank him enough—and he was a Samaritan.

17-19 Jesus said, "Were not ten healed? Where are the nine? Can none be found to come back and give glory to God except this outsider?" Then he said to him, "Get up. On your way. Your faith has healed and saved you."

WHEN THE SON OF MAN ARRIVES

20-21 Jesus, grilled by the Pharisees on when the kingdom of God would come, answered, "The kingdom of God doesn't come by counting the days on the calendar. Nor when someone says, 'Look here!' or, 'There it is!' And why? Because God's kingdom is already among you."

22-24 He went on to say to his disciples, "The days are coming when you are going to be desperately homesick for just a glimpse of one of the days of the Son of Man, and you won't see a thing. And they'll say to you, 'Look over there!' or, 'Look here!' Don't fall for any of that nonsense. The arrival of the Son of Man is not something you go out to see. He simply comes.

24-25 "You know how the whole sky lights up from a single flash of lightning? That's how it will be on the Day of the Son of Man. But first it's necessary that he suffer many things and be turned down by the people of today.

26-27 "The time of the Son of Man will be just like the time of Noah—everyone carrying on as usual, having a good time right up to the day Noah boarded the ship. They suspected nothing until the flood hit and swept everything away.

28-30 "It was the same in the time of Lot—the people carrying on, having a good time, business as usual right up to the day Lot walked out of Sodom and a firestorm swept down and burned everything to a crisp. That's how it will be—sudden, total—when the Son of Man is revealed.

31-33 "When the Day arrives and you're out working in the yard, don't run into the house to get anything. And if you're out in the field, don't go back and get your coat. Remember what happened to Lot's wife! If you grasp and cling to life on your terms, you'll lose it, but if you let that life go, you'll get life on God's terms.

34-35 "On that Day, two men will be in the same boat fishing—one taken, the other left. Two women will be working in the same kitchen—one taken, the other left."

37 Trying to take all this in, the disciples said, "Master, where?"

He told them, "Watch for the circling of the vultures. They'll spot the corpse first. The action will begin around my dead body."

THE STORY OF THE PERSISTENT WIDOW

18 1-3 Jesus told them a story showing that it was necessary for them to pray consistently and never quit. He said, "There was once a judge in some city who never gave God a thought and cared nothing for people. A widow in that city kept after him: 'My rights are being violated. Protect me!'

4-5 "He never gave her the time of day. But after this went on and on he said to himself, 'I care nothing what God thinks, even less what people think. But because this widow won't quit badgering me, I'd better do something and see that she gets justice—otherwise I'm going to end up beaten black-and-blue by her pounding.'"

6-8 Then the Master said, "Do you hear what that judge, corrupt as he is, is saying? So what makes you think God won't step in and work justice for his chosen people, who continue to cry out for help? Won't he stick up for them? I assure you, he will. He will not drag his feet. But how much of that kind of persistent faith will the Son of Man find on the earth when he returns?"

THE STORY OF THE TAX MAN AND THE PHARISEE

9-12 He told his next story to some who were complacently pleased with themselves over

The Persistent Widow

Jesus introduced the persistent widow with his purpose for telling her story: to show that it is necessary "to pray consistently and never quit" (Luke 18:1). Her story motivates us to develop our prayer lives and intentionally bring impossible requests to God.

But there is more.

Jesus asked a question that puts a slightly different spin on the story: "But how much of that kind of persistent faith will the Son of Man find on the earth when he returns?" (Luke 18:8). This question seems a bit out of place—this is a story about prayer, isn't it? Yes, but Jesus also went deeper. His question makes the connection between tenacious prayer and courageous faith in our almighty God.

Widows had absolutely no resources in Jesus' day. This widow was seeking justice from the only one who could help her—a judge who had no interest in hearing her case. Her only tool was persistence, and she employed it until he listened to her predicament rather than get "beaten black-and-blue by her pounding" and badgering (Luke 18:5). She had faith that when the judge understood, he would grant her justice.

Our situations are not terribly different. When we face injustice, God is our unequaled defender, even if we remember this only after we've exhausted our efforts. Courageous faith and persistent prayer are linked, for they both originate in a firm understanding of the almighty power and infinite love of God. No one else has the desire and ability to calm the oceans of injustice in which we cling precariously to lifeboats. Meanwhile, perseverance is not easy; as we hang on, our determination can slip.

The helpless widow persisted with a judge who couldn't be bothered, but our God is different. God hears every prayer, understands our needs better than we do, and willingly responds to us. Sometimes God gives us work to do. Sometimes God brings others with the skill or advice we need. Other times God asks us to wait—and sometimes, wait some more, strengthening our grip.

Only one with stubborn faith will continue to hold on, to pray with perseverance when difficult circumstances remain unchanged. May Jesus find that kind of persistent faith in us when he returns.

their moral performance and looked down their noses at the common people: "Two men went up to the Temple to pray, one a Pharisee, the other a tax man. The Pharisee posed and prayed like this: 'Oh, God, I thank you that I am not like other people—robbers, crooks, adulterers, or, heaven forbid, like this tax man. I fast twice a week and tithe on all my income.'

13 "Meanwhile the tax man, slumped in the shadows, his face in his hands, not daring to look up, said, 'God, give mercy. Forgive me, a sinner.'"

14 Jesus commented, "This tax man, not the other, went home made right with God. If you walk around with your nose in the air, you're going to end up flat on your face, but if you're content to be simply yourself, you will become more than yourself."

▲ ▲ ▲

15-17 People brought babies to Jesus, hoping he might touch them. When the disciples saw it, they shooed them off. Jesus called them back. "Let these children alone. Don't get between them and me. These children are the kingdom's pride and joy. Mark this: Unless you accept God's kingdom in the simplicity of a child, you'll never get in."

THE RICH OFFICIAL

18 One day one of the local officials asked him, "Good Teacher, what must I do to deserve eternal life?"

19-20 Jesus said, "Why are you calling me good? No one is good—only God. You know the commandments, don't you? No illicit sex, no killing, no stealing, no lying, honor your father and mother."

21 He said, "I've kept them all for as long as I can remember."

22 When Jesus heard that, he said, "Then there's only one thing left to do: Sell everything you own and give it away to the poor. You will have riches in heaven. Then come, follow me."

23 This was the last thing the official expected to hear. He was very rich and became terribly sad. He was holding on tight to a lot of things and not about to let them go.

24-25 Seeing his reaction, Jesus said, "Do you have any idea how difficult it is for people who have it all to enter God's kingdom? I'd say it's easier to thread a camel through a needle's eye than get a rich person into God's kingdom."

26 "Then who has any chance at all?" the others asked.

27 "No chance at all," Jesus said, "if you think you can pull it off by yourself. Every chance in the world if you trust God to do it."

28 Peter tried to regain some initiative: "We left everything we owned and followed you, didn't we?"

29-30 "Yes," said Jesus, "and you won't regret it. No one who has sacrificed home, spouse, brothers and sisters, parents, children—whatever—will lose out. It will all come back multiplied many times over in your lifetime. And then the bonus of eternal life!"

I WANT TO SEE AGAIN

31-34 Then Jesus took the Twelve off to the side and said, "Listen carefully. We're on our way up to Jerusalem. Everything written in the Prophets about the Son of Man will take place. He will be handed over to the Romans, jeered at, ridiculed, and spit on. Then, after giving him the third degree, they will kill him. In three days he will rise, alive." But they didn't get it, could make neither heads nor tails of what he was talking about.

35-37 He came to the outskirts of Jericho. A blind man was sitting beside the road asking for handouts. When he heard the rustle of the crowd, he asked what was going on. They told him, "Jesus the Nazarene is going by."

38 He yelled, "Jesus! Son of David! Mercy, have mercy on me!"

39 Those ahead of Jesus told the man to shut up, but he only yelled all the louder, "Son of David! Mercy, have mercy on me!"

40 Jesus stopped and ordered him to be brought over. When he had come near, Jesus asked, "What do you want from me?"

41 He said, "Master, I want to see again."

42-43 Jesus said, "Go ahead—see again! Your faith has saved and healed you!" The healing was instant: He looked up, seeing—and then followed Jesus, glorifying God. Everyone in the street joined in, shouting praise to God.

ZACCHAEUS

19 1-4 Then Jesus entered and walked through Jericho. There was a man there, his name Zacchaeus, the head tax man and quite rich. He wanted desperately to see Jesus, but the crowd was in his way—he was a short man and couldn't see over the crowd. So he ran on ahead and climbed up in a sycamore tree so he could see Jesus when he came by.

5-7 When Jesus got to the tree, he looked up and said, "Zacchaeus, hurry down. Today is my day to be a guest in your home." Zacchaeus scrambled out of the tree, hardly believing his good luck, delighted to take Jesus home with him. Everyone who saw the incident was indignant and grumped, "What business does he have getting cozy with this crook?"

8 Zacchaeus just stood there, a little stunned. He stammered apologetically, "Master, I give away half my income to the poor—and if I'm caught cheating, I pay four times the damages."

9-10 Jesus said, "Today is salvation day in this home! Here he is: Zacchaeus, son of Abraham! For the Son of Man came to find and restore the lost."

THE STORY ABOUT INVESTMENT

11 While he had their attention, and because they were getting close to Jerusalem by this time and expectation was building that God's kingdom would appear any minute, he told this story:

12-13 "There was once a man descended from a royal house who needed to make a long trip back to headquarters to get authorization for his rule and then return. But first he called ten servants together, gave them each a sum of money, and instructed them, 'Operate with this until I return.'

14 "But the citizens there hated him. So they sent a commission with a signed petition to oppose his rule: 'We don't want this man to rule us.'

15 "When he came back bringing the authorization of his rule, he called those ten servants to whom he had given the money to find out how they had done.

16 "The first said, 'Master, I doubled your money.'

17 "He said, 'Good servant! Great work! Because you've been trustworthy in this small job, I'm making you governor of ten towns.'

18 "The second said, 'Master, I made a fifty percent profit on your money.'

19 "He said, 'I'm putting you in charge of five towns.'

20-21 "The next servant said, 'Master, here's your money safe and sound. I kept it hidden in the cellar. To tell you the truth, I was a little afraid. I know you have high standards and hate sloppiness, and don't suffer fools gladly.'

22-23 "He said, 'You're right that I don't suffer fools gladly—and you've acted the fool! Why didn't you at least invest the money in securities so I would have gotten a little interest on it?'

24 "Then he said to those standing there, 'Take the money from him and give it to the servant who doubled my stake.'

25 "They said, 'But Master, he already has double . . .'

26 "He said, 'That's what I mean: Risk your life and get more than you ever dreamed of. Play it safe and end up holding the bag.

27 "'As for these enemies of mine who petitioned against my rule, clear them out of here. I don't want to see their faces around here again.'"

GOD'S PERSONAL VISIT

28-31 After saying these things, Jesus headed straight up to Jerusalem. When he got near Bethphage and Bethany at the mountain called Olives, he sent off two of the disciples with instructions: "Go to the village across from you. As soon as you enter, you'll find a colt tethered, one that has never been ridden. Untie it and bring it. If anyone says anything, asks, 'What are you doing?' say, 'His Master needs him.'"

32-33 The two left and found it just as he said. As they were untying the colt, its owners said, "What are you doing untying the colt?"

34 They said, "His Master needs him."

35-36 They brought the colt to Jesus. Then, throwing their coats on its back, they helped Jesus get on. As he rode, the people gave him a grand welcome, throwing their coats on the street.

37-38 Right at the crest, where Mount Olives begins its descent, the whole crowd of disciples burst into enthusiastic praise over all the mighty works they had witnessed:

Blessed is he who comes,
  the king in God's name!
All's well in heaven!
  Glory in the high places!

39 Some Pharisees from the crowd told him, "Teacher, get your disciples under control!"

40 But he said, "If they kept quiet, the stones would do it for them, shouting praise."

41-44 When the city came into view, he wept over it. "If you had only recognized this day, and everything that was good for you! But now it's too late. In the days ahead your enemies are going to bring up their heavy artillery and surround you, pressing in from every side. They'll smash you and your babies on the pavement. Not one stone will be left intact. All this because you didn't recognize and welcome God's personal visit."

45-46 Going into the Temple he began to throw out everyone who had set up shop, selling everything and anything. He said, "It's written in Scripture,

My house is a house of prayer;
You have turned it into a religious bazaar."

47-48 From then on he taught each day in the Temple. The high priests, religion scholars, and the leaders of the people were trying their best to find a way to get rid of him. But with the people hanging on every word he spoke, they couldn't come up with anything.

20

1-2 One day he was teaching the people in the Temple, proclaiming the Message. The high priests, religion scholars, and leaders confronted him and demanded, "Show us your credentials. Who authorized you to speak and act like this?"

3-4 Jesus answered, "First, let me ask you a question: About the baptism of John—who authorized it, heaven or humans?"

5-7 They were on the spot, and knew it. They pulled back into a huddle and whispered, "If we say 'heaven,' he'll ask us why we didn't believe him; if we say 'humans,' the people will tear us limb from limb, convinced as they are that John was God's prophet." They agreed to concede that round to Jesus and said they didn't know.

8 Jesus said, "Then neither will I answer your question."

THE STORY OF CORRUPT FARMHANDS

9-12 Jesus told another story to the people: "A man planted a vineyard. He handed it over to farmhands and went off on a trip. He was gone a long time. In time he sent a servant back to the farmhands to collect the profits, but they beat him up and sent him off empty-handed. He decided to try again and sent another servant. That one they beat black-and-blue, and sent him off empty-handed. He tried a third time. They worked that servant over from head to foot and dumped him in the street.

13 "Then the owner of the vineyard said, 'I know what I'll do: I'll send my beloved son. They're bound to respect my son.'

14-15 "But when the farmhands saw him coming, they quickly put their heads together. 'This is our chance—this is the heir! Let's kill him and have it all to ourselves.' They killed him and threw him over the fence.

15-16 "What do you think the owner of the vineyard will do? Right. He'll come and get rid of everyone. Then he'll assign the care of the vineyard to others."

Those who were listening said, "Oh, no! He'd never do that!"

17-18 But Jesus didn't back down. "Why, then, do you think this was written:

That stone the masons threw out—
It's now the cornerstone!?

"Anyone falling over that stone will break every bone in his body; if the stone falls on anyone, he'll be smashed to smithereens."

19 The religion scholars and high priests wanted to lynch him on the spot, but they were intimidated by public opinion. They knew the story was about them.

PAYING TAXES

20-22 Watching for a chance to get him, they sent spies who posed as honest inquirers, hoping to trick him into saying something that would get him in trouble with the law. So they asked him, "Teacher, we know that you're honest and straightforward when you teach, that you don't pander to anyone but teach the way of God accurately. Tell us: Is it lawful to pay taxes to Caesar or not?"

23-24 He knew they were laying for him and said, "Show me a coin. Now, this engraving, who does it look like and what does it say?"

25 "Caesar," they said.

Jesus said, "Then give Caesar what is his and give God what is his."

26 Try as they might, they couldn't trap him into saying anything incriminating. His answer caught them off guard and left them speechless.

ALL INTIMACIES WILL BE WITH GOD

27-33 Some Sadducees came up. This is the Jewish party that denies any possibility of resurrection. They asked, "Teacher, Moses wrote us that if a man dies and leaves a wife but no child, his brother is obligated to marry her and give her children. Well, there once were seven brothers. The first took a wife. He died childless. The second married her and died, then the third, and eventually all seven had their turn, but no child. After all that, the wife died. That wife, now—in the resurrection whose wife is she? All seven married her."

34-38 Jesus said, "Marriage is a major preoccupation here, but not there. Those who are included in the resurrection of the dead will no longer be concerned with marriage nor, of course, with death. They will have better things to think about, if you can believe it. All ecstasies and intimacies then will be with God. Even Moses exclaimed about resurrection at the burning bush, saying, 'God: God of Abraham, God of Isaac, God of Jacob!' God isn't the God of dead men, but of the living. To him all are alive."

39-40 Some of the religion scholars said, "Teacher, that's a great answer!" For a while, anyway, no one dared put questions to him.

▲ ▲ ▲

41-44 Then he put a question to them: "How is it that they say that the Messiah is David's son? In the Book of Psalms, David clearly says,

God said to my Master,
"Sit here at my right hand
until I put your enemies under
your feet."

"David here designates the Messiah as 'my Master'—so how can the Messiah also be his 'son'?"

45-47 With everybody listening, Jesus spoke to his disciples. "Watch out for the religion scholars. They love to walk around in academic gowns, preen in the radiance of public flattery, bask in prominent positions, sit at the head table at every church function. And all the time they are exploiting the weak and helpless. The longer their prayers, the worse they get. But they'll pay for it in the end."

21 1-4 Just then he looked up and saw the rich people dropping offerings in the collection plate. Then he saw a poor widow put in two pennies. He said, "The plain truth is that this widow has given by far the largest offering today. All these others made offerings that they'll never miss; she gave extravagantly what she couldn't afford—she gave her all!"

WATCH OUT FOR DOOMSDAY DECEIVERS

5-6 One day people were standing around talking about the Temple, remarking how beautiful it was, the splendor of its stonework and memorial gifts. Jesus said, "All this you're admiring so much—the time is coming when every stone in that building will end up in a heap of rubble."

7 They asked him, "Teacher, when is this going to happen? What clue will we get that it's about to take place?"

8-9 He said, "Watch out for the doomsday deceivers. Many leaders are going to show up with forged identities claiming, 'I'm the One,' or, 'The end is near.' Don't fall for any of that. When you hear of wars and uprisings, keep your head and don't panic. This is routine history and no sign of the end."

10-11 He went on, "Nation will fight nation and ruler fight ruler, over and over. Huge earthquakes will occur in various places. There will be famines. You'll think at times that the very sky is falling.

12-15 "But before any of this happens, they'll arrest you, hunt you down, and drag you to court and jail. It will go from bad to worse, dog-eat-dog, everyone at your throat because you carry my name. You'll end up on the witness stand, called to testify. Make up your mind right now not to worry about it. I'll give you the words and wisdom that will reduce all your accusers to stammers and stutters.

16-19 "You'll even be turned in by parents, brothers, relatives, and friends. Some of you will be killed. There's no telling who will hate you because of me. Even so, every detail of your body and soul—even the hairs of your head!—is in my care; nothing of you will be lost. Staying with it—that's what is required. Stay with it to the end. You won't be sorry; you'll be saved.

THE DAY OF RECKONING

20-24 "When you see soldiers camped all around Jerusalem, then you'll know that she is about to be devastated. If you're living in Judea at the time, run for the hills. If you're in the city, get out quickly. If you're out in the fields, don't go home to get your coat. This is the Day of Reckoning—everything written about it will come to a head. Pregnant and nursing mothers will have it especially hard. Incredible misery! Torrential rage! People dropping like flies; people dragged off to prisons; Jerusalem under the boot of barbarians until the nations finish what was given them to do.

25-26 "It will seem like all hell has broken loose—sun, moon, stars, earth, sea, in an uproar and everyone all over the world in a panic, the wind knocked out of them by the threat of doom, the powers-that-be quaking.

27-28 "And then—then!—they'll see the Son of Man welcomed in grand style—a glorious welcome! When all this starts to happen, up on your feet. Stand tall with your heads high. Help is on the way!"

29-33 He told them a story. "Look at a fig tree. Any tree for that matter. When the leaves begin to show, one look tells you that summer is right around the corner. The same here—when you see these things happen, you know God's kingdom is about here. Don't brush this off: I'm not just saying this for some future generation, but for this one, too—these things will happen. Sky and earth will wear out; my words won't wear out.

34-36 "But be on your guard. Don't let the sharp edge of your expectation get dulled by parties and drinking and shopping. Otherwise, that Day is going to take you by complete surprise, spring on you suddenly like a trap, for it's going to come on everyone, everywhere, at once. So, whatever you do, don't fall asleep at the wheel. Pray constantly that you will have the strength and wits to make it through everything that's coming and end up on your feet before the Son of Man."

37-38 He spent his days in the Temple teaching, but his nights out on the mountain called Olives. All the people were up at the crack of dawn to come to the Temple and listen to him.

THE PASSOVER MEAL

22 1-2 The Feast of Unleavened Bread, also called Passover, drew near. The high priests and religion scholars were looking for a way to do away with Jesus but, fearful of the people, they were also looking for a way to cover their tracks.

3-6 That's when Satan entered Judas, the one called Iscariot. He was one of the Twelve. Leaving the others, he conferred with the high priests and the Temple guards about how he might betray Jesus to them. They couldn't believe their good luck and agreed to pay him well. He gave them his word and started looking for a way to betray Jesus, but out of sight of the crowd.

7-8 The Day of Unleavened Bread came, the day the Passover lamb was butchered. Jesus sent Peter and John off, saying, "Go prepare the Passover for us so we can eat it together."

9 They said, "Where do you want us to do this?"

10-12 He said, "Keep your eyes open as you enter the city. A man carrying a water jug will meet you. Follow him home. Then speak with the owner of the house: The Teacher wants to know, 'Where is the guest room where I can eat the Passover meal with my disciples?' He will show you a spacious second-story room, swept and ready. Prepare the meal there."

13 They left, found everything just as he told them, and prepared the Passover meal.

14-16 When it was time, he sat down, all the apostles with him, and said, "You've no idea how much I have looked forward to eating this Passover meal with you before I enter my time of suffering. It's the last one I'll eat until we all eat it together in the kingdom of God."

17-18 Taking the cup, he blessed it, then said, "Take this and pass it among you. As for me, I'll not drink wine again until the kingdom of God arrives."

19 Taking bread, he blessed it, broke it, and gave it to them, saying, "This is my body, given for you. Eat it in my memory."

20 He did the same with the cup after supper, saying, "This cup is the new covenant written in my blood, blood poured out for you.

21-22 "Do you realize that the hand of the one who is betraying me is at this moment on this table? It's true that the Son of Man is going down a path already marked out—no surprises there. But for the one who turns him in, turns traitor to the Son of Man, this is doomsday."

23 They immediately became suspicious of each other and began quizzing one another, wondering who might be about to do this.

GET READY FOR TROUBLE

24-26 Within minutes they were bickering over who of them would end up the greatest. But Jesus intervened: "Kings like to throw their weight around and people in authority like to give themselves fancy titles. It's not going to be that way with you. Let the senior among you become like the junior; let the leader act the part of the servant.

27-30 "Who would you rather be: the one who eats the dinner or the one who serves the dinner? You'd rather eat and be served, right? But I've taken my place among you as the one who serves. And you've stuck with me through thick and thin. Now I confer on you the royal authority my Father conferred on me so you can eat and drink at my table in my kingdom and be strengthened as you take up responsibilities among the congregations of God's people.

31-32 "Simon, stay on your toes. Satan has tried his best to separate all of you from me, like chaff from wheat. Simon, I've prayed for you in particular that you not give in or give out. When you have come through the time of testing, turn to your companions and give them a fresh start."

33 Peter said, "Master, I'm ready for anything with you. I'd go to jail for you. I'd *die* for you!"

34 Jesus said, "I'm sorry to have to tell you this, Peter, but before the rooster crows you will have three times denied that you know me."

35 Then Jesus said, "When I sent you out and told you to travel light, to take only the bare necessities, did you get along all right?"

"Certainly," they said, "we got along just fine."

36-37 He said, "This is different. Get ready for trouble. Look to what you'll need; there are difficult times ahead. Pawn your coat and get a sword. What was written in Scripture, 'He was lumped in with the criminals,' gets its final meaning in me. Everything written about me is now coming to a conclusion."

38 They said, "Look, Master, two swords!"

But he said, "Enough of that; no more sword talk!"

A DARK NIGHT

39-40 Leaving there, he went, as he so often did, to Mount Olives. The disciples followed him. When they arrived at the place, he said, "Pray that you don't give in to temptation."

41-44 He pulled away from them about a stone's throw, knelt down, and prayed, "Father, remove this cup from me. But please, not what I want. What do *you* want?" At once an angel from heaven was at his side, strengthening him. He prayed on all the harder. Sweat, wrung from him like drops of blood, poured off his face.

45-46 He got up from prayer, went back to the disciples and found them asleep, drugged by grief. He said, "What business do you have sleeping? Get up. Pray so you won't give in to temptation."

47-48 No sooner were the words out of his mouth than a crowd showed up, Judas, the one from the Twelve, in the lead. He came right up to Jesus to kiss him. Jesus said, "Judas, you would betray the Son of Man with a kiss?"

49-50 When those with him saw what was happening, they said, "Master, shall we fight?" One of them took a swing at the Chief Priest's servant and cut off his right ear.

51 Jesus said, "Let them be. Even in this." Then, touching the servant's ear, he healed him.

52-53 Jesus spoke to those who had come—high priests, Temple police, religion leaders: "What is this, jumping me with swords and clubs as if I were a dangerous criminal? Day after day I've been with you in the Temple and you've not so much as lifted a hand against me. But do it your way—it's a dark night, a dark hour."

A ROOSTER CROWED

54-56 Arresting Jesus, they marched him off and took him into the house of the Chief Priest. Peter followed, but at a safe distance. In the middle of the courtyard some people had started a fire and were sitting around it, trying to keep warm. One of the serving maids sitting at the fire noticed him, then took a second look and said, "This man was with him!"

57 He denied it, "Woman, I don't even know him."

58 A short time later, someone else noticed him and said, "You're one of them."

But Peter denied it: "Man, I am not."

59 About an hour later, someone else spoke up, really adamant: "He's got to have been with him! He's got 'Galilean' written all over him."

60-62 Peter said, "Man, I don't know what you're talking about." At that very moment, the last word hardly off his lips, a rooster crowed. Just then, the Master turned and looked at Peter. Peter remembered what the Master had said to him: "Before the rooster crows, you will deny me three times." He went out and cried and cried and cried.

SLAPPING HIM AROUND

63-65 The men in charge of Jesus began poking fun at him, slapping him around. They put a blindfold on him and taunted, "Who hit you that time?" They were having a grand time with him.

66-67 When it was morning, the religious leaders of the people and the high priests and scholars all got together and brought him before their High Council. They said, "Are you the Messiah?"

67-69 He answered, "If I said yes, you wouldn't believe me. If I asked what you meant by your question, you wouldn't answer

The Women on the Way to the Cross

As Jesus was led down the streets of Jerusalem to his death, the crowds of people who had followed him throughout his ministry continued to walk behind him. Among them were female mourners, as was customary. But these devoted women were unusual.

These "companions of Jesus from Galilee" (Luke 23:55) were women Jesus had healed, forgiven, befriended. Perhaps he had healed or even resurrected their loved ones. Their "weeping and carrying on" (Luke 23:27) was needed in that moment, giving voice to Jesus' anguish and the grief of Jesus' followers—who were losing the Savior on whom they had pinned all their hopes.

Jesus had always been progressive where women were concerned, engaging those on the fringes, such as the woman at the well (John 4:1-30, 39-42) or the woman caught in adultery (John 8:1-11). Now, in his final hours, he again reached out to the women around him—but not for words of comfort, as they might have expected. Instead of dwelling on his suffering, he looked to the future: "Don't cry for me. Cry for yourselves and for your children" (Luke 23:28). He gently exhorted them to get their souls in order and prepare for the trials that would surely come. Though he was deep in his own suffering, Jesus did not waste the crucial final moments before his death with these women, his friends.

As this longest day wore on, Jesus breathed his last, and the crowds dispersed. For some, the spectacle was over. For others, their beloved Messiah was dead. But the women stayed with him, no strangers to the profound work of grief, tears flowing from an endless well. They left only to prepare burial spices, a final act of devotion for the one who had embraced them as full participants in the promises of God.

Then these women did what is perhaps the hardest thing to do when all hope seems lost: They "rested quietly on the Sabbath, as commanded" (Luke 23:56). Despite the bleak circumstances, they continued in faithful obedience, seeking comfort in the God-given gift of the Sabbath rest. Fully present in grief and faithful to the end, the women on the way to the cross truly were "companions of Jesus."

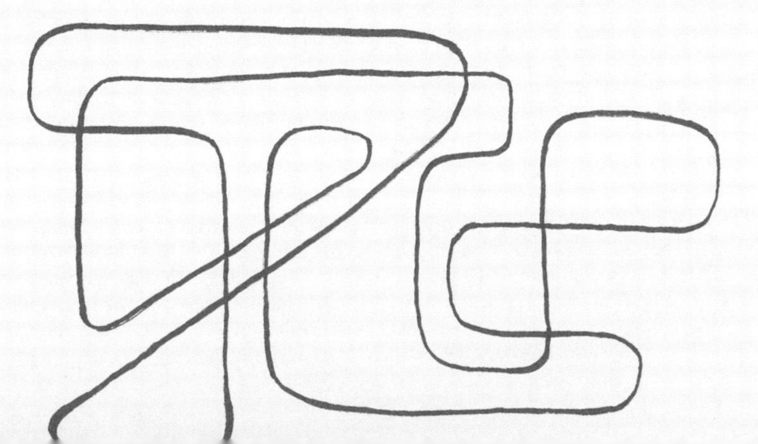

me. So here's what I have to say: From here on the Son of Man takes his place at God's right hand, the place of power."

70 They all said, "So you admit your claim to be the Son of God?"

"You're the ones who keep saying it," he said.

71 But they had made up their minds, "Why do we need any more evidence? We've all heard him as good as say it himself."

PILATE

23 1-2 Then they all took Jesus to Pilate and began to bring up charges against him. They said, "We found this man undermining our law and order, forbidding taxes to be paid to Caesar, setting himself up as Messiah-King."

3 Pilate asked him, "Is this true that you're 'King of the Jews'?"

"Those are your words, not mine," Jesus replied.

4 Pilate told the high priests and the accompanying crowd, "I find nothing wrong here. He seems harmless enough to me."

5 But they were vehement. "He's stirring up unrest among the people with his teaching, disturbing the peace everywhere, starting in Galilee and now all through Judea. He's a dangerous man, endangering the peace."

6-7 When Pilate heard that, he asked, "So, he's a Galilean?" Realizing that he properly came under Herod's jurisdiction, he passed the buck to Herod, who just happened to be in Jerusalem for a few days.

8-10 Herod was delighted when Jesus showed up. He had wanted for a long time to see him, he'd heard so much about him. He hoped to see him do something spectacular. He peppered him with questions. Jesus didn't answer—not one word. But the high priests and religion scholars were right there, saying their piece, strident and shrill in their accusations.

11-12 Mightily offended, Herod turned on Jesus. His soldiers joined in, taunting and jeering. Then they dressed him up in an elaborate king costume and sent him back to Pilate. That day Herod and Pilate became thick as thieves. Always before they had kept their distance.

13-16 Then Pilate called in the high priests, rulers, and the others and said, "You brought this man to me as a disturber of the peace. I examined him in front of all of you and found there was nothing to your charge. And neither did Herod, for he has sent him back here with a clean bill of health. It's clear that he's done nothing wrong, let alone anything deserving death. I'm going to warn him to watch his step and let him go."

18-20 At that, the crowd went wild: "Kill him! Give us Barabbas!" (Barabbas had been thrown in prison for starting a riot in the city and for murder.) Pilate still wanted to let Jesus go, and so spoke out again.

21 But they kept shouting back, "Crucify! Crucify him!"

22 He tried a third time. "But for what crime? I've found nothing in him deserving death. I'm going to warn him to watch his step and let him go."

23-25 But they kept at it, a shouting mob, demanding that he be crucified. And finally they shouted him down. Pilate caved in and gave them what they wanted. He released the man thrown in prison for rioting and murder, and gave them Jesus to do whatever they wanted.

SKULL HILL

26-31 As they led him off, they made Simon, a man from Cyrene who happened to be coming in from the countryside, carry the cross behind Jesus. A huge crowd of people followed, along with women weeping and carrying on. At one point Jesus turned to the women and said, "Daughters of Jerusalem, don't cry for me. Cry for yourselves and for your children. The time is coming when they'll say, 'Lucky the women who never conceived! Lucky the wombs that never gave birth! Lucky the breasts that never gave milk!' Then they'll start calling to the mountains, 'Fall down on us!' calling to the hills, 'Cover us up!' If people do these things to a live, green tree, can you imagine what they'll do with deadwood?"

32 Two others, both criminals, were taken along with him for execution.

33 When they got to the place called Skull Hill, they crucified him, along with the criminals, one on his right, the other on his left.

34-35 Jesus prayed, "Father, forgive them; they don't know what they're doing."

Dividing up his clothes, they threw dice for them. The people stood there staring at Jesus, and the ringleaders made faces, taunting, "He saved others. Let's see him save himself! The Messiah of God—ha! The Chosen—ha!"

36-37 The soldiers also came up and poked fun at him, making a game of it. They toasted him with sour wine: "So you're King of the Jews! Save yourself!"

THE WOMEN AT THE TOMB

It's not just what you know but who you know. That's how you get ahead in the Western world.

But being known by name—Mary Magdalene, Joanna, and Mary the mother of James—didn't give these women any advantage except to be known by us. They represent the other unnamed women who went to the tomb as soon as the Sabbath was over, ready with the supplies needed to embalm the body of their beloved teacher. It's not even clear whether these women had permission to do what they had prepared to do. We only know that they acted to honor tradition, caring for the body of their teacher even in death, even when society had cast him out as a criminal.

These women knew what it meant to create their own community and be cast out; because of their gender, society had placed them in the margins. But they also knew that they could trust one another and do this thing together. There is a solidarity here that we are invited to learn from and replicate, especially those of us from individualistic cultures.

Mary Magdalene and Joanna were both women of financial means. They traveled with Jesus and the other disciples and financially supported Jesus' work. Historically Mary Magdalene has been described as a prostitute, though she was not. Looking at the whole of Jesus' ministry, however, it wouldn't have mattered if she had been. Joanna was married, but the author does not make that relationship primary. It is her presence with and connection to the other women we are invited to consider, not her husband. These women lived out their convictions as the family of Christ beyond blood and legal ties. And in doing so, they became the first witnesses of death's defeat.

38 Printed over him was a sign: THIS IS THE KING OF THE JEWS.

39 One of the criminals hanging alongside cursed him: "Some Messiah you are! Save yourself! Save us!"

40-41 But the other one made him shut up: "Have you no fear of God? You're getting the same as him. We deserve this, but not him—he did nothing to deserve this."

42 Then he said, "Jesus, remember me when you enter your kingdom."

43 He said, "Don't worry, I will. Today you will join me in paradise."

44-46 By now it was noon. The whole earth became dark, the darkness lasting three hours—a total blackout. The Temple curtain split right down the middle. Jesus called loudly, "Father, I place my life in your hands!" Then he breathed his last.

▲ ▲ ▲

47 When the captain there saw what happened, he honored God: "This man was innocent! A good man, and innocent!"

48-49 All who had come around as spectators to watch the show, when they saw what actually happened, were overcome with grief and headed home. Those who knew Jesus well, along with the women who had followed him from Galilee, stood at a respectful distance and kept vigil.

50-54 There was a man by the name of Joseph, a member of the Jewish High Council, a man of good heart and good character. He had not gone along with the plans and actions of the council. His hometown was the Jewish village of Arimathea. He lived in alert expectation of the kingdom of God. He went to Pilate and asked for the body of Jesus. Taking him down, he wrapped him in a linen shroud and placed him in a tomb chiseled into the rock, a tomb never yet used. It was the day before Sabbath, the Sabbath just about to begin.

55-56 The women who had been companions of Jesus from Galilee followed along. They saw the tomb where Jesus' body was placed. Then they went back to prepare burial spices and perfumes. They rested quietly on the Sabbath, as commanded.

LOOKING FOR THE LIVING ONE IN A CEMETERY

24 1-3 At the crack of dawn on Sunday, the women came to the tomb carrying the burial spices they had prepared. They found the entrance stone rolled back from the tomb, so they walked in. But once inside, they couldn't find the body of the Master Jesus.

4-8 They were puzzled, wondering what to make of this. Then, out of nowhere it seemed, two men, light cascading over them, stood there. The women were awestruck and bowed down in worship. The men said, "Why are you looking for the Living One in a cemetery? He is not here, but raised up. Remember how he told you when you were still back in Galilee that he had to be handed over to sinners, be killed on a cross, and in three days rise up?" Then they remembered Jesus' words.

9-11 They left the tomb and broke the news of all this to the Eleven and the rest. Mary Magdalene, Joanna, Mary the mother of James, and the other women with them kept telling these things to the apostles, but the apostles didn't believe a word of it, thought they were making it all up.

12 But Peter jumped to his feet and ran to the tomb. He stooped to look in and saw a few grave clothes, that's all. He walked away puzzled, shaking his head.

THE ROAD TO EMMAUS

13-16 That same day two of them were walking to the village Emmaus, about seven miles out of Jerusalem. They were deep in conversation, going over all these things that had happened. In the middle of their talk and questions, Jesus came up and walked along with them. But they were not able to recognize who he was.

17-18 He asked, "What's this you're discussing so intently as you walk along?"

They just stood there, long-faced, like they had lost their best friend. Then one of them, his name was Cleopas, said, "Are you the only one in Jerusalem who hasn't heard what's happened during the last few days?"

19-24 He said, "What has happened?"

They said, "The things that happened to Jesus the Nazarene. He was a man of God, a prophet, dynamic in work and word, blessed by both God and all the people. Then our high priests and leaders betrayed him, got him sentenced to death, and crucified him. And we had our hopes up that he was the One, the One about to deliver Israel. And it is now the third day since it happened. But now some of our women have completely confused us. Early this morning they were at the tomb and couldn't find his body. They came back with

He Is Risen

The ordinary, familiar roads we travel can become holy ground at any moment.

The Emmaus road offered a path to Jerusalem, the place of the annual Passover. If footprints could speak, the stories of those who had walked it would sound familiar. Women carried infants in their arms or held the tugging, restless hands of tired children. Families and friends chatted about the mundane moments of life—and the celebration-worthy moments too.

Many travelers carried burdens, and some burdens took their lives on unexpected detours. They mourned the loss of family and friends. Marriages and marital statuses changed, as did the lives they'd built around them. Yet the purpose of this trip was to remember the bigger story of which they were part. The Passover festival reminded God's people that the Divine interceded in their lives, meeting them in everyday moments to liberate, protect, and transform.

Some people returning home from this particular trek to Jerusalem carried an exceptionally heavy burden. Their hopes that Jesus was indeed the Divine-made-flesh, their Savior and deliverer, had been dramatically dashed. Now they were filled with confusion and despair. What was anticipated was unrealized.

They were so focused on grief that they didn't notice Jesus' presence.

But he was there. He hadn't abandoned them.

Yes, circumstances had unfolded much differently than they'd expected. But Jesus met them, just as he had promised. They didn't recognize him at first because their disappointment hung so heavy in the air, obstructing their view. But then Jesus interrupted the conversation. As he talked, something clicked. They remarked later during a meal together: "Didn't we feel on fire as he conversed with us on the road, as he opened up the Scriptures for us?" (Luke 24:32).

Jesus had been in their midst all along.

The roads we take may appear insignificant, routes of transportation navigating us from point A to point B. Like for the people who walked the road back home to Emmaus, the experiences we carry on the journey will vary. Life unfolds in ways that leave us feeling confused, grieved, or purely happy.

When we are lost in these moments, Jesus interrupts us in the most unexpected ways. He comes and speaks to the deepest struggles of our humanity. And he celebrates with us as our eyes open and we begin to recognize the hope he offers. Jesus' resurrected life is always intersecting our lives. As we keep our eyes open, we will notice him in our midst—even if it takes a minute to recognize him.

the story that they had seen a vision of angels who said he was alive. Some of our friends went off to the tomb to check and found it empty just as the women said, but they didn't see Jesus."

25-27 Then he said to them, "So thick-headed! So slow-hearted! Why can't you simply believe all that the prophets said? Don't you see that these things had to happen, that the Messiah had to suffer and only then enter into his glory?" Then he started at the beginning, with the Books of Moses, and went on through all the Prophets, pointing out everything in the Scriptures that referred to him.

28-31 They came to the edge of the village where they were headed. He acted as if he were going on but they pressed him: "Stay and have supper with us. It's nearly evening; the day is done." So he went in with them. And here is what happened: He sat down at the table with them. Taking the bread, he blessed and broke and gave it to them. At that moment, open-eyed, wide-eyed, they recognized him. And then he disappeared.

32 Back and forth they talked. "Didn't we feel on fire as he conversed with us on the road, as he opened up the Scriptures for us?"

A GHOST DOESN'T HAVE MUSCLE AND BONE

33-34 They didn't waste a minute. They were up and on their way back to Jerusalem. They found the Eleven and their friends gathered together, talking away: "It's really happened! The Master has been raised up—Simon saw him!"

35 Then the two went over everything that happened on the road and how they recognized him when he broke the bread.

36-41 While they were saying all this, Jesus appeared to them and said, "Peace be with you." They thought they were seeing a ghost and were scared half to death. He continued with them, "Don't be upset, and don't let all these doubting questions take over. Look at my hands; look at my feet—it's really me. Touch me. Look me over from head to toe. A ghost doesn't have muscle and bone like this." As he said this, he showed them his hands and feet. They still couldn't believe what they were seeing. It was too much; it seemed too good to be true.

41-43 He asked, "Do you have any food here?" They gave him a piece of leftover fish they had cooked. He took it and ate it right before their eyes.

YOU'RE THE WITNESSES

44 Then he said, "Everything I told you while I was with you comes to this: All the things written about me in the Law of Moses, in the Prophets, and in the Psalms have to be fulfilled."

45-49 He went on to open their understanding of the Word of God, showing them how to read their Bibles this way. He said, "You can see now how it is written that the Messiah suffers, rises from the dead on the third day, and then a total life-change through the forgiveness of sins is proclaimed in his name to all nations—starting from here, from Jerusalem! You're the first to hear and see it. You're the witnesses. What comes next is very important: I am sending what my Father promised to you, so stay here in the city until he arrives, until you're equipped with power from on high."

50-51 He then led them out of the city over to Bethany. Raising his hands he blessed them, and while blessing them, made his exit, being carried up to heaven.

52-53 And they were on their knees, worshiping him. They returned to Jerusalem bursting with joy. They spent all their time in the Temple praising God. Yes.

John

PUTTING IT ALL TOGETHER

In Genesis, the first book of the Bible, God is presented as speaking the creation into existence. God speaks the word and it happens: heaven and earth, ocean and stream, trees and grass, birds and fish, animals and humans. Everything, seen and unseen, called into being by God's spoken word.

In deliberate parallel to the opening words of Genesis, John presents God as speaking salvation into existence. "The Word was first, the Word present to God, God present to the Word. The Word was God, in readiness for God from day one" (John 1:1-2). This time God's word takes on human form and enters history in the person of Jesus. Jesus speaks the word and it happens: forgiveness and judgment, healing and illumination, mercy and grace, joy and love, freedom and resurrection. Everything broken and fallen, sinful and diseased, called into salvation by God's spoken word.

For, somewhere along the line things went wrong (Genesis tells that story, too) and are in desperate need of fixing. The fixing is all accomplished by speaking—God speaking salvation into being in the person of Jesus. Jesus, in this account, not only speaks the word of God; he *is* the Word of God.

Keeping company with these words, we begin to realize that our words are more important than we ever supposed. Saying "I believe," for instance, marks the difference between life and death. John wrote, "Jesus provided far more God-revealing signs than are written down in this book. These are written down so you will believe that Jesus is the Messiah, the Son of God, and in the act of believing, have real and eternal life in the way he personally revealed it" (John 20:30-31).

Our words accrue dignity and gravity in conversations with Jesus. For Jesus doesn't impose salvation as a solution; he *narrates* salvation into being through leisurely conversation, intimate personal relationships, compassionate responses, passionate prayer, and—putting it all together—a sacrificial death. We don't casually walk away from words like that.

THE LIFE-LIGHT

1 1-2 The Word was first,
the Word present to God,
God present to the Word.
The Word was God,
in readiness for God from day one.

3-5 Everything was created through him;
nothing—not one thing!—
came into being without him.
What came into existence was Life,
and the Life was Light to live by.
The Life-Light blazed out of the darkness;
the darkness couldn't put it out.

6-8 There once was a man, his name John, sent by God to point out the way to the Life-Light. He came to show everyone where to look, who to believe in. John was not himself the Light; he was there to show the way to the Light.

9-13 The Life-Light was the real thing:
Every person entering Life
he brings into Light.
He was in the world,
the world was there through him,
and yet the world didn't even notice.
He came to his own people,
but they didn't want him.
But whoever did want him,
who believed he was who he claimed
and would do what he said,
He made to be their true selves,
their child-of-God selves.
These are the God-begotten,
not blood-begotten,
not flesh-begotten,
not sex-begotten.

14 The Word became flesh and blood,
and moved into the neighborhood.
We saw the glory with our own eyes,
the one-of-a-kind glory,
like Father, like Son,
Generous inside and out,
true from start to finish.

15 John pointed him out and called, "This is the One! The One I told you was coming after me but in fact was ahead of me. He has always been ahead of me, has always had the first word."

16-18 We all live off his generous abundance,
gift after gift after gift.
We got the basics from Moses,
and then this exuberant giving
and receiving,
This endless knowing and
understanding—
all this came through Jesus,
the Messiah.
No one has ever seen God,
not so much as a glimpse.
This one-of-a-kind God-Expression,
who exists at the very heart of
the Father,
has made him plain as day.

THUNDER IN THE DESERT

19-20 When Jews from Jerusalem sent a group of priests and officials to ask John who he was, he was completely honest. He didn't evade the question. He told the plain truth: "I am not the Messiah."

21 They pressed him, "Who, then? Elijah?"

"I am not."

"The Prophet?"

"No."

22 Exasperated, they said, "Who, then? We need an answer for those who sent us. Tell us something—anything!—about yourself."

23 "I'm thunder in the desert: 'Make the road straight for God!' I'm doing what the prophet Isaiah preached."

24-25 Those sent to question him were from the Pharisee party. Now they had a question of their own: "If you're neither the Messiah, nor Elijah, nor the Prophet, why do you baptize?"

26-27 John answered, "I only baptize using water. A person you don't recognize has taken his stand in your midst. He comes after me, but he is not in second place to me. I'm not even worthy to hold his coat for him."

28 These conversations took place in Bethany on the other side of the Jordan, where John was baptizing at the time.

THE GOD-REVEALER

29-31 The very next day John saw Jesus coming toward him and yelled out, "Here he is, God's Passover Lamb! He forgives the sins of the world! This is the man I've been talking about, 'the One who comes after me but is really ahead of me.' I knew nothing about who he was—only this: that my task has been to get Israel ready to recognize him as the God-Revealer. That is why I came here baptizing with water, giving you a good bath and scrubbing sins from your life so you can get a fresh start with God."

The Word Became Flesh

Of all the ways God might have been revealed to the world, God chose to come wrapped in human skin: Jesus, the revelation of God, walking around with blood and bones and sinew. "The Word became flesh and blood, and moved into the neighborhood" (John 1:14).

John makes it clear that Jesus didn't come into existence the hour his human body slipped from Mary's womb. John tells us that Jesus, the Word, was first, present with God. Jesus *has always been* God. John's story about Jesus begins earlier than the Incarnation; it begins in the beginning, before all things came into being, because "nothing—not one thing!—came into being without him" (John 1:3).

John's story isn't a fairy tale. John wrote of what he had seen with his own eyes. Can you imagine? After generations of stories about the coming Messiah, now here he was, standing in the water, a dove descending from heaven—the Spirit of God "making himself at home in him" (John 1:32). John bore witness as another man named John pressed his feet into the hot sand of the desert and proclaimed to the priests and officials the surprise arrival of God's physical presence, "made . . . plain as day" (John 1:18).

Wild-eyed with excitement, John the Baptizer made sure there was no confusion about his role, about who this Word-made-flesh person was. "I am not the Messiah," he told his examiners. "I'm thunder in the desert. . . . I'm doing what the prophet Isaiah preached" (John 1:20, 23). It seems that John was the only one in this story who *wasn't* confused. He knew what he'd seen. He believed what he had heard.

The Pharisees had another question. "If you're neither the Messiah, nor Elijah, nor the Prophet, why do you baptize?" they asked. John responded, "I only baptize using water. A person you don't recognize has taken his stand in your midst" (John 1:25-26). This wasn't the last time Jesus would be present among people who failed to recognize him.

John called out, "Here he is, God's Passover Lamb! He forgives the sins of the world!" (John 1:30).

Until this moment, no one had ever seen God, "not so much as a glimpse" (John 1:18). But there he was, enfleshed, walking around, talking to people, "mov[ing] into the neighborhood" (John 1:14). He began calling the first disciples and inviting people to "come along and see" for themselves what he was up to (John 1:39).

Jesus is both the life and the light of the world. His very real presence is not diminished by those who fail to see him for who he is. Jesus' invitation to would-be disciples then and now is "Come, follow me. . . . You haven't seen anything yet!" (John 1:43, 50).

32-34 John clinched his witness with this: "I watched the Spirit, like a dove flying down out of the sky, making himself at home in him. I repeat, I know nothing about him except this: The One who authorized me to baptize with water told me, 'The One on whom you see the Spirit come down and stay, this One will baptize with the Holy Spirit.' That's exactly what I saw happen, and I'm telling you, there's no question about it: *This* is the Son of God."

COME, SEE FOR YOURSELF

35-36 The next day John was back at his post with two disciples, who were watching. He looked up, saw Jesus walking nearby, and said, "Here he is, God's Passover Lamb."

37-38 The two disciples heard him and went after Jesus. Jesus looked over his shoulder and said to them, "What are you after?"

They said, "Rabbi" (which means "Teacher"), "where are you staying?"

39 He replied, "Come along and see for yourself."

They came, saw where he was living, and ended up staying with him for the day. It was late afternoon when this happened.

40-42 Andrew, Simon Peter's brother, was one of the two who heard John's witness and followed Jesus. The first thing he did after finding where Jesus lived was find his own brother, Simon, telling him, "We've found the Messiah" (that is, "Christ"). He immediately led him to Jesus.

Jesus took one look up and said, "You're John's son, Simon? From now on your name is Cephas" (or Peter, which means "Rock").

43-44 The next day Jesus decided to go to Galilee. When he got there, he ran across Philip and said, "Come, follow me." (Philip's hometown was Bethsaida, the same as Andrew and Peter.)

45-46 Philip went and found Nathanael and told him, "We've found the One Moses wrote of in the Law, the One preached by the prophets. It's *Jesus*, Joseph's son, the one from Nazareth!" Nathanael said, "Nazareth? You've got to be kidding."

But Philip said, "Come, see for yourself."

47 When Jesus saw him coming he said, "There's a real Israelite, not a false bone in his body."

48 Nathanael said, "Where did you get that idea? You don't know me."

Jesus answered, "One day, long before Philip called you here, I saw you under the fig tree."

49 Nathanael exclaimed, "Rabbi! You are the Son of God, the King of Israel!"

50-51 Jesus said, "You've become a believer simply because I say I saw you one day sitting under the fig tree? You haven't seen anything yet! Before this is over you're going to see heaven open and God's angels descending to the Son of Man and ascending again."

FROM WATER TO WINE

2 1-3 Three days later there was a wedding in the village of Cana in Galilee. Jesus' mother was there. Jesus and his disciples were guests also. When they started running low on wine at the wedding banquet, Jesus' mother told him, "They're just about out of wine."

4 Jesus said, "Is that any of our business, Mother—yours or mine? This isn't my time. Don't push me."

5 She went ahead anyway, telling the servants, "Whatever he tells you, do it."

6-7 Six stoneware water pots were there, used by the Jews for ritual washings. Each held twenty to thirty gallons. Jesus ordered the servants, "Fill the pots with water." And they filled them to the brim.

8 "Now fill your pitchers and take them to the host," Jesus said, and they did.

9-10 When the host tasted the water that had become wine (he didn't know what had just happened but the servants, of course, knew), he called out to the bridegroom, "Everybody I know begins with their finest wines and after the guests have had their fill brings in the cheap stuff. But you've saved the best till now!"

11 This act in Cana of Galilee was the first sign Jesus gave, the first glimpse of his glory. And his disciples believed in him.

12 After this he went down to Capernaum along with his mother, brothers, and disciples, and stayed several days.

TEAR DOWN THIS TEMPLE . . .

13-14 When the Passover Feast, celebrated each spring by the Jews, was about to take place, Jesus traveled up to Jerusalem. He found the Temple teeming with people selling cattle and sheep and doves. The loan sharks were also there in full strength.

15-17 Jesus put together a whip out of strips of leather and chased them out of the Temple, stampeding the sheep and cattle, upending the tables of the loan sharks, spilling coins left and right. He told the dove merchants,

"Get your things out of here! Stop turning my Father's house into a shopping mall!" That's when his disciples remembered the Scripture, "Zeal for your house consumes me."

18-19 But the Jews were upset. They asked, "What credentials can you present to justify this?" Jesus answered, "Tear down this Temple and in three days I'll put it back together."

20-22 They were indignant: "It took forty-six years to build this Temple, and you're going to rebuild it in three days?" But Jesus was talking about his body as the Temple. Later, after he was raised from the dead, his disciples remembered he had said this. They then put two and two together and believed both what was written in Scripture and what Jesus had said.

23-25 During the time he was in Jerusalem, those days of the Passover Feast, many people noticed the signs he was displaying and, seeing they pointed straight to God, entrusted their lives to him. But Jesus didn't entrust his life to them. He knew them inside and out, knew how untrustworthy they were. He didn't need any help in seeing right through them.

BORN FROM ABOVE

3 1-2 There was a man of the Pharisee sect, Nicodemus, a prominent leader among the Jews. Late one night he visited Jesus and said, "Rabbi, we all know you're a teacher straight from God. No one could do all the God-pointing, God-revealing acts you do if God weren't in on it."

3 Jesus said, "You're absolutely right. Take it from me: Unless a person is born from above, it's not possible to see what I'm pointing to—to God's kingdom."

4 "How can anyone," said Nicodemus, "be born who has already been born and grown up? You can't re-enter your mother's womb and be born again. What are you saying with this 'born-from-above' talk?"

5-6 Jesus said, "You're not listening. Let me say it again. Unless a person submits to this original creation—the 'wind-hovering-over-the-water' creation, the invisible moving the visible, a baptism into a new life—it's not possible to enter God's kingdom. When you look at a baby, it's just that: a body you can look at and touch. But the person who takes shape within is formed by something you can't see and touch—the Spirit—and becomes a living spirit.

7-8 "So don't be so surprised when I tell you that you have to be 'born from above'—out of this world, so to speak. You know well enough how the wind blows this way and that. You hear it rustling through the trees, but you have no idea where it comes from or where it's headed next. That's the way it is with everyone 'born from above' by the wind of God, the Spirit of God."

9 Nicodemus asked, "What do you mean by this? How does this happen?"

10-12 Jesus said, "You're a respected teacher of Israel and you don't know these basics? Listen carefully. I'm speaking sober truth to you. I speak only of what I know by experience; I give witness only to what I have seen with my own eyes. There is nothing secondhand here, no hearsay. Yet instead of facing the evidence and accepting it, you procrastinate with questions. If I tell you things that are plain as the hand before your face and you don't believe me, what use is there in telling you of things you can't see, the things of God?

13-15 "No one has ever gone up into the presence of God except the One who came down from that Presence, the Son of Man. In the same way that Moses lifted the serpent in the desert so people could have something to see and then believe, it is necessary for the Son of Man to be lifted up—and everyone who looks up to him, trusting and expectant, will gain a real life, eternal life.

16-18 "This is how much God loved the world: He gave his Son, his one and only Son. And this is why: so that no one need be destroyed; by believing in him, anyone can have a whole and lasting life. God didn't go to all the trouble of sending his Son merely to point an accusing finger, telling the world how bad it was. He came to help, to put the world right again. Anyone who trusts in him is acquitted; anyone who refuses to trust him has long since been under the death sentence without knowing it. And why? Because of that person's failure to believe in the one-of-a-kind Son of God when introduced to him.

19-21 "This is the crisis we're in: God-light streamed into the world, but men and women everywhere ran for the darkness. They went for the darkness because they were not really interested in pleasing God. Everyone who makes a practice of doing evil, addicted to denial and illusion, hates God-light and won't come near it, fearing a painful exposure. But anyone working and living in truth and reality welcomes God-light so the work can be seen for the God-work it is."

The Joy of Decreasing

A beloved woman from my community recently passed away at the age of ninety-one. Marilyn was a pioneer in her profession and an anchor in her community. Her insightful faith and deep love of Jesus were legendary among those of us who knew her.

Before she died, Marilyn asked her pastor not to speak about her at the funeral. She didn't want to be celebrated. Rather, she wanted to use the opportunity, when all her friends and family were gathered, to share the love of Jesus.

Marilyn embodied what John the Baptizer meant when he told his disciples that Jesus must "move into the center, while I slip off to the sidelines" (John 3:30). John's disciples were jealous that Jesus was gaining more followers than John. But the very thing that was upsetting John's disciples was what filled John with great joy. John referred to Jesus as "the bridegroom" (John 3:29). John's role as the best man was to prepare the way and point to the central character. With the bridegroom on the scene, John was delighted for Jesus to take center stage and for John himself to fade into the wings.

Seeking to decrease in this way doesn't mean that our self-worth declines. It's actually the opposite: We are so secure in Jesus' love for us that we no longer seek the applause of the world. Our self-esteem no longer depends on our achievements or the size of our following. We can cease all our striving to do more, gain more, and be more. We have nothing left to prove because Jesus has proven his love for us.

As Jesus becomes greater in our lives and we become less, we may speak up more—not for our own glory, but to advocate for what Jesus cares about. We may also take better care of ourselves when we know our value in Christ. Marilyn taught a popular self-defense class where she empowered her students to see themselves as Jesus saw them: valuable and worthy of the utmost care. Her book, *Free to Fight Back*, is based on the motto of that class: "I am a child of the King, and I will not be a victim."

When we seek to decrease so Jesus can increase, we become more like our true selves. We are set free from former idols that falsely defined us. We become less self-focused and more able to love God and others. We experience more joy, peace, and love in our lives.

The pastor honored Marilyn's wishes. Her funeral was a celebration of what Jesus had done in her life, and as a result, someone in attendance accepted Christ that day! Like John the Baptizer, Marilyn discovered the joy of decreasing. Her life was a signpost that pointed to Jesus, the way to a joyful, abundant, and meaningful life.

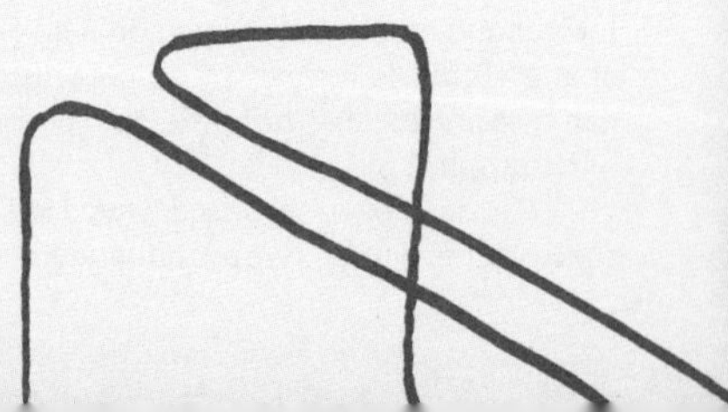

THE BRIDEGROOM'S FRIEND

22-26 After this conversation, Jesus went on with his disciples into the Judean countryside and relaxed with them there. He was also baptizing. At the same time, John was baptizing over at Aenon near Salim, where water was abundant. This was before John was thrown into jail. John's disciples got into an argument with the establishment Jews over the nature of baptism. They came to John and said, "Rabbi, you know the one who was with you on the other side of the Jordan? The one you authorized with your witness? Well, he's now competing with us. He's baptizing, too, and everyone's going to him instead of us."

27-29 John answered, "It's not possible for a person to succeed—I'm talking about *eternal* success—without heaven's help. You yourselves were there when I made it public that I was not the Messiah but simply the one sent ahead of him to get things ready. The one who gets the bride is, by definition, the bridegroom. And the bridegroom's friend, his 'best man'—that's me—in place at his side where he can hear every word, is genuinely happy. How could he be jealous when he knows that the wedding is finished and the marriage is off to a good start?

29-30 "That's why my cup is running over. This is the assigned moment for him to move into the center, while I slip off to the sidelines.

31-33 "The One who comes from above is head and shoulders over other messengers from God. The earthborn is earthbound and speaks earth language; the heavenborn is in a league of his own. He sets out the evidence of what he saw and heard in heaven. No one wants to deal with these facts. But anyone who examines this evidence will come to stake his life on this: that God himself is the truth.

34-36 "The One that God sent speaks God's words. And don't think he rations out the Spirit in bits and pieces. The Father loves the Son extravagantly. He turned everything over to him so he could give it away—a lavish distribution of gifts. That is why whoever accepts and trusts the Son gets in on everything, life complete and forever! And that is also why the person who avoids and distrusts the Son is in the dark and doesn't see life. All he experiences of God is darkness, and an angry darkness at that."

THE WOMAN AT THE WELL

4 1-3 Jesus realized that the Pharisees were keeping count of the baptisms that he and John performed (although his disciples, not Jesus, did the actual baptizing). They had posted the score that Jesus was ahead, turning him and John into rivals in the eyes of the people. So Jesus left the Judean countryside and went back to Galilee.

4-6 To get there, he had to pass through Samaria. He came into Sychar, a Samaritan village that bordered the field Jacob had given his son Joseph. Jacob's well was still there. Jesus, worn out by the trip, sat down at the well. It was noon.

7-8 A woman, a Samaritan, came to draw water. Jesus said, "Would you give me a drink of water?" (His disciples had gone to the village to buy food for lunch.)

9 The Samaritan woman, taken aback, asked, "How come you, a Jew, are asking me, a Samaritan woman, for a drink?" (Jews in those days wouldn't be caught dead talking to Samaritans.)

10 Jesus answered, "If you knew the generosity of God and who I am, you would be asking *me* for a drink, and I would give you fresh, living water."

11-12 The woman said, "Sir, you don't even have a bucket to draw with, and this well is deep. So how are you going to get this 'living water'? Are you a better man than our ancestor Jacob, who dug this well and drank from it, he and his sons and livestock, and passed it down to us?"

13-14 Jesus said, "Everyone who drinks this water will get thirsty again and again. Anyone who drinks the water I give will never thirst—not ever. The water I give will be an artesian spring within, gushing fountains of endless life."

15 The woman said, "Sir, give me this water so I won't ever get thirsty, won't ever have to come back to this well again!"

16 He said, "Go call your husband and then come back."

17-18 "I have no husband," she said.

"That's nicely put: 'I have no husband.' You've had five husbands, and the man you're living with now isn't even your husband. You spoke the truth there, sure enough."

19-20 "Oh, so you're a prophet! Well, tell me this: Our ancestors worshiped God at this mountain, but you Jews insist that Jerusalem is the only place for worship, right?"

21-23 "Believe me, woman, the time is coming when you Samaritans will worship the Father neither here at this mountain nor there in Jerusalem. You worship guessing in the dark; we Jews worship in the clear light of

THE SAMARITAN WOMAN

This unnamed Samaritan woman is best known to us as "the woman at the well." Assumptions abound regarding her life and story: she must have been promiscuous to have had so many husbands; she was living in sin with a man who wasn't her husband; Jesus was judging her when he spoke what he knew. Many of these assumptions have been preached and written about enough times that we've begun to think they are as true as Scripture itself.

However, when we simply read what the story says, we find out who the Samaritan woman was:

- *Grieving.* As any woman who's had a marriage end knows, there is grief no matter what caused the separation. This woman had had five commitments made to her and broken, five intended families that did not pan out.
- *Vulnerable.* Since she was either divorced or widowed (or both), the man with whom she lived may have been a family member who had taken her in as his duty under the law but viewed her as a burden on his household.
- *Self-reliant.* She came to the well without the expectation of help, and she came equipped to help herself.
- *Bold.* Her questions to Jesus demonstrated courage and theological acumen; her answers proved she was not willing to be fooled by the promises of a stranger—especially one who shouldn't be speaking to her.

Most importantly, this woman was an evangelist—one of the first mentioned in John's Gospel—and her proclamation was powerful enough to convince her whole village to come and see Jesus.

This Samaritan woman's story is one of many that God uses to remind us that the good news is often told best by those we wrongly assume are unworthy.

day. God's way of salvation is made available through the Jews. But the time is coming—it has, in fact, come—when what you're called will not matter and where you go to worship will not matter.

23-24 "It's who you are and the way you live that count before God. Your worship must engage your spirit in the pursuit of truth. That's the kind of people the Father is out looking for: those who are simply and honestly *themselves* before him in their worship. God is sheer being itself—Spirit. Those who worship him must do it out of their very being, their spirits, their true selves, in adoration."

25 The woman said, "I don't know about that. I do know that the Messiah is coming. When he arrives, we'll get the whole story."

26 "I am he," said Jesus. "You don't have to wait any longer or look any further."

27 Just then his disciples came back. They were shocked. They couldn't believe he was talking with that kind of a woman. No one said what they were all thinking, but their faces showed it.

28-30 The woman took the hint and left. In her confusion she left her water pot. Back in the village she told the people, "Come see a man who knew all about the things I did, who knows me inside and out. Do you think this could be the Messiah?" And they went out to see for themselves.

IT'S HARVEST TIME

31 In the meantime, the disciples pressed him, "Rabbi, eat. Aren't you going to eat?"

32 He told them, "I have food to eat you know nothing about."

33 The disciples were puzzled. "Who could have brought him food?"

34-35 Jesus said, "The food that keeps me going is that I do the will of the One who sent me, finishing the work he started. As you look around right now, wouldn't you say that in about four months it will be time to harvest? Well, I'm telling you to open your eyes and take a good look at what's right in front of you. These Samaritan fields are ripe. It's harvest time!

36-38 "The Harvester isn't waiting. He's taking his pay, gathering in this grain that's ripe for eternal life. Now the Sower is arm in arm with the Harvester, triumphant. That's the truth of the saying, 'This one sows, that one harvests.' I sent you to harvest a field you never worked. Without lifting a finger, you have walked in on a field worked long and hard by others."

39-42 Many of the Samaritans from that village committed themselves to him because of the woman's witness: "He knew all about the things I did. He knows me inside and out!" They asked him to stay on, so Jesus stayed two days. A lot more people entrusted their lives to him when they heard what he had to say. They said to the woman, "We're no longer taking this on your say-so. We've heard it for ourselves and know it for sure. He's the Savior of the world!"

▲ ▲ ▲

43-45 After the two days he left for Galilee. Now, Jesus knew well from experience that a prophet is not respected in the place where he grew up. So when he arrived in Galilee, the Galileans welcomed him, but only because they were impressed with what he had done in Jerusalem during the Passover Feast, not that they really had a clue about who he was or what he was up to.

46-48 Now he was back in Cana of Galilee, the place where he made the water into wine. Meanwhile in Capernaum, there was a certain official from the king's court whose son was sick. When he heard that Jesus had come from Judea to Galilee, he went and asked that he come down and heal his son, who was on the brink of death. Jesus put him off: "Unless you people are dazzled by a miracle, you refuse to believe."

49 But the court official wouldn't be put off. "Come down! It's life or death for my son."

50-51 Jesus simply replied, "Go home. Your son lives."

The man believed the bare word Jesus spoke and headed home. On his way back, his servants intercepted him and announced, "Your son lives!"

52-53 He asked them what time he began to get better. They said, "The fever broke yesterday afternoon at one o'clock." The father knew that that was the very moment Jesus had said, "Your son lives."

53-54 That settled it. Not only he but his entire household believed. This was now the second sign Jesus gave after having come from Judea into Galilee.

EVEN ON THE SABBATH

5 1-6 Soon another Feast came around and Jesus was back in Jerusalem. Near the Sheep Gate in Jerusalem there was a pool, in Hebrew called *Bethesda*, with five alcoves.

The Place We Feel Most Invisible

Being left out or excluded is common to the human experience. Consider the Samaritan woman, who found herself alone at the common well during the hottest time of day.

Jesus chose to visit that particular well at that particular time of day and chose to speak with that particular woman. Not only did he deliberately travel in that direction, but he intentionally initiated conversation with her. He asked her for water, breaking all sorts of taboos to meet someone who needed him. She pointed out that he had no vessel with which to draw water; would Jesus accept water from the pot of a despised Samaritan woman, perhaps one who was ceremonially unclean? (Spoiler alert: He did!)

Here was a woman who was lonely, outcast, and seeking belonging, and Jesus offered her something she yearned for: living water. He spoke of spiritual life and eternal life, acknowledging her thirst. He told her that this living water was available even to her—a Samaritan, a woman, an outsider, an unwelcome person in the eyes of Jesus' people.

When Jesus spoke of this living water, she wanted it. She asked him straightaway for a drink of the sort of water that relieves a lifetime of thirst.

Jesus met her and directed her attention to what he offers: life, salvation, living water. He demonstrated love by truly seeing her and speaking to her. He focused on compassion and open arms, not exclusion. She was searching for something deep and permanent; he recognized her spiritual hunger and offered a solution. He offered her a place to belong.

The disciples were put off by this scandalous conversation. How could Jesus speak to someone the rest of their people despised? Didn't he know better? Indeed, he *did* know better—and acted this way regardless. He exemplified compassion in his gentle treatment, the gracious acceptance of treating her as one of his own. He treated her as a person worthy of dignity—worthy of a long theological discussion and even of his own self-disclosure.

She responded to his identity reveal with wonder and openness. She believed him, returned to her village, told others of this meeting, and brought them to see for themselves. They, too, came to Jesus, listened, and believed. What an astonishing encounter, first for the woman, then for the many who followed.

Jesus finds us at the places and times we are most lonely, most desiring to belong. He sees those of us on the margins as worthy of dignity and intimate dialogue with God, of receiving a piece of God's self-disclosure—for God invests in those who have been cast aside. Jesus went out of his way to find the Samaritan woman, and he will find us, too. He is waiting at the place we feel most invisible, ready to offer life-giving water.

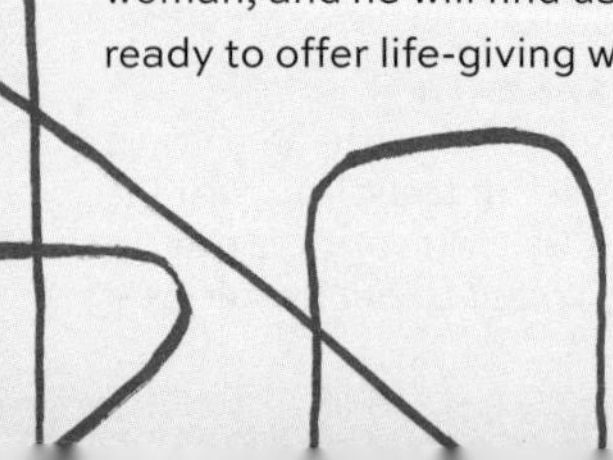

Hundreds of sick people—blind, crippled, paralyzed—were in these alcoves. One man had been an invalid there for thirty-eight years. When Jesus saw him stretched out by the pool and knew how long he had been there, he said, "Do you want to get well?"

7 The sick man said, "Sir, when the water is stirred, I don't have anybody to put me in the pool. By the time I get there, somebody else is already in."

8-9 Jesus said, "Get up, take your bedroll, start walking." The man was healed on the spot. He picked up his bedroll and walked off.

9-10 That day happened to be the Sabbath. The Jews stopped the healed man and said, "It's the Sabbath. You can't carry your bedroll around. It's against the rules."

11 But he told them, "The man who made me well told me to. He said, 'Take your bedroll and start walking.'"

12-13 They asked, "Who gave you the order to take it up and start walking?" But the healed man didn't know, for Jesus had slipped away into the crowd.

14 A little later Jesus found him in the Temple and said, "You look wonderful! You're well! Don't return to a sinning life or something worse might happen."

15-16 The man went back and told the Jews that it was Jesus who had made him well. That is why the Jews were out to get Jesus—because he did this kind of thing on the Sabbath.

17 But Jesus defended himself. "My Father is working straight through, even on the Sabbath. So am I."

18 That really set them off. The Jews were now not only out to expose him; they were out to *kill* him. Not only was he breaking the Sabbath, but he was calling God his own Father, putting himself on a level with God.

WHAT THE FATHER DOES, THE SON DOES

19-20 So Jesus explained himself at length. "I'm telling you this straight. The Son can't independently do a thing, only what he sees the Father doing. What the Father does, the Son does. The Father loves the Son and includes him in everything he is doing.

20-23 "But you haven't seen the half of it yet, for in the same way that the Father raises the dead and creates life, so does the Son. The Son gives life to anyone he chooses. Neither he nor the Father shuts anyone out. The Father handed all authority to judge over to the Son so that the Son will be honored equally with the Father. Anyone who dishonors the Son, dishonors the Father, for it was the Father's decision to put the Son in the place of honor.

24 "It's urgent that you listen carefully to this: Anyone here who believes what I am saying right now and aligns himself with the Father, who has in fact put me in charge, has at this very moment the real, lasting life and is no longer condemned to be an outsider. This person has taken a giant step from the world of the dead to the world of the living.

25-27 "It's urgent that you get this right: The time has arrived—I mean right now!—when dead men and women will hear the voice of the Son of God and, hearing, will come alive. Just as the Father has life in himself, he has conferred on the Son life in himself. And he has given him the authority, simply because he is the Son of Man, to decide and carry out matters of Judgment.

28-29 "Don't act so surprised at all this. The time is coming when everyone dead and buried will hear his voice. Those who have lived the right way will walk out into a resurrection Life; those who have lived the wrong way, into a resurrection Judgment.

30-33 "I can't do a solitary thing on my own: I listen, then I decide. You can trust my decision because I'm not out to get my own way but only to carry out orders. If I were simply speaking on my own account, it would be an empty, self-serving witness. But an independent witness confirms me, the most reliable Witness of all. Furthermore, you all saw and heard John, and he gave expert and reliable testimony about me, didn't he?

34-38 "But my purpose is not to get your vote, and not to appeal to mere human testimony. I'm speaking to you this way so that you will be saved. John was a torch, blazing and bright, and you were glad enough to dance for an hour or so in his bright light. But the witness that really confirms me far exceeds John's witness. It's the work the Father gave me to complete. These very tasks, as I go about completing them, confirm that the Father, in fact, sent me. The Father who sent me, confirmed me. And you missed it. You never heard his voice, you never saw his appearance. There is nothing left in your memory of his Message because you do not take his Messenger seriously.

▲ ▲ ▲

39-40 "You have your heads in your Bibles constantly because you think you'll find eternal life there. But you miss the forest for the trees. These Scriptures are all about *me*! And here I am, standing right before you, and you aren't willing to receive from me the life you say you want.

41-44 "I'm not interested in crowd approval. And do you know why? Because I know you and your crowds. I know that love, especially God's love, is not on your working agenda. I came with the authority of my Father, and you either dismiss me or avoid me. If another came, acting self-important, you would welcome him with open arms. How do you expect to get anywhere with God when you spend all your time jockeying for position with each other, ranking your rivals and ignoring God?

45-47 "But don't think I'm going to accuse you before my Father. Moses, in whom you put so much stock, is your accuser. If you believed, really believed, what Moses said, you would believe me. He wrote of me. If you won't take seriously what *he* wrote, how can I expect you to take seriously what *I* speak?"

BREAD AND FISH FOR ALL

6 1-4 After this, Jesus went across the Sea of Galilee (some call it Tiberias). A huge crowd followed him, attracted by the miracles they had seen him do among the sick. When he got to the other side, he climbed a hill and sat down, surrounded by his disciples. It was nearly time for the Feast of Passover, kept annually by the Jews.

5-6 When Jesus looked out and saw that a large crowd had arrived, he said to Philip, "Where can we buy bread to feed these people?" He said this to stretch Philip's faith. He already knew what he was going to do.

7 Philip answered, "Two hundred silver pieces wouldn't be enough to buy bread for each person to get a piece."

8-9 One of the disciples—it was Andrew, brother to Simon Peter—said, "There's a little boy here who has five barley loaves and two fish. But that's a drop in the bucket for a crowd like this."

10-11 Jesus said, "Make the people sit down." There was a nice carpet of green grass in this place. They sat down, about five thousand of them. Then Jesus took the bread and, having given thanks, gave it to those who were seated. He did the same with the fish. All ate as much as they wanted.

12-13 When the people had eaten their fill, he said to his disciples, "Gather the leftovers so nothing is wasted." They went to work and filled twelve large baskets with leftovers from the five barley loaves.

14-15 The people realized that God was at work among them in what Jesus had just done. They said, "This is the Prophet for sure, God's Prophet right here in Galilee!" Jesus saw that in their enthusiasm, they were about to grab him and make him king, so he slipped off and went back up the mountain to be by himself.

16-21 In the evening his disciples went down to the sea, got in the boat, and headed back across the water to Capernaum. It had grown quite dark and Jesus had not yet returned. A huge wind blew up, churning the sea. They were maybe three or four miles out when they saw Jesus walking on the sea, quite near the boat. They were scared senseless, but he reassured them, "It's me. It's all right. Don't be afraid." So they took him on board. In no time they reached land—the exact spot they were headed to.

22-24 The next day the crowd that was left behind realized that there had been only one boat, and that Jesus had not gotten into it with his disciples. They had seen them go off without him. By now boats from Tiberias had pulled up near where they had eaten the bread blessed by the Master. So when the crowd realized he was gone and wasn't coming back, they piled into the Tiberias boats and headed for Capernaum, looking for Jesus.

25 When they found him back across the sea, they said, "Rabbi, when did you get here?"

26 Jesus answered, "You've come looking for me not because you saw God in my actions but because I fed you, filled your stomachs—and for free.

THE BREAD OF LIFE

27 "Don't waste your energy striving for perishable food like that. Work for the food that sticks with you, food that nourishes your lasting life, food the Son of Man provides. He and what he does are guaranteed by God the Father to last."

28 To that they said, "Well, what do we do then to get in on God's works?"

29 Jesus said, "Sign on with the One that God has sent. That kind of a commitment gets you in on God's works."

30-31 They waffled: "Why don't you give us a clue about who you are, just a hint of what's going on? When we see what's up, we'll commit ourselves. Show us what you can do. Moses fed our ancestors with bread in the desert. It says so in the Scriptures: 'He gave them bread from heaven to eat.'"

32-33 Jesus responded, "The real significance of that Scripture is not that Moses gave you bread from heaven but that my Father is right now offering you bread from heaven, the *real* bread. The Bread of God came down out of heaven and is giving life to the world."

34 They jumped at that: "Master, give us this bread, now and forever!"

35-38 Jesus said, "I am the Bread of Life. The person who aligns with me hungers no more and thirsts no more, ever. I have told you this explicitly because even though you have seen me in action, you don't really believe me. Every person the Father gives me eventually comes running to me. And once that person is with me, I hold on and don't let go. I came down from heaven not to follow my own agenda but to accomplish the will of the One who sent me.

39-40 "This, in a nutshell, is that will: that everything handed over to me by the Father be completed—not a single detail missed—and at the wrap-up of time I have everything and everyone put together, upright and whole. This is what my Father wants: that anyone who sees the Son and trusts who he is and what he does and then aligns with him will enter *real* life, *eternal* life. My part is to put them on their feet alive and whole at the completion of time."

41-42 At this, because he said, "I am the Bread that came down from heaven," the Jews started arguing over him: "Isn't this the son of Joseph? Don't we know his father? Don't we know his mother? How can he now say, 'I came down out of heaven' and expect anyone to believe him?"

43-46 Jesus said, "Don't bicker among yourselves over me. You're not in charge here. The Father who sent me is in charge. He draws people to me—that's the only way you'll ever come. Only then do I do my work, putting people together, setting them on their feet, ready for the End. This is what the prophets meant when they wrote, 'And then they will all be personally taught by God.' Anyone who has spent any time at all listening to the Father, really listening and therefore learning, comes to me to be taught personally—to see it with his own eyes, hear it with his own ears, from me, since I have it firsthand from the Father. No one has seen the Father except the One who has his Being alongside the Father—and you can see *me*.

47-51 "I'm telling you the most solemn and sober truth now: Whoever believes in me has real life, eternal life. I am the Bread of Life. Your ancestors ate the manna bread in the desert and died. But now here is Bread that truly comes down out of heaven. Anyone eating this Bread will not die, ever. I am the Bread—living Bread!—who came down out of heaven. Anyone who eats this Bread will live—and forever! The Bread that I present to the world so that it can eat and live is myself, this flesh-and-blood self."

52 At this, the Jews started fighting among themselves: "How can this man serve up his flesh for a meal?"

53-58 But Jesus didn't give an inch. "Only insofar as you eat and drink flesh and blood, the flesh and blood of the Son of Man, do you have life within you. The one who brings a hearty appetite to this eating and drinking has eternal life and will be fit and ready for the Final Day. My flesh is real food and my blood is real drink. By eating my flesh and drinking my blood you enter into me and I into you. In the same way that the fully alive Father sent me here and I live because of him, so the one who makes a meal of me lives because of me. This is the Bread from heaven. Your ancestors ate bread and later died. Whoever eats this Bread will live always."

59 He said these things while teaching in the meeting place in Capernaum.

TOO TOUGH TO SWALLOW

60 Many among his disciples heard this and said, "This is tough teaching, too tough to swallow."

61-65 Jesus sensed that his disciples were having a hard time with this and said, "Does this rattle you completely? What would happen if you saw the Son of Man ascending to where he came from? The Spirit can make life. Sheer muscle and willpower don't make anything happen. Every word I've spoken to you is a Spirit-word, and so it is life-making. But some of you are resisting, refusing to have any part in this." (Jesus knew from the start that some weren't going to risk themselves with him. He knew also who would betray him.) He went on to say, "This is why I told you earlier that no one is capable of coming to me on his own. You get to me only as a gift from the Father."

66-67 After this, many of his disciples left. They no longer wanted to be associated with him. Then Jesus gave the Twelve their chance: "Do you also want to leave?"

68-69 Peter replied, "Master, to whom would we go? You have the words of real life, eternal life. We've already committed ourselves, confident that you are the Holy One of God."

70-71 Jesus responded, "Haven't I handpicked you, the Twelve? Still, one of you is a devil!" He was referring to Judas, son of Simon Iscariot. This man—one from the Twelve!—was even then getting ready to betray him.

7 1-2 Later Jesus was going about his business in Galilee. He didn't want to travel in Judea because the Jews there were looking for a chance to kill him. It was near the time of Tabernacles, a feast observed annually by the Jews.

3-5 His brothers said, "Why don't you leave here and go up to the Feast so your disciples can get a good look at the works you do? No one who intends to be publicly known does everything behind the scenes. If you're serious about what you are doing, come out in the open and show the world." His brothers were pushing him like this because they didn't believe in him either.

6-8 Jesus came back at them, "Don't pressure me. This isn't my time. It's your time—it's *always* your time; you have nothing to lose. The world has nothing against you, but it's up in arms against me. It's against me because I expose the evil behind its pretensions. You go ahead, go up to the Feast. Don't wait for me. I'm not ready. It's not the right time for me."

9-11 He said this and stayed on in Galilee. But later, after his family had gone up to the Feast, he also went. But he kept out of the way, careful not to draw attention to himself. The Jews were already out looking for him, asking around, "Where is that man?"

12-13 There was a lot of contentious talk about him circulating through the crowds. Some were saying, "He's a good man." But others said, "Not so. He's selling snake oil." This kind of talk went on in guarded whispers because of the intimidating Jewish leaders.

COULD IT BE THE MESSIAH?

14-15 With the Feast already half over, Jesus showed up in the Temple, teaching. The Jews were impressed, but puzzled: "How does he know so much without being schooled?"

16-19 Jesus said, "I didn't make this up. What I teach comes from the One who sent me. Anyone who wants to do his will can test this teaching and know whether it's from God or whether I'm making it up. A person making things up tries to make himself look good. But someone trying to honor the one who sent him sticks to the facts and doesn't tamper with reality. It was Moses, wasn't it, who gave you God's Law? But none of you are living it. So why are you trying to kill me?"

20 The crowd said, "You're crazy! Who's trying to kill you? You're demon-possessed."

21-24 Jesus said, "I did one miraculous thing a few months ago, and you're still standing around getting all upset, wondering what I'm up to. Moses prescribed circumcision—originally it came not from Moses but from his ancestors—and so you circumcise a man, dealing with one part of his body, even if it's the Sabbath. You do this in order to preserve one item in the Law of Moses. So why are you upset with me because I made a man's whole body well on the Sabbath? Don't be hypercritical; use your head—and heart!—to discern what is right, to test what is authentically right."

25-27 That's when some of the people of Jerusalem said, "Isn't this the one they were out to kill? And here he is out in the open, saying whatever he pleases, and no one is stopping him. Could it be that the rulers know that he is, in fact, the Messiah? And yet we know where this man came from. The Messiah is going to come out of nowhere. Nobody is going to know where he comes from."

28-29 That provoked Jesus, who was teaching in the Temple, to cry out, "Yes, you think you know me and where I'm from, but that's not where I'm from. I didn't set myself up in business. My true origin is in the One who sent me, and you don't know him at all. I come from him—that's how I know him. He sent me here."

30-31 They were looking for a way to arrest him, but not a hand was laid on him because it wasn't yet God's time. Many from the crowd committed themselves in faith to him, saying, "Will the Messiah, when he comes, provide better or more convincing evidence than this?"

32-34 The Pharisees, alarmed at this seditious undertow going through the crowd, teamed up with the high priests and sent their police to arrest him. Jesus rebuffed them: "I am with you only a short time. Then I go on to the One who sent me. You will look for me, but you won't find me. Where I am, you can't come."

35-36 The Jews put their heads together. "Where do you think he is going that we won't be able to find him? Do you think he is about to travel to the Greek world to teach the Jews? What is he talking about, anyway: 'You will look for me, but you won't find me,' and 'Where I am, you can't come'?"

37-39 On the final and climactic day of the Feast, Jesus took his stand. He cried out, "If anyone thirsts, let him come to me and drink. Rivers of living water will brim and spill out of the depths of anyone who believes in me this way, just as the Scripture says." (He said this in regard to the Spirit, whom those who believed in him were about to receive. The Spirit had not yet been given because Jesus had not yet been glorified.)

40-44 Those in the crowd who heard these words were saying, "This has to be the Prophet." Others said, "He is the Messiah!" But others were saying, "The Messiah doesn't come from Galilee, does he? Don't the Scriptures tell us that the Messiah comes from David's line and from Bethlehem, David's village?" So there was a split in the crowd over him. Some went so far as wanting to arrest him, but no one laid a hand on him.

45 That's when the Temple police reported back to the high priests and Pharisees, who demanded, "Why didn't you bring him with you?"

46 The police answered, "Have you heard the way he talks? We've never heard anyone speak like this man."

47-49 The Pharisees said, "Are you carried away like the rest of the rabble? You don't see any of the leaders believing in him, do you? Or any from the Pharisees? It's only this crowd, ignorant of God's Law, that is taken in by him—and damned."

50-51 Nicodemus, the man who had come to Jesus earlier and was both a ruler and a Pharisee, spoke up. "Does our Law decide about a man's guilt without first listening to him and finding out what he is doing?"

52-53 But they cut him off. "Are you also campaigning for the Galilean? Examine the evidence. See if any prophet ever comes from Galilee."

[Then they all went home.

TO THROW THE STONE

8 1-2 Jesus went across to Mount Olives, but he was soon back in the Temple again. Swarms of people came to him. He sat down and taught them.

3-6 The religion scholars and Pharisees led in a woman who had been caught in an act of adultery. They stood her in plain sight of everyone and said, "Teacher, this woman was caught red-handed in the act of adultery. Moses, in the Law, gives orders to stone such persons. What do you say?" They were trying to trap him into saying something incriminating so they could bring charges against him.

6-8 Jesus bent down and wrote with his finger in the dirt. They kept at him, badgering him. He straightened up and said, "The sinless one among you, go first: Throw the stone." Bending down again, he wrote some more in the dirt.

9-10 Hearing that, they walked away, one after another, beginning with the oldest. The woman was left alone. Jesus stood up and spoke to her. "Woman, where are they? Does no one condemn you?"

11 "No one, Master."

"Neither do I," said Jesus. "Go on your way. From now on, don't sin."]

Note: John 7:53–8:11 [the portion in brackets] is not found in the earliest handwritten copies.

YOU'RE MISSING GOD IN ALL THIS

12 Jesus once again addressed them: "I am the world's Light. No one who follows me stumbles around in the darkness. I provide plenty of light to live in."

13 The Pharisees objected, "All we have is your word on this. We need more than this to go on."

14-18 Jesus replied, "You're right that you only have my word. But you can depend on it being true. I know where I've come from and where I go next. You don't know where I'm from or where I'm headed. You decide according to what you can see and touch. I don't make judgments like that. But even if I did, my judgment would be true because I wouldn't make it out of the narrowness of my experience but in the largeness of the One who sent me, the Father. That fulfills the conditions set down in God's Law: that you can count on the testimony of two witnesses. And that is what you have: You have my word and you have the word of the Father who sent me."

19 They said, "Where is this so-called Father of yours?"

Jesus said, "You're looking right at me and you don't see me. How do you expect to see the Father? If you knew me, you would at the same time know the Father."

20 He gave this speech in the Treasury while teaching in the Temple. No one arrested him because his time wasn't yet up.

THE WOMAN CAUGHT IN ADULTERY

This entry and the passage it addresses involve highly sensitive topics that might be triggering to some readers. If that is you, be gentle with yourself.

The woman caught in adultery. She was nameless, naked, guilty. She was subject to punishment by stoning, and the man caught with her was not, which indicates that she was probably unmarried. Little else is known about her; but then again, this is not really her story. This woman was a character in a scene, a pawn in the Pharisees' divisive plan to trap Jesus. She was guilt personified, a dehumanized object used to turn eyes back to the law, judgment, and rightness. Dragged to the Temple, she knew death was imminent.

John does not describe the woman's outward emotions. He does not speculate about her thoughts. The woman heard the Pharisees ask Jesus, "What do you say?" (John 8:5). They waited for an answer; so did she. She watched Jesus dismiss their question by stooping to write in the dust. Meanwhile, angry men stooped to grab rocks.

Then Jesus said, "The sinless one among you, go first" (John 8:7). Had she heard him correctly? More importantly, had the men heard him correctly? Would their hypocrisy be as exposed as her guilt had been? She watched each man set down his stone and exit.

Jesus met the woman's gaze and spoke to her, a sharp contrast to the depersonalizing actions of her accusers. Her answer was stripped of superfluous defense or apology, but she used the word *Master* (John 8:11). Was she employing courtesy or reverence? We don't know. But just as Jesus' words had awakened the guilt of her accusers, we can imagine that his mercy also effectively awakened the conscience of the accused woman.

Before Jesus' mercy, the woman had been a nameless adulterer; after it, she became a woman freed from condemnation, free to go and sin no more. Condemnation could not transform her. But being seen through the eyes of mercy may have changed her life.

21 Then he went over the same ground again. "I'm leaving and you are going to look for me, but you're missing God in this and are headed for a dead end. There is no way you can come with me."

22 The Jews said, "So, is he going to kill himself? Is that what he means by 'You can't come with me'?"

23-24 Jesus said, "You're tied down to the mundane; I'm in touch with what is beyond your horizons. You live in terms of what you see and touch. I'm living on other terms. I told you that you were missing God in all this. You're at a dead end. If you won't believe I am who I say I am, you're at the dead end of sins. You're missing God in your lives."

25-26 They said to him, "Just who are you anyway?"

Jesus said, "What I've said from the start. I have so many things to say that concern you, judgments to make that affect you, but if you don't accept the trustworthiness of the One who commanded my words and acts, none of it matters. That is who you are questioning—not me but the One who sent me."

27-29 They still didn't get it, didn't realize that he was referring to the Father. So Jesus tried again. "When you raise up the Son of Man, then you will know who I am—that I'm not making this up, but speaking only what the Father taught me. The One who sent me stays with me. He doesn't abandon me. He sees how much joy I take in pleasing him."

30 When he put it in these terms, many people decided to believe.

IF THE SON SETS YOU FREE

31-32 Then Jesus turned to the Jews who had claimed to believe in him. "If you stick with this, living out what I tell you, you are my disciples for sure. Then you will experience for yourselves the truth, and the truth will free you."

33 Surprised, they said, "But we're descendants of Abraham. We've never been slaves to anyone. How can you say, 'The truth will free you'?"

34-38 Jesus said, "I tell you most solemnly that anyone who chooses a life of sin is trapped in a dead-end life and is, in fact, a slave. A slave can't come and go at will. The Son, though, has an established position, the run of the house. So if the Son sets you free, you are free through and through. I know you are Abraham's descendants. But I also know that you are trying to kill me because my message hasn't yet penetrated your thick skulls. I'm talking about things I have seen while keeping company with the Father, and you just go on doing what you have heard from your father."

39-41 They were indignant. "Our father is Abraham!"

Jesus said, "If you were Abraham's children, you would have been doing the things Abraham did. And yet here you are trying to kill me, a man who has spoken to you the truth he got straight from God! Abraham never did that sort of thing. You persist in repeating the works of your father."

They said, "We're not bastards. We have a legitimate father: the one and only God."

42-47 "If God were your father," said Jesus, "you would love me, for I came from God and arrived here. I didn't come on my own. He sent me. Why can't you understand one word I say? Here's why: You can't handle it. You're from your father, the Devil, and all you want to do is please him. He was a killer from the very start. He couldn't stand the truth because there wasn't a shred of truth in him. When the Liar speaks, he makes it up out of his lying nature and fills the world with lies. I arrive on the scene, tell you the plain truth, and you refuse to have a thing to do with me. Can any one of you convict me of a single misleading word, a single sinful act? But if I'm telling the truth, why don't you believe me? Anyone on God's side listens to God's words. This is why you're not listening—because you're not on God's side."

I AM WHO I AM

48 The Jews then said, "That settles it. We were right all along when we called you a Samaritan and said you were crazy—demon-possessed!"

49-51 Jesus said, "I'm not crazy. I simply honor my Father, while you dishonor me. I am not trying to get anything for myself. God intends something gloriously grand here and is making the decisions that will bring it about. I say this with absolute confidence. If you practice what I'm telling you, you'll never have to look death in the face."

52-53 At this point the Jews said, "Now we *know* you're crazy. Abraham died. The prophets died. And you show up saying, 'If you practice what I'm telling you, you'll never have to face death, not even a taste.' Are you greater than Abraham, who died? And the prophets died! Who do you think you are!"

54-56 Jesus said, "If I were striving to get all

One Hand Alone Cannot Clap

Just as one hand alone cannot clap, neither is adultery committed solely by one person.

Jesus was teaching in the Temple when religion scholars and Pharisees burst in, interrupting to declare that the woman in their custody had been "caught red-handed in the act of adultery" (John 8:4). There was, however, a critical piece of missing evidence: the presentation—or at minimum, the identification—of her abettor.

Have you ever encountered a tattletale? Tattling is snitching, carrying tales for no good, revealing secrets not yours to divulge. There were few greater failings in my childhood than being branded a talebearer—a label that extends as far back as ancient times.

There is so much wrong in John 8:1-11. The scholars and Pharisees disrupted Christ's teaching in the Temple. They publicly shamed and accused a woman, failing to either produce an accomplice or to present evidence. Their sole purpose in barging in was itself hypocrisy; they were trying to trap Jesus into incorrectly applying ancient Jewish law, which said, "If a man is found sleeping with another man's wife, both must die" (Deuteronomy 22:22).

Further pressing their case, they continued: "Moses, in the Law, gives orders to stone such persons. What do you say?" (John 8:5).

Preoccupied with making accusations under the law, they did not abide by the admonishment "Don't spread gossip and rumors" (Leviticus 19:16). The Talmud reinforces this command, forbidding anything negative spoken about a fellow Jew, false or true. This prohibition is of *lashon hara*, "malicious speech"—and the scholars and Pharisees knew it.

Jesus, whom I envision wearing a knowing look, said nothing, preferring to quietly write in the dirt. Aggrieved and sanctimonious, the scholars and Pharisees pressed their case, taunting him to self-incriminate. It didn't work. Finally, he challenged their commitment to malicious behavior, advising, "The sinless one among you, go first: Throw the stone" (John 8:7).

What could they do? Led by the eldest among them, they retreated in silence, one by one.

Jesus was alone then, except for the woman. We have no idea what he wrote. Was it a word from the prophets? Was it a list of names? Was it a revelation specific to each who read it?

He rose from his writing, addressing her directly. "Woman, where are they? Does no one condemn you?"

"No one, Master."

"Neither do I," Jesus said. "Go on your way. From now on, don't sin" (John 8:10-11).

Faith does not promise that we will not suffer from unjust plots and accusations. We do not believe ourselves to be immune to assault. However, the prophet Isaiah declared God's assurance that although weapons might be forged against us, while we are under God's care, they cannot cause us harm (see Isaiah 54:17). As God's beloveds, we know that everything works out ultimately for our good.

Was that the message Jesus sketched on the ground?

the attention, it wouldn't amount to anything. But my Father, the same One you say is your Father, put me here at this time and place of splendor. You haven't recognized him in this. But I have. If I, in false modesty, said I didn't know what was going on, I would be as much of a liar as you are. But I do know, and I am doing what he says. Abraham—your 'father'—with elated faith looked down the corridors of history and saw my day coming. He saw it and cheered."

57 The Jews said, "You're not even fifty years old—and Abraham saw you?"

58 "Believe me," said Jesus, "*I am who I am* long before Abraham was anything."

59 That did it—pushed them over the edge. They picked up rocks to throw at him. But Jesus slipped away, getting out of the Temple.

TRUE BLINDNESS

9 1-2 Walking down the street, Jesus saw a man blind from birth. His disciples asked, "Rabbi, who sinned: this man or his parents, causing him to be born blind?"

3-5 Jesus said, "You're asking the wrong question. You're looking for someone to blame. There is no such cause-effect here. Look instead for what God can do. We need to be energetically at work for the One who sent me here, working while the sun shines. When night falls, the workday is over. For as long as I am in the world, there is plenty of light. I am the world's Light."

6-7 He said this and then spit in the dust, made a clay paste with the saliva, rubbed the paste on the blind man's eyes, and said, "Go, wash at the Pool of Siloam" (Siloam means "Sent"). The man went and washed—and saw.

8 Soon the town was buzzing. His relatives and those who year after year had seen him as a blind man begging were saying, "Why, isn't this the man we knew, who sat here and begged?"

9 Others said, "It's him all right!"

But others objected, "It's not the same man at all. It just looks like him."

He said, "It's me, the very one."

10 They said, "How did your eyes get opened?"

11 "A man named Jesus made a paste and rubbed it on my eyes and told me, 'Go to Siloam and wash.' I did what he said. When I washed, I saw."

12 "So where is he?"

"I don't know."

13-15 They marched the man to the Pharisees. This day when Jesus made the paste and healed his blindness was the Sabbath. The Pharisees grilled him again on how he had come to see. He said, "He put a clay paste on my eyes, and I washed, and now I see."

16 Some of the Pharisees said, "Obviously, this man can't be from God. He doesn't keep the Sabbath."

Others countered, "How can a bad man do miraculous, God-revealing things like this?" There was a split in their ranks.

17 They came back at the blind man, "You're the expert. He opened *your* eyes. What do you say about him?"

He said, "He is a prophet."

18-19 The Jews didn't believe it, didn't believe the man was blind to begin with. So they called the parents of the man now bright-eyed with sight. They asked them, "Is this your son, the one you say was born blind? So how is it that he now sees?"

20-23 His parents said, "We know he is our son, and we know he was born blind. But we don't know how he came to see—haven't a clue about who opened his eyes. Why don't you ask him? He's a grown man and can speak for himself." (His parents were talking like this because they were intimidated by the Jewish leaders, who had already decided that anyone who took a stand that this was the Messiah would be kicked out of the meeting place. That's why his parents said, "Ask him. He's a grown man.")

24 They called the man back a second time—the man who had been blind—and told him, "Give credit to God. We know this man is an impostor."

25 He replied, "I know nothing about that one way or the other. But I know one thing for sure: I was blind . . . I now see."

26 They said, "What did he do to you? How did he open your eyes?"

27 "I've told you over and over and you haven't listened. Why do you want to hear it again? Are you so eager to become his disciples?"

28-29 With that they jumped all over him. "*You* might be a disciple of that man, but we're disciples of Moses. We know for sure that God spoke to Moses, but we have no idea where this man even comes from."

30-33 The man replied, "This is amazing! You claim to know nothing about him, but the fact is, he opened my eyes! It's well known that God isn't at the beck and call of sinners, but listens carefully to anyone who lives in reverence and does his will. That someone opened the eyes of a man born blind has never been heard of—ever. If this man didn't come from God, he wouldn't be able to do anything."

34 They said, "You're nothing but dirt! How dare you take that tone with us!" Then they threw him out in the street.

35 Jesus heard that they had thrown him out, and went and found him. He asked him, "Do you believe in the Son of Man?"

36 The man said, "Point him out to me, sir, so that I can believe in him."

37 Jesus said, "You're looking right at him. Don't you recognize my voice?"

38 "Master, I believe," the man said, and worshiped him.

39 Jesus then said, "I came into the world to bring everything into the clear light of day, making all the distinctions clear, so that those who have never seen will see, and those who have made a great pretense of seeing will be exposed as blind."

40 Some Pharisees overheard him and said, "Does that mean you're calling us blind?"

41 Jesus said, "If you were really blind, you would be blameless, but since you claim to see everything so well, you're accountable for every fault and failure."

HE CALLS HIS SHEEP BY NAME

10 1-5 "Let me set this before you as plainly as I can. If a person climbs over or through the fence of a sheep pen instead of going through the gate, you know he's up to no good—a sheep rustler! The shepherd walks right up to the gate. The gatekeeper opens the gate to him and the sheep recognize his voice. He calls his own sheep by name and leads them out. When he gets them all out, he leads them and they follow because they are familiar with his voice. They won't follow a stranger's voice but will scatter because they aren't used to the sound of it."

6-10 Jesus told this simple story, but they had no idea what he was talking about. So he tried again. "I'll be explicit, then. I am the Gate for the sheep. All those others are up to no good—sheep rustlers, every one of them. But the sheep didn't listen to them. I am the Gate. Anyone who goes through me will be cared for—will freely go in and out, and find pasture. A thief is only there to steal and kill and destroy. I came so they can have real and eternal life, more and better life than they ever dreamed of.

11-13 "I am the Good Shepherd. The Good Shepherd puts the sheep before himself, sacrifices himself if necessary. A hired man is not a real shepherd. The sheep mean nothing to him. He sees a wolf come and runs for it, leaving the sheep to be ravaged and scattered by the wolf. He's only in it for the money. The sheep don't matter to him.

14-18 "I am the Good Shepherd. I know my own sheep and my own sheep know me. In the same way, the Father knows me and I know the Father. I put the sheep before myself, sacrificing myself if necessary. You need to know that I have other sheep in addition to those in this pen. I need to gather and bring them, too. They'll also recognize my voice. Then it will be one flock, one Shepherd. This is why the Father loves me: because I freely lay down my life. And so I am free to take it up again. No one takes it from me. I lay it down of my own free will. I have the right to lay it down; I also have the right to take it up again. I received this authority personally from my Father."

19-21 This kind of talk caused another split in the Jewish ranks. A lot of them were saying, "He's crazy, a maniac—out of his head completely. Why bother listening to him?" But others weren't so sure: "These aren't the words of a crazy man. Can a 'maniac' open blind eyes?"

▲ ▲ ▲

22-24 They were celebrating Hanukkah just then in Jerusalem. It was winter. Jesus was strolling in the Temple across Solomon's Porch. The Jews, circling him, said, "How long are you going to keep us guessing? If you're the Messiah, tell us straight out."

25-30 Jesus answered, "I told you, but you don't believe. Everything I have done has been authorized by my Father, actions that speak louder than words. You don't believe because you're not my sheep. My sheep recognize my voice. I know them, and they follow me. I give them real and eternal life. They are protected from the Destroyer for good. No one can steal them from out of my hand. The Father who put them under my care is so much greater than the Destroyer and Thief. No one could ever get them away from him. I and the Father are one heart and mind."

31-32 Again the Jews picked up rocks to throw at him. Jesus said, "I have made a present to you from the Father of a great many good actions. For which of these acts do you stone me?"

33 The Jews said, "We're not stoning you for anything good you did, but for what you said—this blasphemy of calling yourself God."

34-38 Jesus said, "I'm only quoting your inspired Scriptures, where God said, 'I tell you—you are gods.' If God called your ancestors 'gods'—and Scripture doesn't lie—why do you yell, 'Blasphemer! Blasphemer!' at the unique One the Father consecrated and sent into the world, just because I said, 'I am the Son of God'? If I don't do the things my Father does, well and good; don't believe me. But if I am doing them, put aside for a moment what you hear me say about myself and just take the evidence of the actions that are right before your eyes. Then perhaps things will come together for you, and you'll see that not only are we doing the same thing, we *are* the same—Father and Son. He is in me; I am in him."

39-42 They tried yet again to arrest him, but he slipped through their fingers. He went back across the Jordan to the place where John first baptized, and stayed there. A lot of people followed him over. They were saying, "John did no miracles, but everything he said about this man has come true." Many believed in him then and there.

THE DEATH OF LAZARUS

11 1-3 A man was sick, Lazarus of Bethany, the town of Mary and her sister Martha. This was the same Mary who massaged the Lord's feet with aromatic oils and then wiped them with her hair. It was her brother Lazarus who was sick. So the sisters sent word to Jesus, "Master, the one you love so very much is sick."

4 When Jesus got the message, he said, "This sickness is not fatal. It will become an occasion to show God's glory by glorifying God's Son."

5-7 Jesus loved Martha and her sister and Lazarus, but oddly, when he heard that Lazarus was sick, he stayed on where he was for two more days. After the two days, he said to his disciples, "Let's go back to Judea."

8 They said, "Rabbi, you can't do that. The Jews are out to kill you, and you're going back?"

9-10 Jesus replied, "Are there not twelve hours of daylight? Anyone who walks in daylight doesn't stumble because there's plenty of light from the sun. Walking at night, he might very well stumble because he can't see where he's going."

11 He said these things, and then announced, "Our friend Lazarus has fallen asleep. I'm going to wake him up."

12-13 The disciples said, "Master, if he's gone to sleep, he'll get a good rest and wake up feeling fine." Jesus was talking about death, while his disciples thought he was talking about taking a nap.

14-15 Then Jesus became explicit: "Lazarus died. And I am glad for your sakes that I wasn't there. You're about to be given new grounds for believing. Now let's go to him."

16 That's when Thomas, the one called the Twin, said to his companions, "Come along. We might as well die with him."

17-20 When Jesus finally got there, he found Lazarus already four days dead. Bethany was near Jerusalem, only a couple of miles away, and many of the Jews were visiting Martha and Mary, sympathizing with them over their brother. Martha heard Jesus was coming and went out to meet him. Mary remained in the house.

21-22 Martha said, "Master, if you'd been here, my brother wouldn't have died. Even now, I know that whatever you ask God he will give you."

23 Jesus said, "Your brother will be raised up."

24 Martha replied, "I know that he will be raised up in the resurrection at the end of time."

25-26 "You don't have to wait for the End. I am, right now, Resurrection and Life. The one who believes in me, even though he or she dies, will live. And everyone who lives believing in me does not ultimately die at all. Do you believe this?"

27 "Yes, Master. All along I have believed that you are the Messiah, the Son of God who comes into the world."

28 After saying this, she went to her sister Mary and whispered in her ear, "The Teacher is here and is asking for you."

29-32 The moment she heard that, she jumped up and ran out to him. Jesus had not yet entered the town but was still at the place where Martha had met him. When her sympathizing Jewish friends saw Mary run off, they followed her, thinking she was on her way to the tomb to weep there. Mary came to where Jesus was waiting and fell at his feet, saying, "Master, if only you had been here, my brother would not have died."

33-34 When Jesus saw her sobbing and the Jews with her sobbing, a deep anger welled

When Jesus Disappoints

When my husband was diagnosed with stage 4 cancer and graduated to heaven three short months later, the story of Jesus, Mary, Martha, and Lazarus became deeply meaningful to me. Here we find a comingling of two weighty themes: dealing with disappointment and the power of belief.

Jesus received word from his dear friends Mary and Martha that their brother was gravely ill. He assured his disciples that the sickness Lazarus faced would be "an occasion to show God's glory by glorifying God's Son" (John 11:4).

Given the seriousness of Lazarus's illness, we might have expected Jesus to respond right away. However, he lingered for two more days before heading out to Judea, where his friends lived.

During that time, Lazarus died.

When Jesus arrived on the scene, he was greeted on the road by Martha. She complained, "Master, if you'd been here, my brother wouldn't have died" (John 11:21). Her sentiment is relatable: Disappointment is born of unfulfilled hope.

But Martha's disappointment emerged alongside belief. "Even now, I know that whatever you ask God he will give you" (John 11:22). Her disappointment did not cloud her core belief in who Jesus was and why he came to earth.

Jesus responded: "I am, right now, Resurrection and Life. The one who believes in me, even though he or she dies, will live" (John 11:25).

Jesus underscored the power of belief. There will soon be a whole different life—an eternal life—for those who believe in him. Jesus wanted to be sure Martha heard this.

Then Martha's sister, Mary, ran to meet the beloved teacher and greeted him with similar words. She, too, expressed disappointment that Jesus had not come earlier. Mary's sorrow evoked emotion in Jesus, and he wept with these dear friends.

Jesus knew he was about to perform a resurrection miracle for Lazarus, yet he took time to grieve with the women. This tender sharing of sorrow shows how deeply Jesus cares about our disappointment, our doubts, our discouragement.

Grief and glory are constantly comingling. When my husband was diagnosed with cancer, we prayed fervently for the healing of his body. We believed that God could perform a miracle. Yet God chose to heal my husband in heaven rather than on this earth. I am not grateful for his death or our suffering, but I am grateful for how God transformed our grief. In the midst of loss, God provided me with family and a chapter of our story I would never have imagined. We grieve the loss of my husband while we live out his legacy of faith.

In life, we will experience prayers that are not answered the way we hope. Jesus meets us in our disappointment and sits with us in our tears—then offers us the expansive hope of glory.

up within him. He said, "Where did you put him?"

34-35 "Master, come and see," they said. Now Jesus wept.

36 The Jews said, "Look how deeply he loved him."

37 Others among them said, "Well, if he loved him so much, why didn't he do something to keep him from dying? After all, he opened the eyes of a blind man."

38-39 Then Jesus, the anger again welling up within him, arrived at the tomb. It was a simple cave in the hillside with a slab of stone laid against it. Jesus said, "Remove the stone."

The sister of the dead man, Martha, said, "Master, by this time there's a stench. He's been dead four days!"

40 Jesus looked her in the eye. "Didn't I tell you that if you believed, you would see the glory of God?"

41-42 Then, to the others, "Go ahead, take away the stone."

They removed the stone. Jesus raised his eyes to heaven and prayed, "Father, I'm grateful that you have listened to me. I know you always do listen, but on account of this crowd standing here I've spoken so that they might believe that you sent me."

43-44 Then he shouted, "Lazarus, come out!" And he came out, a cadaver, wrapped from head to toe, and with a kerchief over his face.

Jesus told them, "Unwrap him and let him loose."

THE MAN WHO CREATES GOD-SIGNS

45-48 That was a turning point for many of the Jews who were with Mary. They saw what Jesus did, and believed in him. But some went back to the Pharisees and told on Jesus. The high priests and Pharisees called a meeting of the Jewish ruling body. "What do we do now?" they asked. "This man keeps on doing things, creating God-signs. If we let him go on, pretty soon everyone will be believing in him and the Romans will come and remove what little power and privilege we still have."

49-52 Then one of them—it was Caiaphas, the designated Chief Priest that year—spoke up, "Don't you know anything? Can't you see that it's to our advantage that one man dies for the people rather than the whole nation be destroyed?" He didn't say this of his own accord, but as Chief Priest that year he unwittingly prophesied that Jesus was about to die sacrificially for the nation, and not only for the nation but so that all God's exile-scattered children might be gathered together into one people.

53-54 From that day on, they plotted to kill him. So Jesus no longer went out in public among the Jews. He withdrew into the country bordering the desert to a town called Ephraim and secluded himself there with his disciples.

55-56 The Jewish Passover was coming up. Crowds of people were making their way from the country up to Jerusalem to get themselves ready for the Feast. They were curious about Jesus. There was a lot of talk of him among those standing around in the Temple: "What do you think? Do you think he'll show up at the Feast or not?"

57 Meanwhile, the high priests and Pharisees gave out the word that anyone who knew his whereabouts should inform them. They were all set to arrest him.

ANOINTING HIS FEET

12 1-3 Six days before Passover, Jesus entered Bethany where Lazarus, so recently raised from the dead, was living. Lazarus and his sisters invited Jesus to dinner at their home. Martha served. Lazarus was one of those sitting at the table with them. Mary came in with a jar of very expensive aromatic oils, anointed and massaged Jesus' feet, and then wiped them with her hair. The fragrance of the oils filled the house.

4-6 Judas Iscariot, one of his disciples, even then getting ready to betray him, said, "Why wasn't this oil sold and the money given to the poor? It would have easily brought three hundred silver pieces." He said this not because he cared two cents about the poor but because he was a thief. He was in charge of their common funds, but also embezzled them.

7-8 Jesus said, "Let her alone. She's anticipating and honoring the day of my burial. You always have the poor with you. You don't always have me."

9-11 Word got out among the Jews that he was back in town. The people came to take a look, not only at Jesus but also at Lazarus, who had been raised from the dead. So the high priests plotted to kill Lazarus because so many of the Jews were going over and believing in Jesus on account of him.

SEE HOW YOUR KING COMES

12-15 The next day the huge crowd that had arrived for the Feast heard that Jesus was entering Jerusalem. They broke off palm branches and went out to meet him. And they cheered:

> Hosanna!
> Blessed is he who comes in God's name!
> Yes! The King of Israel!

Jesus got a young donkey and rode it, just as the Scripture has it:

> No fear, Daughter Zion:
> See how your king comes,
> riding a donkey's colt.

16 The disciples didn't notice the fulfillment of many Scriptures at the time, but after Jesus was glorified, they remembered that what was written about him matched what was done to him.

17-19 The crowd that had been with him when he called Lazarus from the tomb, raising him from the dead, was there giving eyewitness accounts. It was because they had spread the word of this latest God-sign that the crowd swelled to a welcoming parade. The Pharisees took one look and threw up their hands: "It's out of control. The world's in a stampede after him."

A GRAIN OF WHEAT MUST DIE

20-21 There were some Greeks in town who had come up to worship at the Feast. They approached Philip, who was from Bethsaida in Galilee: "Sir, we want to see Jesus. Can you help us?"

22-23 Philip went and told Andrew. Andrew and Philip together told Jesus. Jesus answered, "Time's up. The time has come for the Son of Man to be glorified.

24-25 "Listen carefully: Unless a grain of wheat is buried in the ground, dead to the world, it is never any more than a grain of wheat. But if it is buried, it sprouts and reproduces itself many times over. In the same way, anyone who holds on to life just as it is destroys that life. But if you let it go, reckless in your love, you'll have it forever, real and eternal.

26 "If any of you wants to serve me, then follow me. Then you'll be where I am, ready to serve at a moment's notice. The Father will honor and reward anyone who serves me.

27-28 "Right now I am shaken. And what am I going to say? 'Father, get me out of this'? No, this is why I came in the first place. I'll say, 'Father, put your glory on display.'"

A voice came out of the sky: "I have glorified it, and I'll glorify it again."

29 The listening crowd said, "Thunder!" Others said, "An angel spoke to him!"

30-33 Jesus said, "The voice didn't come for me but for you. At this moment the world is in crisis. Now Satan, the ruler of this world, will be thrown out. And I, as I am lifted up from the earth, will attract everyone to me and gather them around me." He put it this way to show how he was going to be put to death.

34 Voices from the crowd answered, "We heard from God's Law that the Messiah lasts forever. How can it be necessary, as you put it, that the Son of Man 'be lifted up'? Who is this 'Son of Man'?"

35-36 Jesus said, "For a brief time still, the light is among you. Walk by the light you have so darkness doesn't destroy you. If you walk in darkness, you don't know where you're going. As you have the light, believe in the light. Then the light will be within you, and shining through your lives. You'll be children of light."

THEIR EYES ARE BLINDED

36-40 Jesus said all this, and then went into hiding. All these God-signs he had given them and they still didn't get it, still wouldn't trust him. This proved that the prophet Isaiah was right:

> God, who believed what we preached?
> Who recognized God's arm, outstretched
> and ready to act?

First they wouldn't believe, then they *couldn't*—again, just as Isaiah said:

> Their eyes are blinded,
> their hearts are hardened,
> So that they wouldn't see with their eyes
> and perceive with their hearts,
> And turn to me, God,
> so I could heal them.

41 Isaiah said these things after he got a glimpse of God's overflowing glory that would pour through the Messiah.

42-43 On the other hand, a considerable number from the ranks of the leaders did believe. But because of the Pharisees, they didn't come out in the open with it. They were afraid of getting kicked out of the meeting place. When push came to shove they cared more for human approval than for God's glory.

MARY AND MARTHA

The Bible lets us peek at several family conflicts created by sibling rivalry. Although Mary and Martha are often seen as pitted against each other, their primary identity was not as quarreling sisters: Rather, it was as close friends of Jesus.

In the moment described in John 12:1-11, both Martha and Mary served Jesus. Martha prepared a meal. Mary anointed Jesus' feet. Both actions were equally valuable acts of worship; after all, everything we do in the name of the Lord is an act of worship. Jesus didn't bring attention to the different ways the sisters expressed their worship. However, when Judas (who would later betray Jesus) claimed that Mary was being wasteful, Jesus defended her extravagant act of devotion.

The sisters remind us that God has given each of us a unique personality that determines how we relate to God and others and how we choose to serve and spend time with Jesus. Martha showed her love with acts of service, honoring Jesus' presence. Mary showed her love by sitting at his feet and listening; she, too, honored his presence.

Martha and Mary reveal the complexity of hospitality and of developing relationships with others. While one sister prepared a meal to show the guests they were welcomed and loved, the other sister paused to give her full attention and make the guests *feel* welcomed and loved. Yes, Mary could have helped Martha with a few things and then returned to sit at Jesus' feet. And yes, Martha could have lessened the workload, dropping a few items off the menu to create time to sit with the guests and join her sister by Jesus.

Neither sister was wrong in her approach to their friend and teacher. These sisters demonstrate that the best way to show love is to approach God as we are and with confidence in God's love for us.

44-46 Jesus summed it all up when he cried out, "Whoever believes in me, believes not just in me but in the One who sent me. Whoever looks at me is looking, in fact, at the One who sent me. I am Light that has come into the world so that all who believe in me won't have to stay any longer in the dark.

47-50 "If anyone hears what I am saying and doesn't take it seriously, I don't reject him. I didn't come to reject the world; I came to save the world. But you need to know that whoever puts me off, refusing to take in what I'm saying, is willfully choosing rejection. The Word, the Word-made-flesh that I have spoken and that I am, *that* Word and no other is the last word. I'm not making any of this up on my own. The Father who sent me gave me orders, told me what to say and how to say it. And I know exactly what his command produces: real and eternal life. That's all I have to say. What the Father told me, I tell you."

WASHING HIS DISCIPLES' FEET

13 1-2 Just before the Passover Feast, Jesus knew that the time had come to leave this world to go to the Father. Having loved his dear companions, he continued to love them right to the end. It was suppertime. The Devil by now had Judas, son of Simon the Iscariot, firmly in his grip, all set for the betrayal.

3-6 Jesus knew that the Father had put him in complete charge of everything, that he came from God and was on his way back to God. So he got up from the supper table, set aside his robe, and put on an apron. Then he poured water into a basin and began to wash the feet of the disciples, drying them with his apron. When he got to Simon Peter, Peter said, "Master, *you* wash *my* feet?"

7 Jesus answered, "You don't understand now what I'm doing, but it will be clear enough to you later."

8 Peter persisted, "You're not going to wash my feet—ever!"

Jesus said, "If I don't wash you, you can't be part of what I'm doing."

9 "Master!" said Peter. "Not only my feet, then. Wash my hands! Wash my head!"

10-12 Jesus said, "If you've had a bath in the morning, you only need your feet washed now and you're clean from head to toe. My concern, you understand, is holiness, not hygiene. So now you're clean. But not every one of you." (He knew who was betraying him. That's why he said, "Not every one of you.") After he had finished washing their feet, he took his robe, put it back on, and went back to his place at the table.

12-17 Then he said, "Do you understand what I have done to you? You address me as 'Teacher' and 'Master,' and rightly so. That is what I am. So if I, the Master and Teacher, washed your feet, you must now wash each other's feet. I've laid down a pattern for you. What I've done, you do. I'm only pointing out the obvious. A servant is not ranked above his master; an employee doesn't give orders to the employer. If you understand what I'm telling you, act like it—and live a blessed life.

THE ONE WHO ATE BREAD AT MY TABLE

18-20 "I'm not including all of you in this. I know precisely whom I've selected, so as not to interfere with the fulfillment of this Scripture:

> The one who ate bread at my table
> Will stab me in the back.

"I'm telling you all this ahead of time so that when it happens you will believe that I am who I say I am. Make sure you get this right: Receiving someone I send is the same as receiving me, just as receiving me is the same as receiving the One who sent me."

21 After he said these things, Jesus became visibly upset, and then he told them why. "One of you is going to betray me."

22-25 The disciples looked around at one another, wondering who on earth he was talking about. One of the disciples, the one Jesus loved dearly, was reclining against him, his head on his shoulder. Peter motioned to him to ask who Jesus might be talking about. So, being the closest, he said, "Master, who?"

26-27 Jesus said, "The one to whom I give this crust of bread after I've dipped it." Then he dipped the crust and gave it to Judas, son of Simon the Iscariot. As soon as the bread was in his hand, Satan entered him.

"What you must do," said Jesus, "do. Do it and get it over with."

28-29 No one around the supper table knew why he said this to him. Some thought that since Judas was their treasurer, Jesus was telling him to buy what they needed for the Feast, or that he should give something to the poor.

30 Judas, with the piece of bread, left. It was night.

A NEW COMMAND

31-32 When he had left, Jesus said, "Now the Son of Man is seen for who he is, and God seen for who he is in him. The moment God is seen in him, God's glory will be on display. In glorifying him, he himself is glorified—glory all around!

33 "Children, I am with you for only a short time longer. You are going to look high and low for me. But just as I told the Jews, I'm telling you: 'Where I go, you are not able to come.'

34-35 "Let me give you a new command: Love one another. In the same way I loved you, you love one another. This is how everyone will recognize that you are my disciples—when they see the love you have for each other."

36 Simon Peter asked, "Master, just where are you going?"

Jesus answered, "You can't now follow me where I'm going. You will follow later."

37 "Master," said Peter, "why can't I follow now? I'll lay down my life for you!"

38 "Really? You'll lay down your life for me? The truth is that before the rooster crows, you'll deny me three times."

THE ROAD

14 1-4 "Don't let this rattle you. You trust God, don't you? Trust me. There is plenty of room for you in my Father's home. If that weren't so, would I have told you that I'm on my way to get a room ready for you? And if I'm on my way to get your room ready, I'll come back and get you so you can live where I live. And you already know the road I'm taking."

5 Thomas said, "Master, we have no idea where you're going. How do you expect us to know the road?"

6-7 Jesus said, "I am the Road, also the Truth, also the Life. No one gets to the Father apart from me. If you really knew me, you would know my Father as well. From now on, you do know him. You've even seen him!"

8 Philip said, "Master, show us the Father; then we'll be content."

9-10 "You've been with me all this time, Philip, and you still don't understand? To see me is to see the Father. So how can you ask, 'Where is the Father?' Don't you believe that I am in the Father and the Father is in me? The words that I speak to you aren't mere words. I don't just make them up on my own. The Father who resides in me crafts each word into a divine act.

11-14 "Believe me: I am in my Father and my Father is in me. If you can't believe that, believe what you see—these works. The person who trusts me will not only do what I'm doing but even greater things, because I, on my way to the Father, am giving you the same work to do that I've been doing. You can count on it. From now on, whatever you request along the lines of who I am and what I am doing, I'll do it. That's how the Father will be seen for who he is in the Son. I mean it. Whatever you request in this way, I'll do.

THE SPIRIT OF TRUTH

15-17 "If you love me, show it by doing what I've told you. I will talk to the Father, and he'll provide you another Friend so that you will always have someone with you. This Friend is the Spirit of Truth. The godless world can't take him in because it doesn't have eyes to see him, doesn't know what to look for. But you know him already because he has been staying with you, and will even be *in* you!

18-20 "I will not leave you orphaned. I'm coming back. In just a little while the world will no longer see me, but you're going to see me because I am alive and you're about to come alive. At that moment you will know absolutely that I'm in my Father, and you're in me, and I'm in you.

21 "The person who knows my commandments and keeps them, that's who loves me. And the person who loves me will be loved by my Father, and I will love him and make myself plain to him."

22 Judas (not Iscariot) said, "Master, why is it that you are about to make yourself plain to us but not to the world?"

23-24 "Because a loveless world," said Jesus, "is a sightless world. If anyone loves me, he will carefully keep my word and my Father will love him—we'll move right into the neighborhood! Not loving me means not keeping my words. The message you are hearing isn't mine. It's the message of the Father who sent me.

25-27 "I'm telling you these things while I'm still living with you. The Friend, the Holy Spirit whom the Father will send at my request, will make everything plain to you. He will remind you of all the things I have told you. I'm leaving you well and whole. That's my parting gift to you. Peace. I don't leave you the way you're used to being left—feeling abandoned, bereft. So don't be upset. Don't be distraught.

28 "You've heard me tell you, 'I'm going away, and I'm coming back.' If you loved me, you would be glad that I'm on my way to the Father because the Father is the goal and purpose of my life.

29-31 "I've told you this ahead of time, before it happens, so that when it does happen, the confirmation will deepen your belief in me. I'll not be talking with you much more like this because the chief of this godless world is about to attack. But don't worry—he has nothing on me, no claim on me. But so the world might know how thoroughly I love the Father, I am carrying out my Father's instructions right down to the last detail.

"Get up. Let's go. It's time to leave here."

THE VINE AND THE BRANCHES

15 1-3 "I am the Real Vine and my Father is the Farmer. He cuts off every branch of me that doesn't bear grapes. And every branch that is grape-bearing he prunes back so it will bear even more. You are already pruned back by the message I have spoken.

4 "Live in me. Make your home in me just as I do in you. In the same way that a branch can't bear grapes by itself but only by being joined to the vine, you can't bear fruit unless you are joined with me.

5-8 "I am the Vine, you are the branches. When you're joined with me and I with you, the relation intimate and organic, the harvest is sure to be abundant. Separated, you can't produce a thing. Anyone who separates from me is deadwood, gathered up and thrown on the bonfire. But if you make yourselves at home with me and my words are at home in you, you can be sure that whatever you ask will be listened to and acted upon. This is how my Father shows who he is—when you produce grapes, when you mature as my disciples.

9-10 "I've loved you the way my Father has loved me. Make yourselves at home in my love. If you keep my commands, you'll remain intimately at home in my love. That's what I've done—kept my Father's commands and made myself at home in his love.

11-15 "I've told you these things for a purpose: that my joy might be your joy, and your joy wholly mature. This is my command: Love one another the way I loved you. This is the very best way to love. Put your life on the line for your friends. You are my friends when you do the things I command you. I'm no longer calling you servants because servants don't understand what their master is thinking and planning. No, I've named you friends because I've let you in on everything I've heard from the Father.

16 "You didn't choose me, remember; I chose you, and put you in the world to bear fruit, fruit that won't spoil. As fruit bearers, whatever you ask the Father in relation to me, he gives you.

17 "But remember the root command: Love one another.

HATED BY THE WORLD

18-19 "If you find the godless world is hating you, remember it got its start hating me. If you lived on the world's terms, the world would love you as one of its own. But since I picked you to live on God's terms and no longer on the world's terms, the world is going to hate you.

20 "When that happens, remember this: Servants don't get better treatment than their masters. If they beat on me, they will certainly beat on you. If they did what I told them, they will do what you tell them.

21-25 "They are going to do all these things to you because of the way they treated me, because they don't know the One who sent me. If I hadn't come and told them all this in plain language, it wouldn't be so bad. As it is, they have no excuse. Hate me, hate my Father—it's all the same. If I hadn't done what I have done among them, works no one has *ever* done, they wouldn't be to blame. But they saw the God-signs and hated anyway, both me and my Father. Interesting—they have verified the truth of their own Scriptures where it is written, 'They hated me for no good reason.'

26-27 "When the Friend I plan to send you from the Father comes—the Spirit of Truth issuing from the Father—he will confirm everything about me. You, too, from your side must give your confirming evidence, since you are in this with me from the start."

16 1-4 "I've told you these things to prepare you for rough times ahead. They are going to throw you out of the meeting places. There will even come a time when anyone who kills you will think he's doing God a favor. They will do these things because they never really understood the Father. I've told you these things so that when the time comes and they start in on you, you'll be well-warned and ready for them.

I Am the Vine

Outside my office window, a thick grapevine grows along the backyard fence. Planted over two decades ago by my husband, this resilient plant has weathered seasons of drought and excessive rainfall, surviving periods of complete neglect and an overeager dog who runs along the fence to bark at the dogs walking on the sidewalk beyond. The visual reminder of this strong vine centers me season after season. From this thick, stately vine, year after year, brand new branches and leaves grow and spread and bear clusters of grapes.

I can picture Jesus at the Last Supper, his final meal with his closest disciples and friends, pointing to a nearby grapevine and using the moment to disclose the most poignant, foundational, and timeless lessons for his followers.

"I am the Real Vine" (John 15:1).

Jesus explains that he is the sole source of life and growth. We would do well to evaluate where we focus and where we find life. Do we find our source of meaning in our accomplishments? Is the value of our lives found in the jobs we have, the money in our bank accounts, the cars we drive, or our educational degrees? Do we look to our families, relationships, or social media followers as our source of life and fulfillment?

Some of us may even mistakenly seek life through Christian ministry and altogether miss the God we serve.

Though none of these things are bad or wrong in and of themselves, Jesus states plainly that he is our source, where true and lasting life is found.

"I am the Vine, you are the branches. When you're joined with me and I with you, the relation intimate and organic, the harvest is sure to be abundant" (John 15:5).

Our part is to be joined with him, to abide or remain in him—to live in close, intimate connection with him. Jesus explains that God is glorified when we bear much fruit, but when our focus moves off the Vine to the fruit, we miss a key lesson of the Christian life. Fruit—what God produces through us and in us—is a natural by-product of being connected to the Vine. The greater our intimate and organic connection with the Vine, the more abundant the fruit. Our surrendered lives release God's Spirit to lead, guide, and supply what we need to grow.

We often think fruit is the blessing. But truly, the blessing is Jesus—knowing him and being known by him. Let Jesus have first place in your life and watch him produce abundance in and through you.

THE FRIEND WILL COME

4-7 "I didn't tell you this earlier because I was with you every day. But now I am on my way to the One who sent me. Not one of you has asked, 'Where are you going?' Instead, the longer I've talked, the sadder you've become. So let me say it again, this truth: It's better for you that I leave. If I don't leave, the Friend won't come. But if I go, I'll send him to you.

8-11 "When he comes, he'll expose the error of the godless world's view of sin, righteousness, and judgment: He'll show them that their refusal to believe in me is their basic sin; that righteousness comes from above, where I am with the Father, out of their sight and control; that judgment takes place as the ruler of this godless world is brought to trial and convicted.

12-15 "I still have many things to tell you, but you can't handle them now. But when the Friend comes, the Spirit of the Truth, he will take you by the hand and guide you into all the truth there is. He won't draw attention to himself, but will make sense out of what is about to happen and, indeed, out of all that I have done and said. He will honor me; he will take from me and deliver it to you. Everything the Father has is also mine. That is why I've said, 'He takes from me and delivers to you.'

16 "In a day or so you're not going to see me, but then in another day or so you will see me."

JOY LIKE A RIVER OVERFLOWING

17-18 That stirred up a hornet's nest of questions among the disciples: "What's he talking about: 'In a day or so you're not going to see me, but then in another day or so you will see me'? And, 'Because I'm on my way to the Father'? What is this 'day or so'? We don't know what he's talking about."

19-20 Jesus knew they were dying to ask him what he meant, so he said, "Are you trying to figure out among yourselves what I meant when I said, 'In a day or so you're not going to see me, but then in another day or so you will see me'? Then fix this firmly in your minds: You're going to be in deep mourning while the godless world throws a party. You'll be sad, very sad, but your sadness will develop into gladness.

21-23 "When a woman gives birth, she has a hard time, there's no getting around it. But when the baby is born, there is joy in the birth. This new life in the world wipes out memory of the pain. The sadness you have right now is similar to that pain, but the coming joy is also similar. When I see you again, you'll be full of joy, and it will be a joy no one can rob from you. You'll no longer be so full of questions.

23-24 "This is what I want you to do: Ask the Father for whatever is in keeping with the things I've revealed to you. Ask in my name, according to my will, and he'll most certainly give it to you. Your joy will be a river overflowing its banks!

25-28 "I've used figures of speech in telling you these things. Soon I'll drop the figures and tell you about the Father in plain language. Then you can make your requests directly to him in relation to this life I've revealed to you. I won't continue making requests of the Father on your behalf. I won't need to. Because you've gone out on a limb, committed yourselves to love and trust in me, believing I came directly from the Father, the Father loves you directly. First, I left the Father and arrived in the world; now I leave the world and travel to the Father."

29-30 His disciples said, "Finally! You're giving it to us straight, in plain talk—no more figures of speech. Now we know that you know everything—it all comes together in you. You won't have to put up with our questions anymore. We're convinced you came from God."

31-33 Jesus answered them, "Do you finally believe? In fact, you're about to make a run for it—saving your own skins and abandoning me. But I'm not abandoned. The Father is with me. I've told you all this so that trusting me, you will be unshakable and assured, deeply at peace. In this godless world you will continue to experience difficulties. But take heart! I've conquered the world."

JESUS' PRAYER FOR HIS FOLLOWERS

17 1-5 Jesus said these things. Then, raising his eyes in prayer, he said:

Father, it's time.
Display the bright splendor of your Son
So the Son in turn may show your
bright splendor.
You put him in charge of everything
human
So he might give real and eternal life
to all in his care.
And this is the real and eternal life:
That they know you,
The one and only true God,
And Jesus Christ, whom you sent.
I glorified you on earth
By completing down to the last detail

What you assigned me to do.
And now, Father, glorify me with your very own splendor,
The very splendor I had in your presence
Before there was a world.

▲ ▲ ▲

6-12 I spelled out your character in detail
To the men and women you gave me.
They were yours in the first place;
Then you gave them to me,
And they have now done what you said.
They know now, beyond the shadow of a doubt,
That everything you gave me is firsthand from you,
For the message you gave me, I gave them;
And they took it, and were convinced
That I came from you.
They believed that you sent me.
I pray for them.
I'm not praying for the God-rejecting world
But for those you gave me,
For they are yours by right.
Everything mine is yours, and yours mine,
And my life is on display in them.
For I'm no longer going to be visible in the world;
They'll continue in the world
While I return to you.
Holy Father, guard them as they pursue this life
That you conferred as a gift through me,
So they can be one heart and mind
As we are one heart and mind.
As long as I was with them, I guarded them
In the pursuit of the life you gave through me;
I even posted a lookout.
And not one of them got away,
Except for the rebel bent on destruction
(the exception that proved the rule of Scripture).

▲ ▲ ▲

13-19 Now I'm returning to you.
I'm saying these things in the world's hearing
So my people can experience
My joy completed in them.
I gave them your word;
The godless world hated them because of it,
Because they didn't join the world's ways,
Just as I didn't join the world's ways.
I'm not asking that you take them out of the world
But that you guard them from the Evil One.
They are no more defined by the world
Than I am defined by the world.
Make them holy—consecrated—with the truth;
Your word is consecrating truth.
In the same way that you gave me a mission in the world,
I give them a mission in the world.
I'm consecrating myself for their sakes
So they'll be truth-consecrated in their mission.

▲ ▲ ▲

20-23 I'm praying not only for them
But also for those who will believe in me
Because of them and their witness about me.
The goal is for all of them to become one heart and mind—
Just as you, Father, are in me and I in you,
So they might be one heart and mind with us.
Then the world might believe that you, in fact, sent me.
The same glory you gave me, I gave them,
So they'll be as unified and together as we are—
I in them and you in me.
Then they'll be mature in this oneness,
And give the godless world evidence
That you've sent me and loved them
In the same way you've loved me.

▲ ▲ ▲

24-26 Father, I want those you gave me
To be with me, right where I am,
So they can see my glory, the splendor you gave me,
Having loved me
Long before there ever was a world.
Righteous Father, the world has never known you,
But I have known you, and these disciples know
That you sent me on this mission.
I have made your very being known to them—

Who you are and what you do—
And continue to make it known,
So that your love for me
Might be in them
Exactly as I am in them.

SEIZED IN THE GARDEN AT NIGHT

18 1 Jesus, having prayed this prayer, left with his disciples and crossed over the brook Kidron at a place where there was a garden. He and his disciples entered it.

2-4 Judas, his betrayer, knew the place because Jesus and his disciples went there often. So Judas led the way to the garden, and the Roman soldiers and police sent by the high priests and Pharisees followed. They arrived there with lanterns and torches and swords. Jesus, knowing by now everything that was imploding on him, went out and met them. He said, "Who are you after?"

They answered, "Jesus the Nazarene."

5-6 He said, "That's me." The soldiers recoiled, totally taken aback. Judas, his betrayer, stood out like a sore thumb.

7 Jesus asked again, "Who are you after?"

They answered, "Jesus the Nazarene."

8-9 "I told you," said Jesus, "that's me. I'm the one. So if it's me you're after, let these others go." (This validated the words in his prayer, "I didn't lose one of those you gave.")

10 Just then Simon Peter, who was carrying a sword, pulled it from its sheath and struck the Chief Priest's servant, cutting off his right ear. Malchus was the servant's name.

11 Jesus ordered Peter, "Put back your sword. Do you think for a minute I'm not going to drink this cup the Father gave me?"

12-14 Then the Roman soldiers under their commander, joined by the Jewish police, seized Jesus and tied him up. They took him first to Annas, father-in-law of Caiaphas. Caiaphas was the Chief Priest that year. It was Caiaphas who had advised the Jews that it was to their advantage that one man die for the people.

15-16 Simon Peter and another disciple followed Jesus. That other disciple was known to the Chief Priest, and so he went in with Jesus to the Chief Priest's courtyard. Peter had to stay outside. Then the other disciple went out, spoke to the doorkeeper, and got Peter in.

17 The young woman who was the doorkeeper said to Peter, "Aren't you one of this man's disciples?"

He said, "No, I'm not."

18 The servants and police had made a fire because of the cold and were huddled there warming themselves. Peter stood with them, trying to get warm.

THE INTERROGATION

19-21 Annas interrogated Jesus regarding his disciples and his teaching. Jesus answered, "I've spoken openly in public. I've taught regularly in meeting places and the Temple, where the Jews all come together. Everything has been out in the open. I've said nothing in secret. So why are you treating me like a traitor? Question those who have been listening to me. They know well what I have said. My teachings have all been aboveboard."

22 When he said this, one of the policemen standing there slapped Jesus across the face, saying, "How dare you speak to the Chief Priest like that!"

23 Jesus replied, "If I've said something wrong, prove it. But if I've spoken the plain truth, why this slapping around?"

24 Then Annas sent him, still tied up, to the Chief Priest Caiaphas.

25 Meanwhile, Simon Peter was back at the fire, still trying to get warm. The others there said to him, "Aren't you one of his disciples?"

He denied it, "Not me."

26 One of the Chief Priest's servants, a relative of the man whose ear Peter had cut off, said, "Didn't I see you in the garden with him?"

27 Again, Peter denied it. Just then a rooster crowed.

THE KING OF THE JEWS

28-29 They led Jesus then from Caiaphas to the Roman governor's palace. It was early morning. They themselves didn't enter the palace because they didn't want to be disqualified from eating the Passover. So Pilate came out to them and spoke. "What charge do you bring against this man?"

30 They said, "If he hadn't been doing something evil, do you think we'd be here bothering you?"

31-32 Pilate said, "You take him. Judge him by *your* law."

The Jews said, "We're not allowed to kill anyone." (This would confirm Jesus' word indicating the way he would die.)

33 Pilate went back into the palace and called for Jesus. He said, "Are you the 'King of the Jews'?"

34 Jesus answered, "Are you saying this on your own, or did others tell you this about me?"

35 Pilate said, "Do I look like a Jew? Your people and your high priests turned you over to me. What did you do?"

36 "My kingdom," said Jesus, "doesn't consist of what you see around you. If it did, my followers would fight so that I wouldn't be handed over to the Jews. But I'm not that kind of king, not the world's kind of king."

37 Then Pilate said, "So, are you a king or not?"

Jesus answered, "You tell me. Because I am King, I was born and entered the world so that I could witness to the truth. Everyone who cares for truth, who has any feeling for the truth, recognizes my voice."

38-39 Pilate said, "What is truth?"

Then he went back out to the Jews and told them, "I find nothing wrong in this man. It's your custom that I pardon one prisoner at Passover. Do you want me to pardon the 'King of the Jews'?"

40 They shouted back, "Not this one, but Barabbas!" Barabbas was a Jewish freedom fighter.

THE THORN CROWN OF THE KING

19 1-3 So Pilate took Jesus and had him whipped. The soldiers, having braided a crown from thorns, set it on his head, threw a purple robe over him, and approached him with, "Hail, King of the Jews!" Then they greeted him with slaps in the face.

4-5 Pilate went back out again and said to them, "I present him to you, but I want you to know that I do not find him guilty of any crime." Just then Jesus came out wearing the thorn crown and purple robe.

Pilate announced, "Here he is: the Man."

6 When the high priests and police saw him, they shouted in a frenzy, "Crucify! Crucify!"

Pilate told them, "You take him. You crucify him. I find nothing wrong with him."

7 The Jews answered, "We have a law, and by that law he must die because he claimed to be the Son of God."

8-9 When Pilate heard this, he became even more scared. He went back into the palace and said to Jesus, "Where did you come from?"

Jesus gave no answer.

10 Pilate said, "You won't talk? Don't you know that I have the authority to pardon you, and the authority to—crucify you?"

11 Jesus said, "You haven't a shred of authority over me except what has been given you from heaven. That's why the one who betrayed me to you has committed a far greater fault."

12 At this, Pilate tried his best to pardon him, but the Jews shouted him down: "If you pardon this man, you're no friend of Caesar's. Anyone setting himself up as 'king' defies Caesar."

13-14 When Pilate heard those words, he led Jesus outside. He sat down at the judgment seat in the area designated Stone Court (in Hebrew, *Gabbatha*). It was the preparation day for Passover. The hour was noon. Pilate said to the Jews, "Here is your king."

15 They shouted back, "Kill him! Kill him! Crucify him!"

Pilate said, "I am to crucify your king?"

The high priests answered, "We have no king except Caesar."

16-19 Pilate caved in to their demand. He turned him over to be crucified.

THE CRUCIFIXION

They took Jesus away. Carrying his cross, Jesus went out to the place called Skull Hill (the name in Hebrew is *Golgotha*), where they crucified him, and with him two others, one on each side, Jesus in the middle. Pilate wrote a sign and had it placed on the cross. It read:

JESUS THE NAZARENE
THE KING OF THE JEWS.

20-21 Many of the Jews read the sign because the place where Jesus was crucified was right next to the city. It was written in Hebrew, Latin, and Greek. The Jewish high priests objected. "Don't write," they said to Pilate, "'The King of the Jews.' Make it, 'This man said, "I am the King of the Jews."'"

22 Pilate said, "What I've written, I've written."

23-24 When they crucified him, the Roman soldiers took his clothes and divided them up four ways, to each soldier a fourth. But his robe was seamless, a single piece of weaving, so they said to each other, "Let's not tear it up. Let's throw dice to see who gets it." This confirmed the Scripture that said, "They divided up my clothes among them and threw dice for my coat." (The soldiers validated the Scriptures!)

24-27 While the soldiers were looking after themselves, Jesus' mother, his aunt, Mary the wife of Clopas, and Mary Magdalene stood at the foot of the cross. Jesus saw his mother and the disciple he loved standing near her.

He said to his mother, "Woman, here is your son." Then to the disciple, "Here is your mother." From that moment the disciple accepted her as his own mother.

28 Jesus, seeing that everything had been completed so that the Scripture record might also be complete, then said, "I'm thirsty."

29-30 A jug of sour wine was standing by. Someone put a sponge soaked with the wine on a javelin and lifted it to his mouth. After he took the wine, Jesus said, "It's done . . . complete." Bowing his head, he offered up his spirit.

31-34 Then the Jews, since it was the day of Sabbath preparation, and so the bodies wouldn't stay on the crosses over the Sabbath (it was a high holy day that year), petitioned Pilate that their legs be broken to speed death, and the bodies taken down. So the soldiers came and broke the legs of the first man crucified with Jesus, and then the other. When they got to Jesus, they saw that he was already dead, so they didn't break his legs. One of the soldiers stabbed him in the side with his spear. Blood and water gushed out.

35 The eyewitness to these things has presented an accurate report. He saw it himself and is telling the truth so that you, also, will believe.

36-37 These things that happened confirmed the Scripture, "Not a bone in his body was broken," and the other Scripture that reads, "They will stare at the one they pierced."

▲ ▲ ▲

38 After all this, Joseph of Arimathea (he was a disciple of Jesus, but secretly, because he was intimidated by the Jews) petitioned Pilate to take the body of Jesus. Pilate gave permission. So Joseph came and took the body.

39-42 Nicodemus, who had first come to Jesus at night, came now in broad daylight carrying a mixture of myrrh and aloes, about seventy-five pounds. They took Jesus' body and, following the Jewish burial custom, wrapped it in linen with the spices. There was a garden near the place he was crucified, and in the garden a new tomb in which no one had yet been placed. So, because it was Sabbath preparation for the Jews and the tomb was convenient, they placed Jesus in it.

RESURRECTION!

20 1-2 Early in the morning on the first day of the week, while it was still dark, Mary Magdalene came to the tomb and saw that the stone was moved away from the entrance. She ran at once to Simon Peter and the other disciple, the one Jesus loved, gasping for breath. "They took the Master from the tomb. We don't know where they've put him."

3-10 Peter and the other disciple left immediately for the tomb. They ran, neck and neck. The other disciple got to the tomb first, outrunning Peter. Stooping to look in, he saw the pieces of linen cloth lying there, but he didn't go in. Simon Peter arrived after him, entered the tomb, observed the linen cloths lying there, and the kerchief used to cover his head not lying with the linen cloths but separate, neatly folded by itself. Then the other disciple, the one who had gotten there first, went into the tomb, took one look at the evidence, and believed. No one yet knew from the Scripture that he had to rise from the dead. The disciples then went back home.

11-13 But Mary stood outside the tomb weeping. As she wept, she knelt to look into the tomb and saw two angels sitting there, dressed in white, one at the head, the other at the foot of where Jesus' body had been laid. They said to her, "Woman, why do you weep?"

13-14 "They took my Master," she said, "and I don't know where they put him." After she said this, she turned away and saw Jesus standing there. But she didn't recognize him.

15 Jesus spoke to her, "Woman, why do you weep? Who are you looking for?"

She, thinking that he was the gardener, said, "Sir, if you took him, tell me where you put him so I can care for him."

16 Jesus said, "Mary."

Turning to face him, she said in Hebrew, "*Rabboni!*" meaning "Teacher!"

17 Jesus said, "Don't cling to me, for I have not yet ascended to the Father. Go to my brothers and tell them, 'I ascend to my Father and your Father, my God and your God.'"

18 Mary Magdalene went, telling the news to the disciples: "I saw the Master!" And she told them everything he said to her.

TO BELIEVE

19-20 Later on that day, the disciples had gathered together, but, fearful of the Jews, had locked all the doors in the house. Jesus entered, stood among them, and said, "Peace to you." Then he showed them his hands and side.

The Garden and the Gardener

She was a compassionate woman, Mary Magdalene. First to the tomb on the third day after Jesus' burial; first to know that Jesus' body was missing. She raised the alarm before the sun had fully risen.

After the other disciples had come and confirmed and gone away again, Mary held vigil alone. She was weeping for insult added to injury: Her teacher, master, hope for the world, had been killed, and now someone had stolen his body. She wept for the loss, wept because she was unsure of what to do or where to go. Mary was inconsolable when the angels appeared and asked why she wept. Preoccupied, she was seemingly unfazed by celestial presence and didn't think to be afraid. Mary turned to a man she didn't recognize—a gardener perhaps—and asked if he'd taken her Lord. She was so lost in her grief, lost in the need to act and fix what was broken, that not until he called her by name did Mary realize that this man in the garden was *not* the gardener.

She knew this voice. She recognized Jesus.

Mary. Just her name. Jesus didn't say, "Silly woman, it's me! Look up from your crying!" No. Only her name, and that was enough. He didn't explain his presence, didn't condemn her shaken faith. Jesus called her by name.

The creator of the world—living, then dead, then living again—was standing by her side. No wonder she'd mistaken him for a gardener, this God who, in death, had been laid in the ground and had now risen with new life. How amazing to wake expecting death and grief only to be shocked by renewed life, by joy. Mary's sadness turned to jubilation and immediate action as she once again ran to tell what she had seen.

Jesus' new life gave hope to Mary's life, and now, to ours. The resurrected Jesus is *still* alive, still calling us by name. With Jesus, we, too, are the creation being made new through the care of the creator.

This story began with an alarm raised of hope lost, with Jesus dead and lying in a tomb, but it ends in a garden—in hope and faith restored beyond measure, with a living God who walks alongside us and knows our names.

Hallelujah! He is risen.

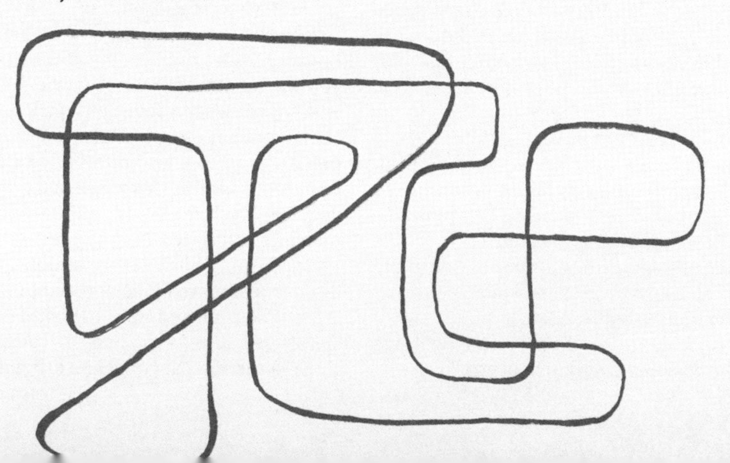

20-21 The disciples, seeing the Master with their own eyes, were awestruck. Jesus repeated his greeting: "Peace to you. Just as the Father sent me, I send you."

22-23 Then he took a deep breath and breathed into them. "Receive the Holy Spirit," he said. "If you forgive someone's sins, they're gone for good. If you don't forgive sins, what are you going to do with them?"

24-25 But Thomas, sometimes called the Twin, one of the Twelve, was not with them when Jesus came. The other disciples told him, "We saw the Master."

But he said, "Unless I see the nail holes in his hands, put my finger in the nail holes, and stick my hand in his side, I won't believe it."

26 Eight days later, his disciples were again in the room. This time Thomas was with them. Jesus came through the locked doors, stood among them, and said, "Peace to you."

27 Then he focused his attention on Thomas. "Take your finger and examine my hands. Take your hand and stick it in my side. Don't be unbelieving. Believe."

28 Thomas said, "My Master! My God!"

29 Jesus said, "So, you believe because you've seen with your own eyes. Even better blessings are in store for those who believe without seeing."

30-31 Jesus provided far more God-revealing signs than are written down in this book. These are written down so you will believe that Jesus is the Messiah, the Son of God, and in the act of believing, have real and eternal life in the way he personally revealed it.

FISHING

21 1-3 After this, Jesus appeared again to the disciples, this time at the Tiberias Sea (the Sea of Galilee). This is how he did it: Simon Peter, Thomas (nicknamed "Twin"), Nathanael from Cana in Galilee, the brothers Zebedee, and two other disciples were together. Simon Peter announced, "I'm going fishing."

3-4 The rest of them replied, "We're going with you." They went out and got in the boat. They caught nothing that night. When the sun came up, Jesus was standing on the beach, but they didn't recognize him.

5 Jesus spoke to them: "Good morning! Did you catch anything for breakfast?"

They answered, "No."

6 He said, "Throw the net off the right side of the boat and see what happens."

They did what he said. All of a sudden there were so many fish in it, they weren't strong enough to pull it in.

7-9 Then the disciple Jesus loved said to Peter, "It's the Master!"

When Simon Peter realized that it was the Master, he threw on some clothes, for he was stripped for work, and dove into the sea. The other disciples came in by boat for they weren't far from land, a hundred yards or so, pulling along the net full of fish. When they got out of the boat, they saw a fire laid, with fish and bread cooking on it.

10-11 Jesus said, "Bring some of the fish you've just caught." Simon Peter joined them and pulled the net to shore—153 big fish! And even with all those fish, the net didn't rip.

12 Jesus said, "Breakfast is ready." Not one of the disciples dared ask, "Who are you?" They knew it was the Master.

13-14 Jesus then took the bread and gave it to them. He did the same with the fish. This was now the third time Jesus had shown himself alive to the disciples since being raised from the dead.

DO YOU LOVE ME?

15 After breakfast, Jesus said to Simon Peter, "Simon, son of John, do you love me more than these?"

"Yes, Master, you know I love you."

Jesus said, "Feed my lambs."

16 He then asked a second time, "Simon, son of John, do you love me?"

"Yes, Master, you know I love you."

Jesus said, "Shepherd my sheep."

17-19 Then he said it a third time: "Simon, son of John, do you love me?"

Peter was upset that he asked for the third time, "Do you love me?" so he answered, "Master, you know everything there is to know. You've got to know that I love you."

Jesus said, "Feed my sheep. I'm telling you the very truth now: When you were young you dressed yourself and went wherever you wished, but when you get old you'll have to stretch out your hands while someone else dresses you and takes you where you don't want to go." He said this to hint at the kind of death by which Peter would glorify God. And then he commanded, "Follow me."

20-21 Turning his head, Peter noticed the disciple Jesus loved following right behind. When Peter noticed him, he asked Jesus, "Master, what's going to happen to *him*?"

22-23 Jesus said, "If I want him to live until I

come again, what's that to you? You—follow me." That is how the rumor got out among the brothers that this disciple wouldn't die. But that is not what Jesus said. He simply said, "If I want him to live until I come again, what's that to you?"

24 This is the same disciple who was eyewitness to all these things and wrote them down. And we all know that his eyewitness account is reliable and accurate.

25 There are so many other things Jesus did. If they were all written down, each of them, one by one, I can't imagine a world big enough to hold such a library of books.

THE TRANSLATOR AND HIS FRIENDS

EUGENE H. PETERSON was a pastor, scholar, writer, and poet. After teaching at a seminary and then giving nearly thirty years to church ministry in the Baltimore area, he created *The Message: The Bible in Contemporary Language*—a vibrant Bible translation that connects with today's readers like no other. It took Eugene a full ten years to complete. He worked from the Greek and Hebrew texts to ensure authenticity. At the same time, his ear was always tuned to the cadence and energy of contemporary English.

For his work on *The Message*, he received the prestigious ECPA Gold Medallion Book Award.

Eugene served as Professor of Spiritual Theology at Regent College in Vancouver, BC, retiring in 2006. He spent his final years in Montana with his beloved wife, Jan.

TRANSLATION CONSULTANTS

Peterson's work has been thoroughly reviewed by the following team of recognized Old and New Testament scholars, who ensured that it is accurate as well as faithful to the original languages.

OLD TESTAMENT TEAM

Robert L. Hubbard Jr., *North Park Theological Seminary* (chair)

Richard E. Averbeck, *Trinity Evangelical Divinity School*

Bryan E. Beyer, *Columbia International University*

Lamar E. Cooper Sr., *Criswell College*

Peter E. Enns, *Eastern University*

Duane E. Garrett, *The Southern Baptist Theological Seminary*

Donald R. Glenn, *Dallas Theological Seminary*

Paul R. House, *Beeson Divinity School, Samford University*

V. Phillips Long, *Regent College*

Tremper Longman III, *Westmont College*

John N. Oswalt, *Asbury Theological Seminary*

Richard L. Pratt Jr., *Reformed Theological Seminary*

John H. Walton, *Wheaton College*

Prescott H. Williams Jr., *Austin Presbyterian Theological Seminary*

Marvin R. Wilson, *Gordon College*

NEW TESTAMENT TEAM

William W. Klein, *Denver Seminary* (chair)

Darrell L. Bock, *Dallas Theological Seminary*

Donald A. Hagner, *Fuller Theological Seminary*

Moisés Silva, *Gordon-Conwell Theological Seminary*

Rodney A. Whitacre, *Trinity School for Ministry*

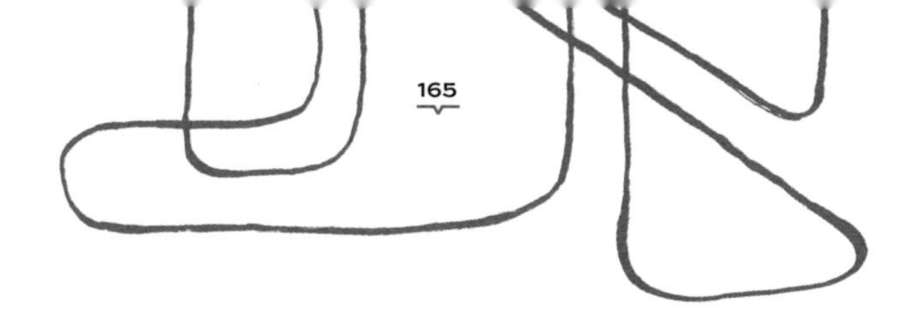

THE MESSAGE WOMEN'S DEVOTIONAL BIBLE TEAM

Olivia Eldredge
The Message Bible Editor

Catherine McNiel
Project Editor

Eva M. Winters
Designer

Ellen Richard Vosburg
Bible Editorial Consultant

Sandra Jurca
Typesetter

Victoria Martin
Product Manager

CONTRIBUTOR BIOGRAPHIES

Olivia Eldredge is the managing editor at NavPress and *The Message* Bible editor. She also serves as a worship leader for Christian organizations and special events.

Catherine McNiel is an author, editor, and speaker seeking the creative, redemptive work of God in our ordinary lives. Catherine has written and edited numerous books, and her articles, devotions, and Bible studies have been featured in various publications and ministries. Catherine is pursuing a master of divinity at North Park Theological Seminary.

▲ ▲ ▲

Judy Allen holds a master's degree in communication and culture from Trinity Graduate School. Her work has been featured in Fathom magazine, ThePerennialGen, Open the Bible, and iBelieve.

Teresa Swanstrom Anderson is the author of several books and Bible studies, the host of the podcast *Living Lighter*, and an entrepreneur.

Connie Armerding is a writer, speaker, and leadership coach. She holds degrees from Wheaton College in communication (bachelor's) and in leadership and evangelism (master's).

Jenny Rae Armstrong is a pastor and author passionate about encouraging women to follow Jesus' call. She has a master of divinity from North Park Theological Seminary.

Kat Armstrong is the author of the Storyline Bible Studies series, has her master's degree from Dallas Theological Seminary, and is pursuing a doctor of ministry degree from Northern Seminary.

Lindsay Banton, author of *Trail Guide: A Simple Manual for Understanding the Bible*, holds a master's degree in practical theology from Regent University. Read more at lindsaybanton.com.

Deborah Beddoe is an author and editor pursuing a master's degree in theopoetics and writing at Bethany Theological Seminary.

Cheryl Grey Bostrom is a former devotional essayist for the *Upper Room Disciplines* and Women of Faith and the author of fiction and nonfiction books.

Rachel Britton holds a master's degree in religion from Gordon-Conwell Theological Seminary. She is the author of several books, devotions, and prayer guides.

Kris Camealy is the founder and director of Refine, a women's retreat in central Ohio. She is a contributor to The Cultivating Project and is an author and devotional writer.

Chelle A. Carter-Wilson is the only daughter of a Black liberation theologist and a Black southern belle. She has contributed to Our Bible App, *The Mudroom*, and the *(in)courage Devotional Bible* and is a member of the Redbud Writers Guild board of directors.

Dorcas Cheng-Tozun is a nonprofit and social-enterprise professional, an editor, the author of several books, and a longtime contributor to *Christianity Today*.

Charity Singleton Craig is the author of several books, articles, and devotions. She writes about faith, art, and nature.

Joyce Koo Dalrymple is a pastor, speaker, podcast host and is the founder of Refuge for Strength, a women's ministry focused on spiritual formation and direction. She is the author of *Women of the New Testament* and *Jesus' Passion Week* in the LifeChange Bible Study series.

Rebecca Detrick is a teacher, music director, and liturgist. She writes regularly in both digital and print publications about education and faith.

Liz Ditty is the author of multiple books and Bible studies, and she leads spiritual formation retreats for Mount Hermon Christian camp. She is completing her master's in theology and master of biblical leadership at Western Seminary.

Xochitl (So-Cheel) Dixon writes about spiritual growth, diversity, and inclusion in her children's books, devotionals, and articles at Our Daily Bread, God Hears Her, and xedixon.com.

Judy Douglass is an author, speaker, and podcaster and the global director of Cru's women's resources. Learn more at judydouglass.com

Melissa Duncan is a pastor and writer of devotional and discipleship materials. She is completing her master of divinity at North Park Theological Seminary.

Dena Dyer is a speaker, a Bible teacher, and the author or coauthor of twelve books, including *Wounded Women of the Bible: Finding Hope When Life Hurts*.

April Fiet is a pastor and the author of *The Sacred Pulse: Holy Rhythms for Overwhelmed Souls* as well as many devotionals and Bible study resources.

Kim Findlay is an author and speaker writing at the intersection of faith and suffering. Her work as been featured on *Facets of Faith*, Ask God Today, and the *Redbud Post*.

Dorina Lazo Gilmore-Young is an award-winning author, Bible teacher, and podcaster. She has published children's books, Bible studies, and devotionals.

Jennifer Grant writes for adults and children. Her picture book *Maybe God Is Like That Too* is a bestseller. Find her online at www.jennifergrant.com.

Dorothy Littell Greco is a photographer and the author of two marriage books. Her writing has been featured in *Christianity Today*, *RELEVANT*, Missio Alliance, and more.

Collette Broady Grund is an ordained pastor and the author of several articles and Bible studies. Her work focuses on grief and people experiencing homelessness.

Ashley Hales is the author of several books and Bible studies, holds a PhD, and researches Christian faith in America at the Willowbrae Institute.

Sarah J. Hauser is a writer, a speaker, and the author of *All Who Are Weary: Finding True Rest by Letting Go of the Burdens You Were Never Meant to Carry*.

Christy Hemphill is a linguist who works in education and minority-language Scripture translation. She has focused her studies on the interpretation of figurative language.

Liuan Huska is a journalist and the author of *Hurting Yet Whole: Reconciling Body and Spirit in Chronic Pain and Illness*. She writes at the intersection of embodiment, ecology, and faith.

Delphina Bedonie Johnson, a Diné, lives in Arizona. Her work with The Navigators encompasses Indigenous people cultivating their God-given cultural identity through a biblical lens.

Rachel Pieh Jones is the author of *Pillars: How Muslim Friends Led Me Closer to Jesus*. She holds a master of theology degree from Fuller Theological Seminary.

Kathy Khang is a writer and podcaster focused on the intersection of faith and culture. She is the author of *Raise Your Voice: Why We Stay Silent and How to Speak Up* and coauthor of *Loving Disagreement: Fighting for Community through the Fruit of the Spirit*.

Diane Dokko Kim serves as a disability-ministry consultant, is a speaker, and is the author of *Unbroken Faith: Spiritual Recovery for the Special Needs Parent*.

Jennifer Kinard writes creative nonfiction and memoir on culture, faith, and family. She serves in the worship-arts and women's ministries at her local church.

Kimberly Knowle-Zeller is an ordained ELCA pastor, writer, and mother. She is the coauthor of *The Beauty of Motherhood: Grace-Filled Devotions for the Early Years*.

Lara Krupicka is an author, essayist, and longtime small-group leader. Her writing has been published in dozens of magazines and newspapers around the globe.

Bronwyn Lea was born in South Africa and currently lives in California. She is a pastor, author, Bible teacher, and leadership coach with Propel Women.

Arianne Braithwaite Lehn is a writer, editor, creator, and PC(USA) pastor. She is the author of *Ash and Starlight: Prayers for the Chaos and Grace of Daily Life.*

Vivian Mabuni is a national speaker, author, and podcast host and is completing her master's in biblical and theological studies at Denver Seminary.

Alice Matagora has worked in disciplemaking ministry, cultural-competency training, and leader development with The Navigators. Alice is a speaker and the author of *How to Save the World: Disciplemaking Made Simple*.

Lucinda Secrest McDowell (d. 2023) was a seasoned mentor and the award-winning author of sixteen traditionally published books. She received her master of theological studies from Gordon-Conwell Theological Seminary.

Rebecca Florence Miller is a writer and editor. She holds a master of divinity from Luther Seminary in St. Paul, Minnesota.

Vina Bermudez Mogg is an artist and writer. Her work has been featured on She Reads Truth, Fathom magazine, and *The Mudroom*.

Michele Morin is a Bible teacher, writer, and gardener. Her work has been featured on Desiring God, (in)courage, ThePerennialGen, SheLoves Magazine, Living by Design Ministries, The Gospel Coalition, and more.

Carrie Morris is a licensed marriage and family therapist. A Wedgewood Circle Artist, her work has appeared in *The Mudroom*, Patheos, and the *Redbud Post*.

Michelle E. Navarrete is a scholar-in-residence at World Outspoken and a current doctoral student of Hebrew Bible at Emory University.

Nilwona Nowlin (MNA, MACF, MDiv) is a licensed minister and the author of several devotions, Sunday school curricula, and small-group studies.

Carolyn Miller Parr is an author and blogger, retired judge, Christian nonprofit leader, and occasional preacher. She's a mother, grandmother, and great-grandmother.

Tammy Perlmutter is founder and curator of *The Mudroom*, a collaborative blog for women, and cofounder of Deeply Rooted, an annual faith and creativity gathering for women. She is a poet and essayist.

Katherine Willis Pershey is a pastor, author, and member of the first doctor of ministry cohort sponsored by the Eugene Peterson Center for Christian Imagination at Western Theological Seminary.

Christiana N. Peterson is the author of books and essays on Christian spirituality. She has a master's degree in theology and the arts from St. Andrews University.

Heather Peterson, PhD, is the senior editor at the Colson Center for Christian Worldview and former associate professor of English. Her work has been featured in *The Mudroom* and InterVarsity's The Well.

Arlisia Potter is a graduate of the University of Central Florida and the UCLA Extension Writers' Program. An author and blogger, her work has been published by Black America Web and the *Redbud Post*.

Paula Frances Price is the Georgia-area director for InterVarsity Christian Fellowship, where she directs ministries that lead missional Bible studies on college campuses.

Alyson Pryor holds degrees in psychology from both the University of Southern California and Fuller Theological Seminary. She is a writer, therapist, spiritual director, and mother of five.

Michelle Ami Reyes is the author of *Becoming All Things: How Small Changes Lead to Lasting Connections across Cultures* and coauthor of *The Race-Wise Family: Ten Postures to Becoming Households of Healing and Hope*.

Traci Rhoades is a Bible teacher and the author of *Not All Who Wander (Spiritually) Are Lost: A Story of Church* and *Shaky Ground: What to Do After the Bottom Drops Out*. Connect with her on X @tracesoffaith.

Amber Mann Riggs is the director of OneStory, where she writes and publishes homeschool curriculum and devotions that help families explore the Bible.

Caryn Rivadeneira is the award-winning author of twenty-five books both for children and for adults. Caryn recently earned her master's degree from Northern Seminary.

Lisa Rodriguez-Watson is the national director of Missio Alliance and a pastor at Christ City Church. She writes, speaks, and leads at the intersection of formation, justice, and mission.

Maggie Wallem Rowe is a national speaker, dramatist, and author who holds a master's degree in biblical studies from Wheaton College Graduate School.

Sheila Wise Rowe, MEd, is a Christian counselor, spiritual director, and speaker and the author of the award-winning books *Healing Racial Trauma: The Road to Resilience* and *Young, Gifted, and Black: A Journey of Lament and Celebration*.

Aubrey Sampson is a church planter, a teaching pastor, and the author of several books, and she has a master's degree in evangelism and church leadership.

Michelle T. Sanchez is the author of *Color-Courageous Discipleship: Follow Jesus, Dismantle Racism, and Build Beloved Community* and *God's Beloved Community* and the former senior discipleship leader of the Evangelical Covenant Church.

Whitney R. Simpson writes about embodied spirituality, combining spiritual direction and yoga. She studied at Garrett-Evangelical Theological Seminary and is a deaconess in the United Methodist Church.

Michelle Stiffler is a certified trauma specialist, trauma-informed trainer, experienced mentor of women in crisis and abuse, former teen mom, and widely published freelancer.

Stephanie J. Thompson is a writer whose work can be found on Crosswalk, *The Mudroom*, The Art of Taleh, Her View from Home, and the *Redbud Post*. She is an ordained pastor in the Evangelical Covenant Church.

Michelle Van Loon is a speaker and the author of seven books and numerous articles, all focusing on themes of spiritual formation and the life of the church.

Prasanta Verma is a writer and speaker with numerous published essays, poems, and devotions, and she is the author of a book about ethnic loneliness.

Leslie Verner holds a master's degree in intercultural studies from Wheaton College Graduate School. She is the author of *Invited: The Power of Hospitality in an Age of Loneliness*, and her work has been featured in the *Christian Century*, *Plough*, the *Englewood Review of Books*, and more.

Nicole T. Walters is the author of the essays, devotions, and sermons at nicoletwalters.com. She holds a master's degree in practical theology and is pursuing her doctor of ministry from Winebrenner Theological Seminary.

Melanie Weldon-Soiset is a master of divinity graduate, former pastor, published poet, poetry editor, and #ChurchToo spiritual abuse survivor. Originally from Georgia, she lives in Washington, DC.

Nina Whang is a therapist and coach in California working at the intersection of church and mental health. She is earning her master's degree in counseling from Western Seminary.

Darcy Wiley is a writer and spiritual director cultivating peaceful spaces for healing, growth, and creativity. Her essays, devotions, and book projects explore spiritual and cultural transformation.

Melie Williams is a writer, editor, worship leader, and Christian audiobook narrator. She holds a master's degree in English from Southern New Hampshire University and a master's degree in religious studies from Southern California Seminary.

Tricia Lott Williford is the author of several books, including *This Book Is for You: Loving God's Words in Your Actual Life*.

Nichole Woo is a writer, editor, and podcast producer. She is the managing editor at *The Mudroom*, and her writing has been featured on Red Tent Living, SheLoves Magazine, the *MOPS Blog*, Patheos, and more.

Lydia Wylie-Kellermann is a writer, activist, and mother. She is the editor of *Geez* magazine and the director of Kirkridge Retreat and Study Center in Bangor, Pennsylvania.

April Yamasaki is a pastor, an editor, and the author of *Sacred Pauses: Spiritual Practices for Personal Renewal*; *Four Gifts: Seeking Self-Care for Heart, Soul, Mind, and Strength*; and other books on living with faith and hope.

INDEX OF DEVOTIONAL ENTRIES

INDEX OF BIBLICAL CHARACTER PROFILES

Character profiles marked with an asterisk (*) and the characters they address involve highly sensitive issues that might be triggering for some readers. We encourage you to be gentle with yourself as you move through this devotional Bible.

NOTES

Matthew 4, "Watch Out for Twisted Truth"

Eugene Peterson writes: Eugene H. Peterson, *Tell It Slant: A Conversation on the Language of Jesus in His Stories and Prayers* (Grand Rapids: Eerdmans, 2008), 58.

Matthew 5, "Flipping the Script on Blessing"

God-shaped voids only God can fill: Blaise Pascal, *Pensées*, trans. A. J. Krailsheimer (London: Penguin, 1993), 45.

Matthew 28, "The Worship of Women"

Frederick Dale Bruner observes: Frederick Dale Bruner, *Matthew: A Commentary*, vol. 2, *The Churchbook: Matthew 13–28*, rev. ed. (Grand Rapids: Eerdmans, 1990), 780.

John 3, "The Joy of Decreasing"

***Free to Fight Back*:** Marilyn Scribner, *Free to Fight Back: A Self-Defense Handbook for Women* (Wheaton, IL: Harold Shaw Publishers, 1988).

John 8, "One Hand Alone Cannot Clap"

The Talmud reinforces this command: Talmud Arakhin 15b, The William Davidson Talmud, trans. Rabbi Adin Even-Israel Steinsaltz, accessed March 24, 2024, https://www.sefaria.org/Arakhin.15b.7?lang=bi.

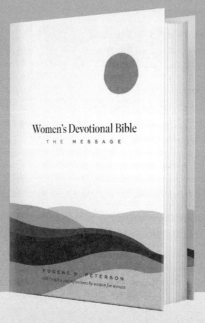